Six Machine

I Don't Like Cricket . . . I Love It

CHRIS GAYLE

with Tom Fordyce

VIKING

an imprint of

PENGUIN BOOKS

VIKING

UK | USA | Canada | Ireland | Australia

India | New Zealand | South Africa

Viking is part of the Penguin Random House group of companies
whose addresses can be found at global.penguinrandomhouse.com

First published 2016

001

Copyright © Chris Gayle, 2016

The moral right of the author has been asserted

'Dugu Dugu', words and music by Dave Kelly, copyright © 1996, Dave Kelly Music/EMI
Music Publishing Ltd, London W1F 9LD; 'Dreadlock Holiday', words and music by
Eric Stewart and Graham Gouldman, copyright © 1978, reproduced by permission of EMI
Music Publishing Ltd, London W1F 9LD; 'Warlord Walk', composed by Rodney Price
(PRS), administered by Downtown Music UK Ltd (PRS) obo Abood Music Ltd (PRS)

Typeset in 13.5/16 pt Bembo Book MT Std by Thomson Digital Pvt Ltd, Noida, Delhi
Printed in Great Britain by Clays Ltd, St Ives plc

A CIP catalogue record for this book is available from the British Library

HARDBACK ISBN: 978–0–241–27342–5
TRADE PAPERBACK ISBN: 978–0–241–25634–3

www.greenpenguin.co.uk

This book is dedicated to all those people out there who have stood with me in the struggle: through the good, the bad and – well, there hasn't been much ugly. Know from me that you can achieve what you want. Understand too that you should live the life you love, and love the life you live. Thank you to my family, friends and fans. One love.

Contents

Prologue

Into the Light

Beep. Beep. Beep.

A dark hospital room in a foreign country. I am flat on my back, wires and sensors attached to my chest and coming out of my groin. I feel like I'm coming to the surface after a deep dive. My breath is short and my head thick. It takes seconds of blinking and coughing to remember where I am.

All alone. None of those closest to me know I am here. Not my mum, not my dad, not my five brothers or big sister or my best friends. I haven't told them what's happening, because I don't want to worry them. Halfway round the world, they think I'm playing cricket.

The cricket is going on without me. I am in Melbourne, in a ward on Bridge Road, just a lofted six from the giant pylons of the MCG. The rest of the West Indies squad have flown west to Adelaide. I am all alone.

Beep. Beep. Beep.

It started in when I was 16. Feeling a little bit out of breath when I hadn't done anything to get out of breath about. You feel difficult. It's like breathing but not breathing. You try to catch the air but it won't come. You lift up your shirt and with a lurch you can see it, your heart ticking and jumping under the skin.

I ignore it and carry on. A sudden movement, and it knocks on the door again. Breathing but not breathing. The skin ticking and jumping.

There is something wrong with a valve. It scares me thinking about it, so I keep playing cricket as if all is smooth and easy. Playing Test matches, feeling like a king, the World Boss, the Six Machine, only for it to come again and again. I have to stop games, signal to the umpire. Down on my haunches, calling for water. Trying not to show any weakness to the opposition, to the leery bowlers, but inside scared scared scared.

Always in my mind. I speak to the West Indies Cricket Board about it, about getting money for surgery. They are hesitant. I speak to the players' association; they step in.

We travel round Australia, and my heart haunts every hot mile. We come to Melbourne and I make the decision. I've never before had any sort of surgery, never been put to sleep. My team-mates move on and I stay back, all alone.

Beep. Beep. Beep.

So here I am, lying in the hospital bed, a drip in my arm, the heart monitor showing green lines. Wires and patches. I'm not allowed to lift anything or have something to drink. I'm not allowed to move.

I was happiest when I was young, when I was carefree. You don't know the danger and you don't know responsibility. As life catches you up there is more and more to it: worries, pressures, bills upon bills.

As a kid you just carry on living. Go out and have fun, play cricket and football in the street, talk about girls, shoot birds for breakfast. You don't know how free you are. You don't think about what's ahead of you. You don't worry about what's down the road, where you're going to be, what you're going to become. You just think about playing cricket, because that's all you want to do.

And now I am cheating death.

We have a saying in Jamaica: *Use sleep an' mark death*. Sleep foreshadows death. You get warnings in life, and the wise man heeds them.

In that moment I realize I have changed. Looking down at the wires, the patches, my heart no longer jumping under my skin, I make the vow.

From this day on, I'm going to enjoy life endlessly. Whenever – God's will – I get better, I'm going to do everything to the fullest. No waiting, no hedging, no compromises, no apologies. Night won't stop me, dawn won't stop me. Wherever I go, I'm going to have fun.

I call my family. Things start to happen. Jamaicans in the city bring me soup and home-cooked specials. My strength comes back, and the vow remains.

I fly home. On my first night I go straight to a club. On my second night I go to a club. On my third night I can't remember my second night.

I picture a green graph like the ones I've been watching on the cardiograph, except this time showing parties per week rather than heartbeats. In Melbourne I'm flatlining. In Kingston there's a spike that won't calm down.

And I have a new philosophy to go with my newly mended heart. Just breathe. Breathe. Get out in the air and breathe.

Define yourself, what you want to do. Breathe and let the stress and anger go. And you will be guided accordingly. Your mind will take you places.

It comes to me naturally. You can't live in the darkness. You must come into the light.

1. 100 Not Out

I'm weird. I'm a weirdo.

You think you know me? You don't know me.

Yuh cyaan read me. Yuh cyaan study me. Doh' even try study me.

You think you know Chris Gayle. World Boss. The Six Machine. Destroyer of bowlers, demolisher of records, king of the party scene.

You're right. You also wrong. I am complicated. I am all you see and much more you don't. My name in lights, my true self hidden away. Sometime the main man, sometime quiet and chill. Sometime the life and soul, sometime the silent man. Confident. Shy. The joker, the observer. All mouth and sweet talk, all silence and down come the shutters.

I'm a man who can grind out a Test triple century and then do it again, a man who on a different day can smash 100 runs off 30 balls. I have hit more T20 sixes than any other man in history; I have stood invincible on a ground for two days while every one of my team-mates fell. I've opened a strip bar in my own house; I've started a foundation for poor kids in my home city.

Complicated.

You think you know me? I party harder than any other cricketer yet I'm strong and mighty when the pretenders have retired. I blow big cash on big nights but saved my sweetest payday for my brother's heart operation. I hate to run and I love to bat. I speak English to the world and *patwah* with my friends, the kid from the bad part of town who made it good.

People think I'm arrogant. No attitude towards the game of cricket. That I'm *facety* – rude, disrespectful. That I don't care about the sport that brought me up, that I only care about the money.

Maybe they misinterpret things. Maybe it's the way I bat. I play a lot of shots, and sometimes I get out. Maybe they think I don't care. Maybe that's how it looks on television, or through the pages of an old coaching manual. I play my shots and I get out. I get out on 40 so they say I don't care as much as the man who gets out on five.

Trus' mi, dem nuh know wah dem a chat 'bout.

I play with smiles and good times, so they think I'm not serious about the game. You see me drop a catch and laugh? You take a bad thing and make a joke of it. That's how you deal with it. That's me.

Maybe it's the women. Girls love me. I love the girls. I'm a hot boy. Arrogant? Nah. This is how we do it in Jamaica, up front and honest. No pretending or stalling. And with the girls I'm good – serious good.

Maybe it's jealousy. I am the Six Machine. Twice as many T20 sixes as the next man, the highest score, the highest average, the most runs. More international one-day centuries than Brian Lara, more Test matches than Ian Botham, more Test catches than Clive Lloyd. I enjoy every day, and I make people happy.

Who wouldn't want to be me?

That word is right. Complicated. And I am moody. That's how I am. My disposition can shift like a storm coming down off the Blue Mountains and swirling round the Kingston plains.

In the dressing-room I'm the biggest clown. In the West Indies team I'm the biggest clown. Most guys say I should do a stand-up show. You're going to laugh. It's naturally who I am. I love to mess around and I love to run jokes. If I'm in a franchise team and chatting it, players will just kill themselves with laughter. The way I am, really and truly. I talk a lot of crap. I have fun. I make fun of everything.

Catch me in the bars and clubs and I'm alive.

Shot a 'ennessy. Bounty Killer an' Vybz Kartel an' Mavado 'pon da sound system. Bashment music. Beenie Man – 'Di girls dem sugar . . .'

Sometime those shutters come down. Too many blaggers, too many after my money and name. I'm a human being as well. I have to keep a piece of me for myself. Sometime I'll have to say, sorry, I can't take a photo now. You take millions of photos, sign everything in sight, but for that one particular person, you're the worst person in the world. They might be a fan but they'll change into a hater. They wouldn't understand. People get the wrong concept of you, until they get close.

Because no one gave it to me. Everything I have came through the fight. Coming up hard, coming up hungry. From a young age I'm one of the hardest workers in the game of cricket, something amazing that you wouldn't believe. Most people don't even know me like that. But once you get close and talk to me you realize: you're meeting a total different concept, in every way.

Everybody will talk. Everyone will have something to say. Just know in life you will never please everyone. Even when you score a triple century. There will be someone out there who won't be happy for you, and won't be happy you get 300. Maybe they want you to get 400. And they still wouldn't be happy.

Most of my career I've spent time looking out for people, and sometime what do you get in return? A slap in the face. Not everyone is appreciative of what you have done for them. So I'm learning. Now I think, it's your life, and you live it as you want. You have to satisfy yourself first and then others after, for in these days and times no one will look out for you. Try to please someone else and you will lose your true self in the trying.

As a youngster coming up I've been facing those things all my days. I know it won't stop. This is where I am. That's the way of living, and just understand it. And know not to take it on, because what can you do?

Jus' breathe. Breathe. Get out in the air an' breathe. Define yourself, what you want to do. Breathe an' let the anger go.

It can be hard for me, but it's become a natural part of my life. We have to deal with it. And don't get me wrong. It is good fun being me. Runs and girls. Partying across the continents, seeing bowlers shake and stutter. Big nights and big bats and bigger sixes. World Boss and Six Machine. Oh, such fun! And they all know that. They all know that . . .

I wake up before the sun. Rollington Town, east side of Kingston, half a mile or so from the coast, Sabina Park a mile to the west. Cockerels loosening their throats, not always waiting till dawn shows his nose.

Birds chirp in the trees. From the chalk factory next door the rumble of machinery. From inside this small bedroom, grunts and snores. Two single beds, five kids: sister Michelle in one, four brothers sharing the other and the floor below. We know the sleeping pattern, whose turn it is for springs and whose for cold concrete. Maybe little Wayney will go next door with Mum and Dad, curl up on the chair and leave a little more room for his bigger siblings.

I wait for the next noise, the one that will soundtrack the sticky day through to dusk: the sound of ball hitting zinc fence. Somewhere, every second, someone is bowling and someone is batting. Street, yard, tennis ball, compress ball. A bat made from bamboo, shared around, stumps chalked on the corrugated iron.

A yawn and a pace outside. Breeze-block walls, wooden boards or flapping cloths over the windows, more corrugated zinc up on the roof, held in place with lumps of concrete. Pale pink paint and faded turquoise. The bathroom in the yard, the step up to it another loose breeze-block.

Into the kitchen, narrow and dark, one wash basin and more concrete in slabs, big cooking pots on either side. Maybe there'll be water, maybe there won't. Have we matched up to the bills? Maybe I'll have to take a bucket and see if there's an unguarded tap up the road, a hose that somebody forgot to tuck away.

I'm a skinny boy. Just as well. This is a house built for the slight and silent – one storey, sectioned into thirds, a family in each. All of us number one, us the 'C' part. Soon Marlene in 'B' will turn on her television, and I can watch in secret through a crack in the wall.

Past the zinc fence and into the quiet street. Only stray dogs and cats on the move, slinking into bushes and under beaten-up cars jacked up on bricks. The bottom end of St James Road, just wide enough for a car and a half, potholes and weeds taking over. Turn right and it bends round the corner into Preston Road, turn left and it opens up the tight grid of streets beyond – Fernandez Avenue running east–west, Van Street further on, Giltress Street one more on. All small and narrow and dusty, more lights showing now if they've stretched to the bills for the electric. Lots of trees, because Kingston is a green city as well as a tough one. Looming over us to the east, steep and dark and forested, the Wareika Hills, where bad men go to hide out.

I stand and stretch. Directly opposite, five quick steps across the bumpy concrete, is a hole in a wall, the secret passage leading to my favourite place in the world: the cricket ground.

The family behind. Father Dudley, already 50 years old when I was born, raised in St Thomas out on the south-eastern tip of Jamaica, into the capital like so many other rural boys to look for work. Mother Hazel, running the ship. Wayne, three years younger than me, Andrew three years older. That's the Gayles. Then Michelle Crew, four years before Andrew, from a different relationship of Mum's, and Michael Crew, nine years older than me. Two more brothers, Lyndon Johnson and Vanclive Paris, from Mum's side again, both old enough to be away working.

The rest of us all jam-pack into 1C. We have our little differences coming up, have our fights, a talk here and there. It's tight. Andrew and Wayne louder than me, no one louder than Michael Crew. Anywhere.

Michael Crew is like no one else. Natural talent with a cricket bat, natural talent with the good times. So the first sound in the room each morning is Michael Crew coming back from a party at five o'clock, into our bedroom, onto the floor. His cricket kit is already left at the club from the night before. Preparation. At seven o'clock he will spring awake and stroll over to the ground to play. All he might drink will be a beer left over from the night before. Warm beer for breakfast, then go out there and smoke the bowling. He will hope Dad is on the late shift, because

Dad is a policeman at Harman Barracks on East Queen Street in the middle of town, and if he's been on the overnights he'll be coming in at the same time as the night-clubbers, and if he's on the earlies he won't take pleasure in being woken before the hot and dusty beat calls.

We look out for one another. In the struggle coming up, that's the way it has to be. We bicker but we watch each other's backs.

You might think your mum has favourites. If she want something to cook and you have to go to the shop to buy, she'll call one particular name all the time. 'Christopher? Com 'ere!' And so you say, hey excuse me, he's not doing anything, why you calling me? Why can't she do it? And she say, 'If yuh nah go to shop, yuh nah getting anyting fi eat.' So you have to cry and suck it up, and get to the shop and walk. If she's going to the market on a Saturday, you don't want to go there. Early in the morning, 6 a.m., carrying the bags. 'Please doh be me today . . .'

Strict? We get hit with anything she grabs. It's not so much the crime, it's if you get caught. Then you're getting it. One time I said something under my breath about liking my dad more. She heard. Licks followed. Proper licks. As she beat me she say, 'Yuh like yuh dad more? How 'bout now? An' now?'

As a youngster you know when you're going to get beaten. You don't want to go in the house. You wait until late, late, late. You don't even go for your dinner. You stay by the neighbours' house a long time, but you can't hide. *Di morning yuh wake up, sun be over you, yuh get a beatin' same way.* Sometimes you just got to man up and take it. Get it over.

I get licks with slippers, the broomstick. Trust me, you name it. *Proper licks*. As soon as she loses her grip, you run. You gone. I never try to retaliate. Just take your licks, because that's the respect you have for your family. You can't raise your hand. You try it, you get more beaten. Keep it simple, keep your eyes shut and your teeth clenched.

People think we grow up in Jamaica on rice and peas. Maybe in some other parts of town. Rice and peas is the Sunday treat, maybe with yam on the side. Rice and peas is out of reach on a normal day, because the coconut cream and the bacon you need to cook it proper are also out of reach. Saturday you look forward to, because Saturday might mean chicken foot soup. The other five days you hope. You hope, because sometimes dinner is just a ball of flour and water, squashed into a puck, fried and served with a lump of margarine on top. You don't forget that, once you've eaten it for a while. You don't forget those hard dry pucks at the end of a long hot day. *Yuh don' know struggle till yuh live dis life.*

Birthdays come and go. There are no cards and no cake, not where we come from. *A birthday jus' another day you hungry.*

You learn instead to await the seasons. You look forward to the rain coming in May, and then again and much harder in September and October, when it is sticky and humid all day long, because then you can play in the rain, and when the tropical storms strike and the water is pouring off the roof like a wall, then you are even happier, because that is how you shower. And you can run into the yard for your bucket and pots and pans and try to grab as much as you can, because the bills come round too fast. We all learn to improvise. When the electricity gets cut for the same reason, lots of families hook up to the overhead wires to take it for free, bridge-lighting, not safe and definitely not legal but often the only way. We make bottle torches, filling a beer empty with kerosene and jamming a rag or roll of paper in the neck. A dangerous game, but we all need a light in the darkness sometimes.

Christmas is the big deal. Christmas is the big one. Because Christmas you're going to get a good meal. Not just one meat kind but sometimes, if you can afford it, two – some chicken, maybe some ham too. I used to look forward to that ham all year. I'd eat it alone even now. *Two meat kind on yuh plate!* You wished every day could be Christmas, so that every day you could have meat on your plate.

Someone boils up a Caribbean speciality called Sorrel. Ginger, sliced thin. Cloves. Dried sorrel buds. All in a pan with water, to the boil, then cover it and let it alone to steep over Christmas Eve. Strain it off, pour it over ice. Maybe a little lime juice, definitely some sugar, maybe a little rum for the adults. A deep red, a sweet taste.

The smell of Sorrel is the smell of Christmas. The sound of Christmas is firecrackers in the street. Getting the older boys to buy some from Mr Lenny's shop on the corner of Fernandez Avenue. Out in the street, lighting the clappers, throwing them and running like a *duppy*, a ghost, chasing you. You'll hear the entire street going off – duh-duh-duh-duh – and then the entire city. Duh-duh-duh-duh! Leaping around, fingers in ears, lighting more, throwing more. All the way from Christmas to New Year, you have to have something to light.

I am still a quiet boy. I don't say much. I watch and I listen and I learn. I see Dad go out to work with a whistle rather than a gun, a small man, and already I am growing tall. He is a foot shorter than his own father, and the genes seem to have jumped a generation. From Dad there is no sport. He has never held a cricket bat. He has never played a match. Without me being aware of it, he has already given me enough of a gift: before he settled with my mum, a lady friend from the old days who had moved to England wanted so much for him to join her that she sent him the fare from Kingston to Birmingham. When he returned it she sent it again. When he returned that too she sent it a third time. Three tempters outside off stump, and he refused to play a shot at any of them. And so I grow up next to a cricket ground in tropical Jamaica, rather than in cold and wet England. I play outside every minute of the warm day rather than being trapped inside by the wind and sleet. If you're going to be short of money for bills, better be so in a country where no one needs heating. If you're going to be hungry each day, better be so on a street where you can climb mango trees to grab a little extra, or jump the neighbour's fence to smash and grab on their ackee tree for more.

Outside is where we want to be. Running races down the street. Football on the corners, this end of the road against that one. Making *bingie* catapults and firing stones at the birds in the trees in the hope of bagging a little skinny meat for the plate later on.

Our first wicket: bowl with your back to the zinc fence, stumps on the wall opposite. About 10 feet in length, the ball pitching on the lumpy street, perfect for working your reactions. That sound of ball pinging off fence – four if you drill it along the ground, six if it hits flush, but out if you clear it entirely. Pushing a ball into the toe of an old sock that's no longer fit for service, tying the other end to a branch and just hit it hit it hit it.

There are other thrills. Riding the bus out to Norman Manley Airport to watch the big planes bumping down and roaring away. A morning trip to Hope Botanical Gardens, north on Mountain View Road past the floodlights of the National Stadium, turn right on Old Hope Road rather than the left that takes you to Bob Marley's old house. Bumper cars and a little zoo. *Lion could be meagre, doh matter. We seeing a lion!*

This is my world. And the centre of it is through that little hole in the wall opposite the house: Lucas Cricket Club.

Lucas Cricket Club, 100 years old. Lucas Cricket Club, the first in the country where poor black men could play the ruling whites. Lucas Cricket Club, the starting point for so many, the schooling ground, the scruffy university of the beautiful game. Lucas, the reason I made it in cricket, the reason I escaped.

Nobody knows who made the hole in the wall. You could climb up and over, but the wriggle through is easier. And then you are onto the outfield – not a pristine rolled green like you might find in England or Australia, but a lot of dry dirt and sand and little patches and smears of tired grass in between. There are trees around the boundary, shade trees planted by the government 60 years before, and there are more zinc fences, marking the back of more one-storey sections, dirty red where the rust has kicked in and sometime whitewashed to smarten them up and break the monotony.

The wicket is another Jamaican speciality. Rolled brown mud, not a blade of grass on it, wetted and rolled and wetted and rolled until it looks and plays like polished stone, the strip cut north to south so no batsman is ever playing directly into the sun. The scoreboard is wooden and rickety, a low black-painted platform with the big white letters marking the total, the wickets fallen, the target score and the overs completed. On top a tall board with numbers 1 to 11 running vertically down, an old rusted ladder leaning against it so boys can shin up and keep each batsman's tally up to date. I love scoring the board when the games are running. If I get to score the book, even better. Definitely worth getting in early for.

The pavilion is a mustard-coloured concrete block in the south-west corner, just in that bend from St James Road to Preston Road. The pillars are painted pale blue, and so are the metal security grilles that are locked down when only the bad men are about and hunting the bats in the storeroom or the bottles of rum in the small bar. In front of it, under a tin-roofed veranda, is a concrete terrace, the ideal place for pick-up games with just a bat and wet tennis ball so it skids on high and fast. There are no other buildings and there are no seats, just the thick grey boundary rope and the grass under the trees beyond. Nets? One concrete strip on the far side, looking east, nothing around it but grass and dust. Our nets have no nets.

George Headley, one of the finest of all West Indian batsmen, learned his skills here. Frank Worrell, the first black man to captain the islands' Test team, finished his career on the same wicket. Now it is me, and I am raw talent. Doesn't seem to matter that Dad can't catch and Mum never dug in a stump – I can just pick up a bat and play. Something is naturally there, just as it's there in Michael Crew, and in Andrew, and later in Wayne. Michelle too. From barren soil all of us can play. All of us have the gift; given a bat and a moving ball, we can make the sweetest of contacts.

I'm always a leftie, and I'm always bowling right-handed. That's just the way it comes. I can bat right-handed, and I can still make that sweet contact, but leftie feels so natural only a fool would question it. Six brothers, three left-handers, three right-handers. A well-balanced line-up from Mum. What a six-a-side team we would make! Perfect combinations all the way through.

Maybe it was unavoidable. It was like growing up next to the Maracanã, and being allowed to play football on the pitch whenever we wanted. St Andrews, and having the run of the Road Hole. You start life with the game in your eyes, and you have to get involved, because it is all around you every day. Each morning, the same start: *look out at Lucas an' see if anyone about.* Elder brothers playing. Friends playing. Every kid in Rollington Town. And so everything that goes with it becomes instinctive as well: feeling so at ease with a cricket bat and a ball that you carry them wherever you go, whether being taken for a haircut up the road or sent to Mr Lenny's for flour, hanging around the score-board hoping to carry up the numbers, hanging round the pavilion to see if you can blag the job of pushing the water cart out to the players when the drinks break calls. And when I use that bat, the reaction from anyone nearby is always the same: 'Oi-yoi! Yuh time dat ball so sweet for a young skinny kid!'

You might think us lucky to have one of the great spir-itual homes of West Indian cricket on our doorstep. Well, we don't. We have two. Off that bottom corner of St James Road, maybe 50 metres from my shared bedroom, is Ken-sington Cricket Club – the Everton FC to our Liverpool, just the width of Preston Road separating it from Lucas, no more than an underarm throw from one pavilion to the other. So close, and so far apart, the fiercest of rivals. The home of fearsome fast bowler Patrick Patterson, famous for his 'perfume ball' – the delivery that passes so close to the batsman's nose that he can smell the leather. The home of Wavell Hinds, who I will open with so many times for the West Indies. Beat Kensington and all the empty bottles from the celebrations will be thrown over the road from one outfield to the other. Lose and they will send back their own.

You cannot escape it. Cricket is like a father to me, there from birth. And I love it back because I am good at it.

Cricket in the air, cricket in every view. Sometimes there's trouble when we transgress from outfield onto cut strip. At the centre of Lucas is a man named George Watson – player, chairman, groundsman, security all rolled into one. He may as well be the owner of the club because he's so protective, and he is on to us all the time. Everyone is scared of him. Doesn't matter who you are – *he fight you, he beat you.* He is married to my aunt, but don't think that gets me special treatment. If 'Sorro' catch you – and he spots you so easy we think he's got 10 eyes – you got to go, because he's coming for you with some big stones, and that man has got an arm that's fierce strong and nasty accurate. So we leave someone on lookout duty for him, and as soon as his bicycle is spotted, his legs pumping on it, the shout goes out – *'Tek 'way yuh self!'* – and we scarper. And because they can't afford to have the hole in the wall patched up, we are back as soon as his tyres disappear back inside or up the road.

A little gang of us has grown, from St James Road and Preston Road and then Jackson Road and Madison Avenue running up the east side of Lucas and Fernandez Avenue completing the square around the ground to the north. There is Kevin Murray, nice with bat in hand. There is Popeye, and there is Rambo and Tiddler, and there is

Fanny-Boy, and all you need to know about Fanny-Boy is that he has that name because his mum is called Fanny. All of us tight, none tighter than me and John Murphy. We do it together: pulling out lumps of clay from the outfield when the rainy season churns it up, making gun shapes out of it and chasing each other round the pavilion. Playing ninjas, jumping over walls, stealing ackees, grabbing mangoes. Serious fun.

Together we head off to Rollington Town primary school, left out of my house and two streets north. At three storeys high it is the tallest building in the low-lying district, the same pale blue and yellow as Lucas, and the other critical institution in our young lives. A fence around it topped with barbed wire, and then inside a quadrangle with the names and faces of great Jamaicans painted on the wall – Alexander Bustamante, Norman Manley, Marcus Garvey. Wooden slats for windows rather than glass, the multiplication tables for each number inscribed beneath them so you can't miss the education even if you wanted to.

We start early, in for register at 7.30 a.m., so if Dad is on the earlies we get ready together. He doesn't wear a uniform unless he's on the beat, so it's me looking smart, in khaki shorts and short-sleeved shirt, the same as all kids across the city. The big excitement of the early morning comes with the government truck stopping by to let off supplies of milk and Nutribun, a special bread roll dosed up with protein and energy to get the kids through the day. We love those trucks. As a youngster in Grade One you time the truck every morning and every minute you want to be the one who actually helps unload it. If you miss out on unloading, you compete to push the trolleys up to the rooms, because occasionally you might get a free milk or a free bun. Everyone loves Nutribun something special. It is the unofficial national dish for kids, and when you have to run home for your lunch and your lunch is only cornmeal porridge, you love them even more. Some of the milk might make it home with your dad, and maybe a bulla too – a simple little flat pastry, another Jamaican staple, to throw down the hatch at express pace.

The school knows we like to run free and it imposes its rules upon us. On the blue-and-yellow-painted gates is a hand-drawn code of conduct, 15 red NOs to warn you before you enter: NO bare feet, NO explicit language, NO shouting. NO exposed undergarments, NO midriff blouse skirt, NO hair rollers. NO weapons allowed.

Inside it is just as strict. In Grade Two we have a teacher named Mrs McKenzie. She is feared not only because she is strict but because she backs it up with a *t'ick belt*, a huge leather one that she wears around her waist not for holding her dress in place but for dishing out the hurt. Her big thing is you coming into her class after lunch break with sweaty clothes. So when you come back in from your break, she'll go around and check your back to see if your shirt is wet. And if your shirt is wet, off come the belt, back go the arm and smack! *Yuh get spank on yuh back!*

She love to hit you on the back. So what we learn to do when we're playing is take off our shirt and put it aside and run around half naked. And then two minutes before it is time to go back to class, everyone will try to dry off – flashing our shirts around, blowing on each other's backs, making sure everything is in order. When that doesn't always work, we come up with a strategy: if it do happen that we go into class and your shirt is actually wet, put a school book down your back. She'll still lick you, but this time when she's hitting she's hitting a book. And then we fake the reaction – 'Aaaagh! No miss, no!' *An' wiggle an' grimace an' screaming out fi her to stop.* And when she looks the other way we will turn around and smile and wink and laugh.

I take a liking to English and to social studies, geography, history. Maths I struggle with, although of course I have a soft spot for the numbers four and six, and I know that two hurts a bowler more than one, that four hurts him more and six hurts a bowler more than he can bear.

The education that counts comes from a special lady, a teacher named Miss Hamilton.

She is not my grade teacher, but she coaches cricket and football, and in each other we rapidly understand there is promise and knowledge. She soon spots that I don't like to run, that I will just hit it to the fence so I can save my energy. I spot that she can bowl and bat as well as any man.

The playground gritty asphalt. Although they have painted sections of the breeze-block wall green and blue and red there is nothing pretty about it, a few palm trees leaning over from one side and the wires from the telegraph poles getting in the way of any lofted hits. No shade and certainly no chance of a true bounce, but that tightens our reflexes still further. When Miss Hamilton comes in with her full pace, you are ducking and swaying like those palms in a November hurricane.

She puts out cones for us to shuttle through, in and out, working our agility, rearranging them and telling us to clip our shots precisely between them. She teaches us the long barrier when the ball comes to you fast in the field and how to soften up your hands for the catch when it comes in the air. She hangs a ball in an old stocking of hers to make it come further and faster than in the sock, making us move our feet according to the swing and angle, stepping into it to drive and keeping the head still when it comes in sharply to our skinny legs.

They talk about the strength of a woman. Miss Hamilton teaches me that too. She understands everything about the technical side of the game, and she makes all of it fun. She knows I can bat, and she knows I have rough edges. Because of my hand—eye coordination, because I can hit it so well, I don't bother moving across to the ball. I'm tall and lanky so I can reach out and send it away. She knows too that it's a cultural thing, that all Caribbean kids do it because the big stars do it, going back to calypso cricket. We're thinking, why do we need to bother with this when the big names are not?

There are shouting matches. They finish 10-0 to her. Because of my height she makes me her centre-back in the football team, but I won't run: even if I have the ball and there is no striker on me I will call my team-mate over to clear the ball for me. She lets me off because I will bring her a nice glass of fruit punch at half-time.

And 25 years later I still call on her. I still call her Miss Hamilton when I do.

Each day becomes all about sport from sunrise to bed. As soon as you come in from school, you put down your bag and head straight back out onto the Lucas field. Your parents might want you to stay back and pay more attention at school. But it is a big cricket field, there is football and cricket action, and you can't wait to reach it. So that's it – you jump the wall, you're gone to play. Only when Mum calls you in for a good tea do you come, a treat like fried-egg sandwich or maybe even stewed peas, beautiful and hot with steam coming off it. But we don't eat together. I want to play cricket so as soon as the food is finished I'm gone. As soon as I eat I'm out of the house until late.

Brothers will sometime fight. When you get your own bamboo bat, and something goes wrong in your innings that you think is right, you take your bat and take it away and say the game is finished, because you want the best of everything. Brothers follow you with mouths wailing and fists flying. Sometime you come back with bruises, and Mum grab one and Dad grab one and say, I tell you not to fight, and your mum beats you on top of it as well. Unbelievable. Double blow.

But most of the time we are free to run. This is the Caribbean, and there are no limits on where we go and what time we have to be back. Trust kids to play out. There are so many of us, what harm could come? No child is staying indoors, not when so few have televisions. All the fun is outside.

So many different games. *Mama Lashie* a favourite. One boy get a stick, he plays the mama. His stick plays the lashie. If he catches you, you get licks. You have the whole of Lucas and the whole of Kensington outfields to run and hide, and run you will, because Mama Lash wants to lick you good. All the kids in the grid of streets playing, all running from the lash. *If him catch yuh, yuh get lick.* You just don't let him get you. Once you're running, you don't stop running. *And di lick a pain into yuh heart, it no a play lick. It wail up yuh skin.* Real Mama Lashie.

Stuckie is another simple one. Stuckie for Stuck and Pull. Two sides, as many players as you want. You have to get back to your base, and they have to stop you. If they touch you, you're stuck on the spot, and only your partner can pull you free.

You pick mangoes from trees when the owner is looking elsewhere. If someone has some bottles at the back of the house, you jump the wall and grab them as well, because you can take them back to Mr Lenny's or Lecky's on the opposite corner and get a few cents for the deposit. It's a two-man job: one is on the lookout, one is up the tree. I'm never the climber. I'm the lookout; I've got the height. There are two main flaws. Sometimes someone gets stuck up the tree – *di lookout see someone com', him a gone, you still stuck up tree* . . . Second flaw: you hear the rattle of the dog chain. Then you better get out. No stealth getaway. *Better jump a fence fas'!*

Every cent we can find we spend on food. Up to Mr Lenny's, his shop painted sunshine yellow with a green door, Jamaica colours, up to Lecky's store and bakery, the exterior walls bands of purple and yellow and green paint; on the yellow, hand-painted in square block capitals, 'Home of the famous Lecky's CRUST & CHEESE'.

It's a treat to dream of. A thick fold of pastry, dyed yellow by egg yolk and turmeric, wrapped around a big chunk of cheese the same colour. Sit out on the rusty metal chairs on the terrace when the iron security grilles are opened up and pulled back, take shade under the parasol and blow your fingers as the heat from the crust burns the tips and sizzles on your tongue.

We make a drink called suck-suck. Mix up fruit syrup with water, maybe lemon or cherry or strawberry. Pour it into little clear plastic bags, tie each one up, freeze it. Your own bag-juice. Take it out when time is hot, go and sell it on the street for funds or take them back to Lucas, drinking in the shade of the scoreboard.

Best of all is when we *run a boat*. You might call it a cookout, or a barbecue. We run a boat. Under the big shade tree at the deep-midwicket boundary, making a pit from a few stones and rocks with firewood burning inside, pot on top. Everybody will trump up and put some money together, see if we can stretch to some curried chicken back or dump-ling, real rich persons' food. You might break off to go to the wicket to bat. Between overs the smell is drifting over and tickling your nose and stomach. You shout out. *'How far da boat reach?'* When will it be ready?

At times we want to run a boat but we don't have the funds. If it's a weekend we might wake early, go out with our *bingie* slingshots made from a nice bit of elastic and y-shaped piece of wood and see what we can find perched in the trees around the boundary. There might be ground doves or squits, the best stones or a choice marble saved for the biggest birds. There is a knack to it that only some have – creeping up quiet, get as close as possible. If you have it, like John Murphy, you're known as a marksman. Me? I'm no good. If I make any contact I've done well. Only one time do I ever shoot one out of the air, and then not only is it a nice big pigeon but it comes from a Ken-sington tree as well. One-shot wonder!

You might have to hop a fence to pick up your bird. You might have to stare down a guard dog to grab it, and then fly like the winged beauty you've just downed to get away from that dog without him downing you. When you do, what a breakfast! Seasoned up like chicken, fried up with bread, a crispy bird in your stomach to set you up for what's ahead.

We hustle in the streets to get some money. Unguarded backyards aren't the only places you can find empty bot-tles. They're there in the Lucas pavilion as well, only you have to get past George Watson and his 10 eyes to reach them.

John Murphy is the brave one. He's the one who jumps the fence while I keep the lookout. If we have success, we can run a boat. If we just grab a few, it'll be a crust and cheese or maybe sneaking into the movie theatre for the big picture.

But Sorro loves to fight. And Sorro knows that when our water is cut off we sometimes take our buckets to the cricket club taps, and sometimes we even stretch his hose from the pavilion to our house and hope he doesn't spot us.

Now George Watson is a good man. An aggressive man, but a lovely man. He'll look out for you too. He will be influential in my career, pushing me in the club, helping me to play at the highest level. *Him also know everybody afraid a him.* And he is the man who knows the spot where we hide.

When he catches you he gives you hell. He rides at you with his bicycle. He locks you up in the changing-room. Then he lets you go, and as you race past he beat you with anything to hand – a switch, a stick, a stray front pad. *Lock up four or five, me an' Wayne an' Tiddler, pull the grille an' you have fi run pas' da switch.*

All the while, you eat, you sleep, you get up and you play cricket again. And now my cricket is serious as well as my easy passion.

I'm still skinny. The muscles won't come till later. My bat a light one. But the timing is still there too. I can pick up the line of the ball as soon as it leaves the bowler's fingers. My head just knows where to go, and my arms and hands follow and then the bat. So I caress the ball away. I ease it through the 'V' between mid-on and mid-off. I'm not lumping it over the ropes, I'm persuading it. I have confidence in my ability, and when you have confidence you can persuade anything to do whatever you want.

I discover that I can bat and bat and bat. I can just carry on when others get tired or bored or make mistakes and get out. If I turn sideways I'm so lanky I almost disappear, but when I'm at the crease I'm like a brick wall.

We'll play from morning straight back to it gets dark. Cricket early, then you play football, then you switch back again. Always busy, every day.

Sometimes you'll bat on the concrete in front of the pavilion, sometimes in the nets that don't have nets. There are always people to bowl to you, but it's not every day you're going to bat, so you grow to love the other side of it, and I become a bowling freak too. Of course! I don't want to be standing around with nothing to do, I want to be involved all the time. At school I'll open out fast with the new ball, then when the shine come off I'll continue to bowl spin – some off spin to start, some authentic leg spin to monkey with their minds. I will bowl straight through the innings. One end is basically mine. I control it. And I field first slip at the other end, and then I'm opening the batting.

There are models everywhere to follow. Every weekend there are matches at Lucas. Minor Cup, a nationwide competition, played on a Saturday. Junior Cup, the next level up, played across Saturday and Sunday. Senior Cup, the top level on the whole island, also across both days. I watch these men and I learn from everything I see.

I watch my brother Michael Crew too. He is the most talented cricketer there is. He's got all the shots, can play all round the ground, bat left-handed. Can bowl fast, bowl spin, keep wicket. He can field close under the bat or far from it. Wherever you put him he's made for the game. He is also a crazy man. He is dangerous. He has a tongue that can lash like his bat. I see him taking on all the big names, up in their faces, always talking. *Him always a mouth yuh.* And he will get worse.

In some ways his routines make it easier for me. Mum and Dad go to church every Sunday. They like me to go too, but when you're playing cricket every hour you have, church is going to slip away. Yet Mum won't be too hard on you, because you're following your brother's trail. Lucas is in the family. Then, when you want to look smart and you don't have a wardrobe to choose from, and all you hear about clothes from your mum is, 'Doh put a hole in dem chowziz!' you can take a loan from the playboy brother. If my brother has a nice pair of shoes, I borrow his shoes. You got a class party, you need nice jeans, you borrow it. You share it around. We get through. We manage. We know how to survive, that's the good thing about it.

Lucas is just a different type of church anyway. You are taught how to act, and your elders there pull you up if you play down the wrong line. When you start to get picked for the Minor Cup team, maybe when there's an injury in the Junior Cup XI and an adult moves up to leave a last-gasp place available, it gains you respect in the community. A Lucas man.

You are on the correct side of the Rollington Town divide. In the battle of the faiths, Lucas against Kensington, you are in the ranks of the righteous. When the derby game comes round, it is like a war – Lucas in blue and white if it's a one-day match, Kensington in green and white. The whole area is split down the middle. You're one or the other, and the congregation turns out like it's Easter Sunday; the grassy patches beyond the boundary rope are packed with the faithful.

The wise words come from our elders. There is Brian Breese, known to all as Briggy, a Welshman from Newtown who arrived in Hanover parish at the far north-west of Jamaica in 1967 to teach and never went home. He is sharp – educated at Cambridge University and then Lough-borough – and he is so in tune with Lucas, having been here since 1987, that his accent is stuck somewhere strange between Powys and Kingston. There is Spike Rhoden, who will stand me at one end of the concrete strip and throw balls at me – great technical stuff, a tennis ball so you learn to control the bounce, a wet one that skids so you get in position early, a hockey ball so it's hard and nasty and you watch it like a wasp. My cut shot becomes a serious weapon, but I'm developing the range. Sometime they'll have four people running in to bowl at you, and you don't know which one has the ball. Every day a challenge, every day an education.

We play on the cut strip in the middle when George Watson and his bike are pedalling elsewhere. We know how to prepare the pitch and we know how to patch it up again when we're done so that Sorro never guesses and never has to reach for his switch. On the netless net in the south-west corner of the ground they will bowl at me, and since if you hit it over the fence at square leg into the yard of Josephine Glasspole Basic School you are out, I fizz the ball through the grass until it clatters off those zinc fences. When they bowl at my legs to tempt me, I learn to step away and cream it through the offside so that the ball chases away over the rolled mud wickets in the distance.

My reputation grows. As I bat, people will gather under the lignum tree at third man and watch and *mmm* and *yeesss* and 'Dat bwoy . . .' I even start to straddle the divide; if someone else is on the track, the groundsman at Ken-sington will let me sneak into his nets. No one else gets the privilege, but it is still enemy territory – the bowlers will queue up to have a crack at me, everyone taking an extra stride or two past the single stump to release it from 18 yards instead of the full 22, everyone wanting to get me hopping and hit.

We make it spicier. Rambo and Lindi, two of the fastest bowlers in our little grid of streets, take on the wager: every time they get you out, you owe them $100 Jamaican. It's not much – maybe 30p at the time – but you don't have it, and if they keep rattling your timbers or nibbling at your outside edge, it mounts up. My friend Kevin Murray is catching up fast, but these two guys are proper express. By the end of one day his bill is up to $1,200 Jamaican. We laugh at each other. 'Now yuh see losin' yuh wicket cost yuh dear . . .'

Practice practice practice. Most people who devote more time to practice are not the super-talented ones. Me with the natural talent, I can just pick it up and go. I still put in the practice.

You'll definitely have weaknesses. It can be harder clipping it off my legs, but you practise it. Although this is the West Indies and everyone wants to be a fast bowler like Malcolm Marshall or Pat Patterson or Curtly or Courtney, there are plenty of spinners too, as later in the day the Lucas track will take some turn. John Murphy's big brother Brian can rip it. His googlies will take him into the national side, but I don't have a problem facing him, since at least he's not bowling fast enough to take off my head.

Yes. I still have a little fear about the short sharp one.

A Sunday, just finished a proper dinner, and like normal as soon as you eat you're out the door. Chicken bone in my hand, straight to the cricket ground. Batting batting batting. Brother Andrew coming in at me on the concrete, in his hand a hockey ball which always is bouncing like a brute. Maybe it's the taste of jerk chicken on my lips, but I lose concentration when he serves up his spiciest one. And crack! Straight in the eye it hits me.

I'm seeing stars. I'm seeing the thunder clouds, because I'm on my back. My mum comes over with the commotion and takes one look. No tenderness, just a full attack on Andrew. 'Did you hit him? *Oh-kay.* You lick him, you carry him. *Yuh tek him to doctor.*' So he has to get his shoulder under my arm and drag me to the public hospital. A huge fat black eye, like a right hook to the head.

You get toughened up. Again the examples are all around you. Michael Crew is scared of no one and nothing. He is out all night and he is out partying hard but he is still the Lucas hero the next morning, taking wickets, scoring runs, doing it consistently. Derby day against Kensington, the toss taking place. Michael Crew jumps the fence and strolls to the pavilion, fresh out of the nightclub.

He'll bat at three. Oh, so much talent! He just has that sweet, sweet timing. He loves to square cut. He loves to hurt the bowlers. Viv Richards, the Master Blaster, the swagger in the most dominant team the West Indies will ever have, used to love to torment his opponents. Every time he hit a six he would glare back at the bowler and shout, 'Shit ball!' Michael Crew has that swagger. He can't keep still. He'll crash a boundary and then walk down the pitch, as if to tap the turf. Then the mouth. 'Get back to yuh mark! I'm gonna kill yuh with licks today!'

It can't last for ever. He is known all over the country and all over the Caribbean, but not always for good reasons. He is in the newspapers. Umpires threaten to boycott Lucas because of his behaviours.

He gets suspended. He's not getting picked for Jamaica because of his attitude and his background. In Rollington Town we don't have the tidy accents and the good education of the private schools they favour. So he starts enjoying himself more. A wicket falls and we're waiting for him to stroll out to bat, only we can't find him. He's smoking a pack of cigarettes somewhere.

Indiscipline costs him the way forward. He is still protective of me, still protective of our area, but he's spending more time at the bar than the crease. There is a little rum shack up on Giltress Road, a little hand-painted sign outside it, and Michael Crew is always inside. Rather than beating the ball he's beating the liquor.

His favourite bat increasingly becomes mine to use. Equipment is thin on the ground because the funds are not there. You borrow it, you share it around. We get through, we manage. School has one helmet that you pass around between you. It is just a simple side-piece one without a grille, and although it offers only a little protection it looks a little like the ones the best West Indian players use, so we like it. *A style ting*. The balls are donated, one each, by two legends of the Jamaican scene. Mr Jackie Hendriks was a great wicketkeeper in the 1960s and managed the West Indies team of Viv Richards when they blackwashed England across two different Test series. Mr Chester Watson was a rapid fast bowler who took the new ball for the West Indies with the mighty Wes Hall. Together they now own a sports shop by the Port Authority buildings, down at the container terminal off Marcus Garvey Drive. Each promising young player gets given one shiny cherry each. I get given two. Kevin Murray goes down to the shop and nicks a whole box. Because the funds are not there.

We practise running in pads. Legs out wide, laps of the boundary. Got to do it so we can maximize our shots when we're in the middle. Cash in when you can.

★

I start to work my way up. More and more Minor Cup, men against the 14-year-old boy. Runs come. Up the Junior Cup, really, really challenging, the runs still coming. Big runs, centuries. Then gaps and glimpses above: a Lucas man from the Senior Cup side called in to play for Jamaica, a spot free for a young hungry kid.

The debut comes against Manchester, out at Kirkvine sports ground, almost two hours in a shared car from my familiar streets, out west past Portmore and Spanish Town on the A2. I bat all day, or at least that's what it feels like. Fierce bowling, heavy outfield. Hard to get the ball away. I make 35, and it has started.

More chances come. Batting back on home soil, facing Kirk Powell, a fast bowler who will shortly be picked for Jamaica. I hit him for nine consecutive fours.

Now people are not only coming to sit under the lignum tree and the tin-roofed pavilion veranda to watch me play. They're walking away from the ground when I'm out.

Half-centuries come, then St Catherine Cricket Club, from out at Spanish Town, arrive at Lucas. St Catherine always bring a strong team, and for a Senior Cup match like this they have packed out the attack: fast bowler Audley Sanson, who plays first-class cricket for Jamaica; Bevan Brown, an all-rounder who has played alongside him in the national team; Ephraim McLeod, excellent leg-spinner.

The crowd piles in all day, because this is Senior Cup and young Gayle is playing. People are drinking beer, running a boat, drinking rum. But the game is drifting towards a draw as I prepare to walk out for the second innings. I look out from the pavilion at the eating and drinking and talking. Lucas people everywhere. John Murphy, Kevin Murray, Popeye. George Watson, Miss Hamilton, Briggy Breese.

Time for some licks. Time for some entertainment.

Our captain is a man called O'Neil Cruickshank. Fast bowler, big hitter. Will go on to be president of the club. For now he has a huge bat, a lovely English-made New-bery. It's twice the size of my borrowed one, but it feels good in your hands. *It feel powerful.*

I look at him and it.

'Mi can borrow yuh bat?'

'Yuh aalways askin' fi mi bat!'

A pause. 'Yuh know what? Yuh score a 100, yuh keep di bat.'

Nothing to lose. A kid from Rollington Town never has anything to lose. So I go for it – smoking it, just smoking it. Oh, that bat is sweet! Four following four. A six into Preston Road, bouncing onto the walls of Kensington. More fours. Up past my fifty.

The place is on fire. Now the crowd aren't talking, they're chanting and shouting. Michael Crew is on the march round the rope. 'Chris gonna destroy dem! Him mash dem up!'

The whole ground alive. Smoking it, smoking it. More than 20 fours now, that magic wand in my hand laying beautiful waste.

Seventy-one balls and I'm on 94. A fast full one on my legs, the same legs that are a weakness until I practise practise practise. I flick it up and away for six.

And that's how I won myself a cricket bat. Back home, I watch the 7.30 p.m. sports news on the neighbour's TV, and they will talk about the innings, talk about the game. 'Chris Gayle get a 72-ball hundred!' The next day it's in the papers. And at school in the morning, I walk in feeling like a king, feeling happy, walking like a king.

I didn't brag about it. In your mind you get ready for the next one. Someone had to make it with those surroundings and skills and techniques and coaches and obsession, no?

Here's the strange thing: I never have dreams about cricket. I dream of bad things happening – falling off a building, crashing a car, a wall collapsing. I always wake up as that terrible something is happening, and I'm serious glad, because I know that if you die in your dream, you die in your sleep. And as I wake I get the strangest feeling, a whoosh running through me. Like my spirit went somewhere for real, and just came back into me as I woke up.

Where I'm at today, I've done everything to be here. Scored runs at all levels, straight up to the next level, score some more. Dominating whatever tournament I've played in. I've been scoring hundreds since a baby. *A customary ting.*

Yeah, I knew I was something special. Wherever I go I do well. But I work to be where I am today. Never did anyone say, 'I like Chris Gayle, I'll give him some opportunity, I'll trust his ability.'

I had to perform and perform in the middle like no one else to make it. Why? Because of my background. Most people wouldn't even recognize it like that, but that's how it is. You come from somewhere nice, you speak well, your school carries a reputation, you get the chances. Your skin a nice light colour, you get the chances.

No one can say I was helped like that. Yet I delivered.

I was the kid who people said had no classical technique, who didn't have the focus or drive to make it, whose attitudes to the game stank. And yet here I am today, still playing, one of the world-beaters in international cricket, and wondering what they're saying now. And sometimes the same one who blocked your path and threw doubt upon you is praising you now, wanting to work with you now, wanting to talk to you.

Toughness comes from having to be tough. Determination to stick it out comes from doing it every day. Motivation comes from it always being fun, always being games.

You don't survive in Rollington Town unless you're tough. You don't prosper at Lucas unless you have total commitment. You don't keep coming back unless you love it.

The older guys might try to chase us off, but when they're not here, the ground is our ground. Playing on concrete, the ball coming for your head, showing no fear. *Yuh have to stand up to 'ard pace. Nobody wan' fi get lick.* Bowling at the big kids, them wanting to smoke you around to prove the ranking, having to bowl as hard and tricky as you can to win your right to play. If there are no gloves, you bat without gloves. If there is only one pad, you strap it to your front leg. If there are no pads, you trust your eyes. The sun might be hot and the sweat pouring. You still do it, because that's where you have your fun.

Hey pickney! Yuh gonna get lick so 'ard!

You wonder why we're competitive? It's coming at us every day. St James Road against Portland Road. These games are cut-throat, because round here there's always beef, always kids at it.

Sometimes it's football. Street football we call scrimmage. Three-a-side, four-a-side, a league made up of the different street corners. You play intense. It can get dirty sometimes, and no one is surprised when a little fight breaks out here and there. We love the skills and the swagger. We play a game we call Shift: the man with the ball runs at his opponent, fools him with some crazy skill to leave him hanging, and everyone has a laugh at him.

Simple things, and such a joy. Ground Stroke is a version of cricket you can play with anything from two players to 20, in the street or on a patch of dirt, wickets or no wickets. One rule: hit the ball in the air, and you're out. Perfect coaching, a perfect accident.

Wrong Stroke. Play the correct shot and you bat on. Play the wrong one – shape for a drive through cover but send it through mid-on, look like you want to pull in front of square but take it too fine – and a fielder can appeal. Majority decision then rules: if a Wrong Stroke is decreed, you're out. The bowler becomes the batsman; the fielder who called Wrong Stroke, or the one who takes a catch if it's a straightforward dismissal, becomes the bowler. Everyone wants to bat, so there's always a hustle to get the ball. Fighting under catches, people calling Wrong Shot for all sorts, appealing like crazy men. Our love for the game, our skills and our tactics, grow with every battle.

We play hard on the street. No one ever backs down. No one ever goes home because you might be short of time or not have the space or gear to play it normally.

We play something we call Rankin Cup, named after a cousin of mine. We come over to Lucas evening time, we pick up two teams, look at the light left in the day and make a decision: 'Oh-kay, dis one a Test, we play fi two nights, bat till you out . . . Oh-kay, this an ODI, twenty-five over a side.' We will work down to 10 overs, five overs some-times, to make it sharp. Night can catch you, but you want to get a contest in.

There are no umpires, for no one wants to stand around without a bat or ball in their hand or a chance of a catch or appeal. So decisions are mutual: lick it over the fence, you're out; lbws, little snicks behind, majority decision. *One man say hedge, two or tree say not out, yuh get di benefit.*

I love to bat. I hate being out. Very little makes me angry, but getting out does. Tears are not unknown if I feel I've been sawn off and robbed. When I am given out too early, it makes me even more determined to fill my boots the next time. I'll show them. Watch me now. *Him full of heart, yuh can see. It plain on him, vex as hell.*

It is all fun, all pure fun, but we understand there are real dangers all around. The big thing is to own a pair of Travel Fox trainers. I don't. Mine have got 'Montego Bay' printed on them. The kids who do own them walk with their chins on their chests, looking down at their own feet with pride and wonder. *You ain't wearin' Travel Fox, you ain't wearin' nuttin'.* They would be better off looking around them, because Travel Fox are so prized that if you bump into the wrong person on the wrong street at the wrong time, they will take them off you. Pull a knife, pull a gun, goodbye shoes.

Shoes are the code. You see a man wearing Clarks shoes and your heart starts going, for Clarks shoes are not the geeky comfort as in Britain but the shoes of gangsters. You keep looking up. Diamond pattern socks. Ratchet knife in belt. Rag in back pocket, long-sleeve shirt over a mesh vest known as a merino, although there is no soft wool any-where near it. This man is a bad man. He might have newspaper in his wallet to fill it out, but only a fool makes fun of him.

I'm lucky. Being recognized for sport gives you some sort of protection. No one wants to mess with you. But there are kids with knives all over, let alone the adults with guns. McGregor Gully, where Miss Hamilton lives. Jarrett Lane, a few minutes' walk north up Mountain View Ave-nue. Jacques Road, a different gang, literally right across that narrow road.

In quiet times it simmers. Other time the pot explodes. Street turn against street. Guns, always lurking, come out to make hell. When the hell breaks loose, intersec-tions and street corners become no-man's-land, and bullets fly – potshots across streets, breeze-block getting pockmarked, ricochets off the fences. Schools get shut. You keep your head down and you watch where you step.

One gang to our west in Tivoli Gardens. Another east in the Wareika Hills. Nasty in Nannyville, two miles to the north of us by the National Stadium, on the doorstep of our secondary school. So some kids will carry knives to defend themselves on the way home. Others will flash guns and play the scary big man.

As small ones we had played shooting games round the Lucas pavilion, firing our pretend guns made from outfield clay. Boom boom boom! You catch a man in a target, he has to drop. You soak up your surroundings.

Kevin Murray, who goes to Rollington Town primary with me, bats at three or four to my opener and keeps wicket to my off breaks, loses three uncles to the gunfights. His father has to go into hiding; when he eventually returns to Kingston in our later teens, he can't even come watch us play at Lucas in case he winds up with a bullet just like his brothers.

We all grow up in music. On Saturdays, when your mum goes to the market, the *bashment* party music is on the radio. You take your cassette, put it in the player, press play and record at the same time, and it is something beautiful.

We swap tapes between us and buy home-mixed cassettes on the streets. Using a pen and spinning the little wheels round to rewind it without burning up your batteries, long strings of unspooled tape blowing round the streets, tangled round trees. Bounty Killer sings 'Warlord Walk'.

'*Nuh bwoy can chat when di Warlord walk/Fool caan chart when di Warlord talk/Place lock dun when di Warlord rock/Bomb juss when Warlord waan shot.*

'*Tough like a stone that a Warlord heart/Shot bwoy dome dat a Warlord knack/Copper plus chrome dat Warlord pack/Tell mi, gunshot when Warlord want.*'

Then, when the darkness passes, it will settle. A truce will be called. The rival sound systems that supply the music for the *bashment*, often run by strongmen to make themselves money, will call a peace dance, and neighbours will be back to being neighbours again, at least until the next time.

Sometimes you can avoid trouble. Sometimes you can't.

Lucas was a club formed to give poor black men a chance. When the first players came together in Kingston at the end of the nineteenth century, club cricket in Jamaica was organized and played only by whites. Lucas opened its arms and changed that, and changed the perception of what black cricketers could do: within three years of being granted entry into the Senior Cup in 1901, the club had won it, and would win the next two too. That's 17 Senior Cups we've bagged now, 10 Test players we've produced for the West Indies.

But poor black men still have battles to fight. I have captained every team I've played for, all the way up – primary school, high school. *Him a natural leader*. I've won a few trophies. As I come into the Jamaica youth team in my teens the expectation is the same. Big brother Andrew in the side in 1995, my old Kensington friend Wavell Hinds in 1996, me being groomed by the coach, Roy McLean, another Kensington stalwart who can see quality in a particular player, for the 1997 tournament in Guyana.

But already there are stories about me floating around. I'm the laziest player in the camp. I've got the worst technique. A man called Lynden Wright, who will go on to become president of the Jamaica Cricket Association, is the team manager. We're now good friends, and we joke on each other, but he is a strict man who loves rules. Tuck your shirt in. No flip-flops. No earrings. I find it tough, because it's not me or where I come from. I try to abide by most of the rules, even the ridiculous ones, but I'll still get picked on. Before one match he stands watch outside the team hotel and catches eight of us coming back late. The next morning only I am dropped from the starting XI.

On the outside I say nothing. On the inside I think if this was an important game, *yuh ain't runnin' dat*. I still do my job. I still play flat-out. But I know I am being judged on my background. On where I come from.

The Jamaica youth team captaincy comes up. I'm ready for it. I'm the leader, the main man, the one the team want.

It doesn't happen. Instead they give it to a kid named Llewellyn Meggs – nice kid, but he isn't a player, and he isn't a leader. He will go on to play just four first-class games for the island, average 21 with the bat and fail to take a wicket. Nice kid, wrong man.

The selectors know he isn't the man to captain the team, but they go for him all the same. Judged on your background, on where you come from. There are schools in Jamaica that have the reputation and the influence – Campion College, Wolmer's, St George's and Kingston College. If you go to Excelsior, some people will look down on you. They'll think you can't be a bright person. And if your skin is not as light-coloured as your rival's, they've got the biggest advantage of all over you.

It seems extreme, but this is what happens. If you check the history of it, of who is captain at those representative levels, it often comes down to the lightness of your skin colour and your school.

It's not just me. A lot of players suffer in youth cricket for that same reason. The best talent is from the lower schools and the countryside, but the background and the assumptions keep killing it. *Dem poor ones 'ave to fight 'arder.*

Kids from the posh schools already have the advantages – the equipment, the facilities, the funds. And since those schools also have big names as ex-students, they can prosper from that legacy too. As a kid from the tastier part of town you have to be exceptional, to perform outstandingly in the trials to get picked, because the selectors know their favourites.

A lot of talent I've seen heartbroken. A lot of kids who should have made it but couldn't, and so changed their minds from cricket. Out there in the wilderness now, doing nothing. Some of them bring cause on themselves, but too many super talents they let slip away. These years on, I'm still angry about it.

Sometimes you can avoid trouble, sometimes you can't. The blackness of my skin I expect to be an issue in Jamaica, but I experience it across the cricketing world.

In Australia, going out. Never a player on the field, but going to a nightclub, and you hear it – 'You black bastard . . .' Then it will come again – 'Nigger . . .'

You just keep moving. It's not spoiling my night. I'm out to have fun. I'll go somewhere else. But you can see it in the stares sometimes. The stares mean no good.

Sometimes in England, they won't even let you into a club. They will find some excuses — those shoes aren't allowed, that shirt is wrong. Always an excuse. It doesn't make sense to fight over what you can't handle. There are plenty more clubs to go to. You venture on.

'Jus' breathe. Get out in the air and breathe. Breathe an' let the stress an' anger go. You can't live in the darkness . , .'

I use those things as motivation. Some crumble under it. It gives me extra drive. You want to prove those people wrong.

Just the same as sniping and slating of your technique. Maybe you have to be criticized to excel. You definitely have to be able to use it.

They used to look at Viv Richards' famous front-foot flick to leg, playing right across his pad.

'What happens if you miss it?'

'I ain't missing it, man. It's in the stands . . .'

I had already played Test matches and Test series when someone high up in West Indies cricket decided I should step down to the 'A' team that was touring England. 'Your technique needs the help. You can't play the swinging ball. You won't score any runs.' This to a batsman who will average 50 in his first series there, who will average 52 in one-day internationals on English grounds against English swing bowlers.

The guy with the conventional technique is seldom the one who excels. The men who have changed cricket in my lifetime are the mavericks: King Vivi, Shane Warne, Virender Sehwag, Murali.

Sometimes you have to leave people alone, work with what they have, guide them along the line of their strength. Don't try to change them, because that's how they get here. Celebrate what they have rather than moaning what they don't have. If the sight of it doesn't please you, please yourself. Ask any Test batsman in the world: you rather make a pretty 30 or an ugly century? Then search the scorebooks. There's no asterisk next to an innings and a note saying 'This one a pretty hundred' or 'This one an ugly one.'

The strong mind is what allows you to score big runs and dismantle big attacks, not the perfect front elbow or the back-lift that points straight to second slip or a stance that match a manual from the times when Queen Victoria is on the throne and wickets are mowed by grazing sheep.

The determination to deliver. Being ready to endure whatever it takes to get the job done. Using those barbs to spur you on. Then you will make it, no matter what they put in your way. *Trus' mi.*

Am I ready when the call comes? In some ways yes, in others still raw.

Picked as a reserve for the West Indies squad at the under-19 World Cup, I open the batting in the Plate final and stroke an unbeaten 141 in the team's total of 243 all out. Cricket all day, all night; this is what you get from it.

The senior West Indies team, the actual men, Brian Lara and Curtly Ambrose and Courtney Walsh, the true heroes, are in Canada playing a triangular one-day series against India and Pakistan. They've just arrived from another competition in Singapore, so they are rotating squad members. I'm still not expecting to answer my phone to this: 'Chris, you have to come to Toronto.' *Whaat?*

When you dream about your West Indies debut, you dream about Sabina Park or Lord's or the MCG. You don't dream about the Toronto Cricket, Skating and Curling Club. Dreams can wait for another dawn. I'm excited just to be flying.

Jump on a plane, land in the evening darkness. As I reach the hotel, I see a couple of the senior players heading out.

I've brought my Lucas chat and confidence. 'Yow! Weh yuh a go?

'Inna town.'

'Oh-kay, gimme two minute, I tro' mi bag an' com' . . .'

We start in the bars, we take in a proper nightclub, we continue at a strip club. This is my first night with the West Indies team, and nobody is stopping me, nobody says anything. They seem happy for me to go and party, so I shrug and think, 'Good times!'

You see the big guns, Curtly and Courtney and Brian Charles Lara. I don't fool around in those corners. I stay in my range – Wavell Hinds, Sherwin Campbell. And they say, 'Okay youngster, com' have a beer an' chill.' So you smile, and you kick on, and you start to get in the groove, in the limelight, and girls start to flock you. *An' those sorta tings*.

Now normally a youngster shouldn't do that. You're just reaching land. I'm trying to be natural and play my own style, not knowing what lies ahead, not understanding the eyes now on me, but international cricket is a total different scenario. What you might get away with playing for Lucas, or Jamaica, at the next level it bites you.

And I get bitten. First game, India the opponents, Rahul Dravid and Sourav Ganguly in their ranks. I'm too thrilled just being there. There is a big crowd and there is a lot of noise, although for sure there aren't a lot of West Indians. I get sent to field out on the boundary, and I'm not a person to field on the boundary, but everything is different. I try signing autographs to look like the cool man. Except my hands are trembling so much I can't write my name. I've been practising my signature since I was 14 years old, and now I'm blowing it. A fan looks at me dismissively: 'You can't even sign properly!'

I get sent in at four. I last eight balls and score one run before Robin Singh bowls me. He also bowls Brian Lara for two, but Brian Lara is already the greatest batsman in the world, so no consolation.

Next game, sent in at four again. Fifteen runs this time, including my first international boundary, before Ganguly pins me lbw. Next game, seven off 22 balls.

So dis di top, yeah?

Dropped down to seven when we play Pakistan, Wasim Akram and Waqar Younis coming in like runaway trains. Six runs in 15. Next match, Shabbir Ahmed bowling flat-out and swinging the old ball round corners, me reaching out for my first delivery, reaching out . . . Clatter. *Mi off stump mebbe still travellin' now . . .*

It's not all gloom and golden ducks. Sharing a dressing-room wide-eyed with Curtly and Courtney, I think I've got connections. Me and Curtly born on the same day, 21 September, Courtney another kid out of Excelsior High School. One bowling from either end, Chris Gayle as first slip, waiting for an edge. I take a few, I drop a few, but they don't moan or glare. I love being around them. Ambrose is fun – the way he talks, the expressions he pulls. Sometimes when you look forward to something too hard it can be disappointing when it comes. Not playing with those two.

Against Pakistan, Lara comes over and says, 'You opening the bowling.' So I bowl the first over with my darting off spin, and ah, what a beautiful ball! The best delivery Saeed Anwar will ever get in his life. Pitches on middle and leg, hits off stump, plays all round it. Beauty. *Prappa prappa beauty.* And then I get a young man's revenge against Ganguly – snagged in the giant hands of Carl Hooper at cover.

You get a few big fish early, you start to enjoy life on the high seas.

I'm a kid, not yet out of my teens. Most great careers start slow. Master Blaster Viv made four and three in his first Test. Graham Gooch went for a pair of ducks. A lot of guys who score hundreds on their debut fade away.

And yet I know. It's a weak start, and I have so much to learn. I'm barely aware of what I'm getting involved in. I'll end up learning the hard way, and it'll be very good for me. It will make me think about working even harder, rather than just doing the parties and having fun. But oh, I do so much love those parties! Sometime after the games, sometime before the games. *Yuh do sum tings . . .*

On to Sharjah for a series against Pakistan and Sri Lanka. I'm batting down. My Jamaica team-mate Nehemiah Perry, known me since knee-high, walks up to captain Lara.

'Lissen, sen' Chris to bat early man, him an opener!' In my mind I'm thinking, 'Whoah, didn't he see the fast bowlers out there? Shoaib Akhtar, fastest ever, Mohammad Akram slick and fast, Shabbir Ahmed, swing and fast, Abdul Razzaq rapid on his own?' I try to mouth at Perry – 'Lissen mi – shut up. Shut up!'

Lara nods. 'Okay, I'll try him.' So they send me to bat at three, and now this feels more like it despite the heat and the pace, getting a good start, a couple of boundaries, into the 20s, quick quick quick. Then I get out, but I know now I can live in this world, and so do they. Batting early, building it, building it.

And so, that spring, the Test team calls. Time to fly to Trinidad. Time to jump the next fence.

Zimbabwe are waiting in Port-of-Spain, and I feel ready. I've been scoring big runs for Jamaica, I've had my taste against India and Pakistan. The start of a new beginning, a fresh maroon cap in my hand, seven Jamaicans in the squad, me and Wavell Hinds making our Test debuts. The next kid from Lucas to represent the West Indies; I can be the next person out of the community and club to excel, the next one to show those left behind that they can still escape too.

People can't travel to watch, because it costs and we're pretty much laid back; we're not going to be fussy. Tests in Jamaica will come. But parents are all happy, your friends are all glued to the TV, even if Kevin Murray will get smashed on cheap whisky in all the excitement and spend his best mate's Test debut asleep on the toilet.

You have to be humble in the dressing-room. You're a youngster, so you hold your corner and stay quiet. What you want to learn, you ask. I'm a person who gets on well with everybody, and I don't step on anyone's toes.

You also have to be a big man. You give respect, you get it. Everybody wish you well, and they know the type of player I am. *Jus' go out dere an' do your ting*. Do what you've been doing to get here.

I'm batting three but I'm striding to the crease in the first over after Adrian Griffith is lbw to Heath Streak. Nervous and excited at the same time, but when I stand in my stance and the first ball comes down – ooooh, I'm seeing it so big, and I'm hitting it so sweet, and here comes the confidence, and here come the runs . . .

A four, a four, another four. The ball seems huge and slow and my bat keeps crashing it away. Four. Four. Sherwin Campbell at the other end, a big grin on his face. Four.

A tickle off the pads. A shout from the other end. 'YES!'

What? There's no single there, Sherwin, but by the time I think that he's halfway down the wicket and I'm halfway down the wicket and I hate to run, but I'm running now, and the ball is fizzing past me and it's in the bowler's hands and there go the stumps, and there goes the umpire's finger . . .

I walk back to the dressing-room, and I cry like a baby. The most painful moment of my cricketing career, run out for 33. Run out when I was in the sweet groove, run out when I am certain, from the way I'm seeing the ball and the way it's going to the ropes, that I'm going to score a century.

With my off-spin darts I take three wickets in Zimbabwe's reply. Heath Streak then shuts down my celebration by bowling me for a golden duck in our second innings. Curtly and Courtney, aided by the third quick, Franklyn Rose, take their own revenge in bowling out Streak and his team-mates for just 63 when they need only 99 to take the win.

Already I was working it out. Be hungrier. Don't be satisfied with a 30 or 40. Set yourself to get some runs. Fill your boots, and prepare to be weary – hours in the outfield, get up in the morning and field again, then six overs in the night to bat, straight away the new ball coming at you.

I know what it is like. There will be times when I am dropped, when I have to fight again to get back in, but I am used to fighting. I will get injuries, and I will have to battle, but I am used to the battle. I will wake up and put the work in again, but when did I ever not?

I'm not taking this second chance for granted. I'm not blowing the escape. *Yuh gonna cement dis spot.* That's what I think, and that's what I will do.

And I learn one more thing, one thing from the streets of east Kingston. When a fast bowler come for you, sometime it's like shooting a gun. You have to control your breathing, or else your hands will be moving up and down. So sometime when the fast bowler comes I literally stop my breath. For those split seconds, the body virtually closes down. *Everyting still*. Control your breathing. *Jus' feel*.

See your target, and just feel.

3.   208 Not Out

You think you know me for my cricket. You might also think you know me for the girls. *So lissen mi*. Let me handle this.

Doh judge mi. Jamaica is not the same as England or Australia. We're more relaxed about sex. We're not so hung up about it. This is what people like doing. It's no big deal.

I'm a natural with the bat in hand. I grow and discover I can just find the middle of the bat every time I swing. And so it becomes with girls. I didn't learn from watching some older guy or trying to imitate anyone, it just comes naturally as you grow.

Everybody wants to have a good time. Some people want to have it easy ways, some people want it the longer route. And you've got to be careful out there, because not everyone talks to you for the right reason. If you're smart you'll pick up on these things, but you have to learn from your experiences. You have to know the game, just as in the middle. You have to know your opponent's moves. What's this bowler trying to do? How can he get you?

The pitches you play on are different. When you're chatting up a girl on Jamaican soil it's very different to chatting up an English girl.

You know instinctively when a lady's into you. And you know when she wants to listen to you. A woman who doesn't want to listen to you will just get up and leave. Once they stick around, they're interested.

Sometimes I wear my hair in braids. With girls, it doesn't matter about the braids. *Dyamn*, they look at my baby face and my eyes, they don't get as far as the hair.

That's why I always wear dark glasses. They say, 'Cyaan Chris tek dem off?'

I say, 'Lissen, if you look in my eyes, it game over.'

They protest it. 'No way, no way, no way.'

I say, 'Lissen mi. I tek it off, it game over.'

'Yeah? Oh-kay – try me try me try me!'

Glasses up. 'Ooop! Oh my Gaad! It true!'

'Whoops, too late, you get caught! See? Yuh lookin' trouble!'

Sometimes now I have to play the leave-alone game. A nice juicy half-volley pitched up on off stump and you take a step towards it, head still as always, hands coming down, and then at the last moment pulling the bat out of the way. Leave alone. *Well bowl mate. Cyatch yuh next time! Com' here again I hit yuh bowling all over!*

It's up to you what shot you play. Don't hate me just because I'm not what you want me to be. Don't hate me because I'm not who you are. It's just me, you know?

We grow up pretending to know more than we do. There is a game we play when we are 11 or 12 called Dolly House. *Dalli-Ooos*. Kids across Jamaica have played it for ever; it's when boys and girls fool around before they know what fooling around is, hanging out together, starting to get curious, not really knowing what there is to be curious about.

On the same little derelict plot where the trees grow tall and we creep in with our *bingie* slingshots to hunt birds for breakfast, the grass is long and thick. It's so dense you can make dens in there, little green rooms where you stamp down the fronds and lie there on your own, all quiet and no one bother you.

A girl invites you in. You invite a girl. And when you're in there you experiment. What's this? What does that do?

We know nothing about sex, and this is nothing like sex. It's a fumble here and a fumble there, winding up like we know the bigger kids do, pretending we're expert at what we're not. We call it *dugu dugu*, because there's a track by a dancehall artist, Dave Kelly, called 'Dugu Dugu Riddim' and it's on all our *bashment* tapes, and everyone is singing it and dancing to it.

'Beneat' the star (me wan' dugu dugu)/An inna me car (me wan' dugu dugu)/'Pon da wall (me wan' dugu dugu)/From wi small (me wan' dugu dugu)/All inna me room (me wan' dugu dugu)/All 'pon de roof (me wan' dugu dugu)/Rockin' chair (me wan' dugu dugu)/With foot inna air (me wan' dugu dugu) . . .'

Our friend Fanny-Boy — you remember, his mother's name was Fanny — is our bank. He always has small change when we have none, so he will buy us all snacks — biscuits, suck-suck drinks, crust and cheese from Lecky's. The snacks go into the long grass with the girls, but Fanny-Boy will not follow. At first we think he's shy, but lots of us are shy, and we still go in to see what the fuss about.

Weeks go past. 'Dugu Dugu Riddim' is across the radio. Fanny-Boy still hasn't followed his biscuits. 'Com' Fanny-Bwoy. Wah mek yuh scare?'

Eventually, after much huffing and puffing, he agrees to go in. Biscuits in one hand, suck-suck in other. We wait outside. Silence. Minutes roll by. Then a commotion, a thrashing of the grass and Fanny-Boy shoots out of there like marble from a *bingie*.

'Fanny-Bwoy! Fanny-Bwoy! Wah gwaan?'

He runs past screaming. 'Na! Na go! Dat ting! It have teet'!'

As we grow Fanny-Boy is persuaded those things do not actually have teeth, and we start to find out what we can and can't do. I'm very shy around the girls, just as I'm quiet at home and watchful at school. I'm more into my cricket. I don't talk to girls much, I'll just observe. And then I observe that silence sometime seems to work just as well as the brash boys and the big mouths, because when you do say something, you have their attention and they will listen to you. 'Oh, I didn't know you could talk!'

Then I find the cricket reputation helps. First year at Excelsior High School, first day. Our form teacher, Mr Haynes, is telling us all where to sit. A girl called Trudy goes up to him. 'Sir, I want to sit next to Christopher.' She gets her way, which is bad news only for Kevin Murray and Popeye and Garrick and the rest of the boys, because Trudy is a girl who can make a shy boy blush.

It moves on. A Pro League is set up in the country, where each club is allowed to include a couple of overseas talents as well as the best Jamaica can offer. Batting for Lucas, I come up against an attack with riches all over: Kensington express-man Patrick Patterson, West Indies quick Patterson Thompson, Laurie Williams, who plays ODIs with him, Jamaica fast bowler Kirk Powell and two leggies who also represent the nation. And I take them for a century, and I'm the talk of the town, and suddenly even big women want a piece of a young boy.

From now on there is always the ladies' eyes on me, *always 'ere and dere about*, and that will never stop. My eyes are opened to new things. In Jamaica we start everything at a younger age, because hardships force you to grow up fast, but there are compensations.

I am 16 the first time. I am in a go-go club, and she is a stripper from Guyana. I'm nervous, but I feel the pressure to get some experience, to break my duck and get off the mark.

You pay some money, she takes her clothes off. This much I know. I tip her. We start talking. We have a few drinks, and I make a discovery: sometimes they like you a lot, and you're good to go. *Ya man*. If they like you, you're good.

She is older than me by far. 'This is your first time?'

'Erm, yeah.' In a little shy voice. 'Yeah . . .'

Will I be a natural at this too? Not on this first trip to the crease. We do our *ting* and so forth, a few false shots and edges, few more thick edges into the pads. But it's good fun, and I start to find some form, and in my head I'm a legend, and the legend is starting to work! *An' the legend work work, an' the legend get a riddim and jus' work work work . . .*

And then, boom! Legend is . . . out! Innings over! Gone for a quick 28, lots of boundaries, no staying power, wave goodbye to the crease.

Oh, my knees are weak. *Mi body get weak out!* Then I fall asleep like a baby, at least until she wakes me up. Whaat! I'm a man now? 'Yuh wan' gwaan again?'

Life changes. Cricket is still the obsession, but it has competition. Playing under-19 cricket for Jamaica, I start opening with a crazy kid from the sticks called Leon Garrick.

He is a superstitious boy. The night before a match he insists we go to the movies together, because he believes that if we go to the movies together we make runs together the next day. He also likes to party. We make a good pair, because both of us are shy with girls, have no money to buy clothes and have no money to buy drinks. We can't even get into the places we want to get into, not least for those reasons, but against logic each of us still acts like a *gyalis*, a ladies' man. Playboys in borrowed shirts, playboys in your big brother's shoes.

And it's fun. Opening for Jamaica together, runs starting to flow. Getting into the nightclubs whose doors open because of those runs. Easing into the party groove, starting to find girls, starting to convince them that we're not penniless kids from the country or Rollington Town but somehow men with the world wanting to welcome them in.

Beenie Man is on the sound systems, singing about the girls and sugar, how he's a world-class lover, and these girls we see are like sugar, even if we're not yet the rest of it.

You take back girls to your room. Sometimes you have to say to your roomie, 'Hey roomie, need a likkle 'arf an hour.' And roomie say, 'Oh-kay, do yuh ting man.' Sometimes you can have a difficult room-mate who will never move, and you might just have to improvise.

On and on. You're now partying all the time. Leon is a good wingman, and I'm a good talker. Still shy, but with a couple of shots of Hennessy out comes Flamboyance Gayle. *Shot a 'ennessy, boss di dancefloor.*

The way I'll talk and come across, I'll be rude and sweet at the same time, and girls seem to just gravitate to it. A woman loves a compliment. They love to hear how good they look. I learned that early. Just spill it out. You see some men thinking exactly as men. It's not, 'You want a car, baby?' *Simple likkle tings.* Think as a woman. Counsel them. Pay attention to them, and you're good to go.

In my later days, if a girl throws herself at me, I'm not interested. Too easy, no fun. When you're young, anything comes, you go. You have so much energy. It's all new. It's all an adventure. Enjoyment everywhere you look.

My first tour to England comes in 2000. I'm not playing in many games, so I can have some fun. And what a nice experience! I'll be in the club and buy a bottle of champagne, and the girls will just come over to you. Party animals, in every town from Worcester to Cardiff to Nottingham to Leeds. If they like you, they're coming for you. If a girl wants you, there's nothing stopping her from getting you. That's how it goes.

The Port Authority back in Kingston pay for me and a few other young talents – Daren Ganga, Jermaine Lawson, Ramnaresh Sarwan – to spend the winter at the Australian Cricket Academy in Henley Beach, Adelaide. The cricket is fantastic – very intense, very well organized. Rod Marsh runs it with a firm hand. With me in the ranks are future Aussie skipper Michael Clarke and his long-time teammates Shane Watson and Nathan Hauritz.

The social life is extraordinary. My first time Down Under, and what an experience. At no point do I go out looking for any woman. They look for me.

I walk into a club and I get my arse pinched. 'Whaat! Who did that?' And then you see a girl just wink at you. Me thinking, 'Is this for real?'

I go to the bar, and the bartender brings my drink before I order one, points to the other end of the bar and says, that lady over there sent it to you. 'Whaat? Is this serious?' Andre Richards with me, both of us whistling in shock. 'Is this what Australia is like?'

We don't work it out until later, but it seems a lot of girls in Australia have something for the dark-skinned guy. I'm standing there scratching my head. If you are talking to one girl and she goes to the bathroom, the next one come take her place. *They cyaan slip up!*

Girls buying you drinks, girls pinching your arse. You feel like you're playing a game – eeny-meeny-miney-mo.

We're staying in academy accommodation, so you can't take girls back. Rod's rules. So you have to go where the girl is going. They'll even come pick you up from the academy, which is fine until morning comes, and you don't know where you are in this new city. Time to hustle. Time to get back quickly. Oversleeping, running into the street whistling as loud as you could. 'TAXI!' Me and Jermaine Lawson, waking up in the same house, different bedrooms, different girls, me having to wake him up, him dead to the world.

Sometimes the sun will come up and it will be *aw, man* . . . But it is all such fun. And the girls want to have even more fun than we do.

Leon Garrick and I and adventure just go together. We're an odd couple; me from the big city, him from the backwoods, me tall and skinny, him short and muscles. He can't sit still, I don't like to run, but things happen.

We'll be at Sabina Park, playing for Jamaica. I'll be on the pavilion balcony, feet up, hearing his footsteps. He'll be walking towards you, and then without any warning he'll just jump over the balcony. As you come off your chair like a man on a bungee he'll turn in mid-air, grab back on to the railings and hang there by his fingertips, laughing at you. *Trus' mi. He a skill man. Super super skill. Unbelievable.*

A training camp at Sabina Park, all staying the night there. The joke has been running that when someone is asleep, someone else will fill a bucket of water, sneak up and drench him. So far, so average. When it's Leon Garrick's turn to do something, he takes it to balcony-jumping levels − stealing the groundsman's hose, turning it on strong, putting it through the window and flooding the entire room.

Trouble comes his way for that, consequences and punishment. He can't help it. His brain is always going. One moment when you are fielding he's doing backflips between overs. The next, fielding in close at bat-pad, he'll flick the ball back before anyone has had the chance to move and run the non-striker out. Keeping wicket he is an outrageous cheat, knocking the bails off with his gloves when the ball passes close and yelling, 'He's out!' at the half-asleep umpire.

As a cricketer he is a joy to open with, an education as well as an entertainment. Normally as a batter when you tuck the ball to fine leg and set off at a stroll for a single, the fielder will see what you are doing and just jog around to lob the ball in. So we come up with a plan that if they shape up to lob the ball in, we're going to sprint another run. Always we're on the alert and the awareness of how to score runs.

If you're standing at the non-striker's end, he will tell you, 'Chris man, just go a bit wider from the stump.'

'Why? Why go wider?'

'Okay, when yuh go wider, 'oos fielding at mid-on? Dem will have fi go wide because yuh blockin' dem. Yuh create a gap fi me to straighter!'

A lot of people think he's weird. And he's done a lot of crazy stuff, and he talks a lot of crazy things. He will bat, for example, in two different sorts of shoes. He's a right-hander, and on the left foot he'll wear a rubber-soled trainer; on the right, a standard cricket spike. He says the back foot is his anchor, and the front foot is to slide out and play his cover drives. *He jus do tings an' we talk tings an' just crazy.*

He's annoying at times. Always in the ears, *ninga-ninga-ninga.* Always talking crazy stuff, stupid stuff. When you're batting with him, he'll count the balls left in the over and steal the strike. Every fifth ball he's off to want a single.

T'ief di strike. But he makes you laugh, running down the pitch for those stolen singles, making you watch those movies with him, playing the *gyalis* with the girls, and he's a super talent, one of the best batsmen you'll see, talent in everything he does.

And then one day we do something special that marks it all, that Jamaica cricket will never forget, that West Indies cricket has never seen before.

It's the Busta Cup, that season's name for our first-class competition. Leon Garrick and me opening for Jamaica against a West Indies B team skippered by Richie Richardson, up at Jarrett Park on Montego Bay. Rain clouds have come in off the sea and it's damp, the wicket a sticky dog. We lose the toss and get inserted, we get skittled for 129. The pitch starts to dry out, they reply with 184.

And then it happens. Leon and I start to bat again, and we bat, and we bat. The pitch is drying, the demons are leaving and the two good friends are making hay. We close the second day on 87 and 82 not out, come back on the Sunday and just bat, and bat, and bat, and they just toil, toil, toil.

I get to my hundred first, despite his strike-thieving. He follows fast, overtakes me, gets overtaken back, and then we start to race. Fours, sixes, laughing, driving, cutting, laughing, batting.

I have never batted for so long. Neither has Leon. But I have Lucas in my blood – all those long knocks on the concrete, all those day-long sessions, all the surviving and prospering against the big boys. The double hundred comes up for me, the double comes up for him.

At 425-0 we declare. 208 not out for me, 200 for him. Twenty years old, the first quadruple-century opening partnership in West Indian first-class history, and we have no idea. We were just batting, having fun. Just playing, just playing, just playing.

We bowl them out for 204. We both get man of the match.

The party back to Kingston is a proper one, through to 6 a.m. We're so young and fresh and green. We feel like rockets. Nothing can slow us down.

The world I'm in now has changed. Those sorts of things don't happen so much any more. Now the parties are finishing at 2 a.m. or 3 a.m. And that's way too early.

These days my reputation is known. I can't be the carefree kid of old. Some of the best nights of my life came in India when I was just starting out, some of the best moments of my partying career. Going to the fashion shows, models everywhere, having a ball. Now, in the IPL, it's more cutthroat. Women trying to make money out of you, women making up stories. Cheerleaders banned from talking to players because some were selling stuff to the newspapers.

My reputation is known, and people make assumptions. They're wrong. *Tink yuh know me? Yuh don't know me.*

The T20 World Cup in Sri Lanka, 2012. Three of us in the West Indies squad go out one night, and three of us come back, with three English girls coming with us. The clubs are closing, so we head to the hotel bar, and then that shuts too. Shall we go upstairs? Now security is tight. Any guests coming in have to sign in on the floor they're going to, but when we got to my floor the security just waves us through. I don't know if that's because it's me, but there's no need to sign in, on you go, big grins. All of us into one room, a few drinks, some nice conversation.

All of a sudden I hear a knocking on the door. I open it to see Dwayne Bravo on the lookout, looking seriously worried.

I pop my head further out. Cops all over the floor! What's happening here?

'We've heard you have some girls here. Some prostitutes.'

Now these girls are certainly not prostitutes. They've just come to Sri Lanka to watch the World Cup.

More cops arrive. 'We're going to lock these girls up!'

Now the girls are crying. 'Nah man, dem not gonna lock you up, just show a dem passport. Who you are an' who is it, you know what I mean?'

We're sitting among ourselves. 'This is going to hit the media now. Ahh fock!'

So I think, I'd better phone my girlfriend. 'Lissen me. Someting happen.'

I break it down to her and tell her. 'I was in the room with the guys, we talking, no dramas, this and that.'

'Okay, no problem.'

But when the thing actually hits the news, and hits the Caribbean, the story has changed. Only my name is now mentioned. Now there are five girls. In some reports there are seven. No reference to the other players, or the fact that these were nice girls, or that we were just enjoying a drink and some conversation. I'm the scapegoat. I'm the only goat. I'm in big trouble at home. 'Ah look at dat Chris Gayle. Wit' tree girls an' more!'

The morning after the overblown night before, a big team meeting is called. The manager speaks about not being distracted. And we go on to win the tournament. Perhaps we should have done it more often.

So the girl adventures are different to how they used to be, and the girl adventures don't feature Leon in these days. He lives in the US now, seeking work like so many Jamaicans, his cricket career long since gone. He did get a chance for the West Indies in the end, playing a practice match against South Africa at the same Montego Bay ground where we had filled our boots, and he filled his again, scoring so many so well that he was called up for the next Test against South Africa at Sabina Park. All seems set: Jamaican cricket's spiritual home, him and I opening again together, Leon in some tremendous form, his talent ready to flower and progress. Both of us serious excited.

When we open together for Jamaica, he'll take the first ball. But I've been playing Test cricket for a while, so I say to him, 'You wan' me tek first ball?'

'No no no no. Same ting we do fi Jamaica. I'll tek di first one.'

'Oh-kay . . .'

So we walk out, home crowd loving it. He takes his guard, mark it again, ready now. Allan Donald in for his first ball, short and loose outside off stump, and Leon Garrick cuts – straight into Shaun Pollock's hands at gully.

First ever Test match, first ever ball, a golden duck. The place, so noisy and expectant, now silent. And he just stand at the crease and mark his guard again like he's still going to bat again. He can't process it. He can't believe it. All he wants is the earth to open and just take him in. 'Oh, I'm so ashamed!'

He never played another Test. He got picked for a couple of ODIs, but even that went wrong. In one of them we batted together at the Recreation Ground in Antigua. I played a ball away and straight away he's running, always looking for those cheeky singles.

'Run one!'

'No!'

'Yes one!'

And he got run out, run out through his obsession with stealing runs. Just seven to his name, and anger mixed in with the dismay this time.

'Okay, you run me out, dat will never happen again! Yuh should run! Dat an easy single!'

And on an' on. I was never a relationship guy when I was young. The only one I've ever had is with my girl now.

I always said to myself, Christopher Henry Gayle, if you find a nice girl, settle down with her. And that's what I've done.

We met on an inter-island ferry as she went home to St Kitts. She then sent a letter via her brother, with a photo inside and her phone number, telling me to call. So I did, and we would talk, talk, talk. Nothing more. She had never dated a guy, so it was all new and different. She'd come to watch the cricket in Jamaica sometimes, but at the same time I wasn't really studying her. I was still doing my own thing and this and that. That's how it started, nine years ago.

Because it's my first proper relationship, it's pretty challenging. We've had a lot of ups and downs, a lot of ins and outs. Sometimes we haven't talked for an entire year. Because of me, making trouble, not listening, always tweeting shit, always talking stuff about a woman on Instagram, having some fun.

Have I been with other girls in the time I've been seeing her? In the break-up periods. You don't speak for a year, I'm in Jamaica, she's in St Kitts, *tings will 'appen.* But I have my favourite type of girl now. She got the booty, she got the looks, height, perfect. Natural. Kind, caring and sweet. That's my baby.

In the wide world a man has to be careful. It's not the fame; you travel the world and maybe they haven't seen you in Jamaica, yet you'll always have women out there who'll want to touch you, want to throw themselves at you. That's something you have to handle out there.

You get honey traps in cricket too. As part of the game's regulations we have to attend anti-corruption lessons. They let us be aware that there are stings on the prettiest flowers. *Not everyting good be great, okay?*

They tend to hunt the bars for you. You can see. You can see from afar. The eyes. The look. They wear the sexiest thing, just for you to look at them. And you're going to look; you're human, so you're going to look. You've got to be careful out there.

I've changed, but I haven't changed completely. I mean, you look at a woman, and you're going to lust over a woman for sure. You're not going see a good-looking girl pass and no thought appear. And I'm sure women do the same as well. A woman look at guys, a woman think like guys. It's just nature. It's part of something we all have to understand.

It's who's gonna bite the bait, that's the thing. Everybody look these days. Men look at women. Women look at men. You just have to live as works for you, and make sure you don't bite. And if you're going to bite, make sure you bite the right trap. Because the trap might be sprung, and you might get caught. *Big time . . .*

How do you end up with a strip bar in your own house? It's easier than you might imagine.

I built my house up in the green hills high above Kingston from scratch, and there was nothing in the initial plans for a basement. Home cinema, yes, wood-panelled office, yes, pool level, pool table and the nine bedrooms, including one for my dad, one for Mum and spares for the siblings and any of the gang needing it – Kevin Murray, Popeye, whoever requires a roof and plush mattress. No more five to a room, no more sleeping on concrete floors.

Then the contractor said we shouldn't waste the space down below, that we could dig out two extra rooms. So then I started thinking, what should I do with these bonus rooms?

Initially they were bedrooms. That just felt a little tame, so one became a gym. And then the other one of them had a peculiar set-up that felt it needed something else: a king-sized bed, and then a shelved platform in the rest of the room. It looked like the stage in a nightclub.

My first notion was to put in a barbershop – a barber's chair surrounded by mirrors, so I could have my hair cut and be shaved in proper style. Then I was in there one evening, and talking with friends in the decorating business, and we looked at the stage and the bed and the space, and a thought popped up: a nice little strip club could just fit in there.

'You want it, jus' say the word.'

'Okay, just do it.'

'Yeah man, it's done.'

So I left it to him, and he got everything organized, and then the work started with the mirrors and the pole in the centre of the stage, and when it turned out as perfect as it is, I walked in and, 'Wow!' Then he put some lighting in there, and some sound, and it looked the real deal.

There was one issue. At the time I was doing it I didn't tell my girlfriend what was happening. She was in the house when it was being built, but no one was going to go down to the basement with all that building work going on, and it was locked up in between workmen coming and going, so the right time never came up. And then she went down there one day to use the gym with her friend, and the door was open and she just walked in.

I suppose I was expecting a reaction. It's a strip bar in your boyfriend's basement. Yet the two of them just sat there and carried on talking, as if they've walked into a bathroom or the garage. Nothing.

To this day she's never said anything about it. She's also never danced for me in there. I have no idea whether she likes it. I hope so. It's a great strip bar.

I had guests christen it for me. If they want to be entertained, it's their room. Entertained in there, sleep in there, have fun in there. One time I went down there, didn't even know anyone was using it, stuck my head in and saw a friend having a good time with two other new friends. Shut the door, left them to their fun. Whatever happens in that room stays in that room.

And that's how the strip club comes in, and it turned out really nice.

The swagger, or the attempt at swagger, starts early in Rollington Town. Across the streets kids will pull the dry twigs off a calabash tree, set light to one end and puff smoke through it. You don't know what you're doing but you want to do it, just as when you first get a taste of liquor.

The beverage of choice is Red Label wine, a Jamaican speciality that's sickly sweet to an adult but perfect for the tender tongue, a little cinnamon kiss on it as well. The big kids can get it from Mr Lenny's, and we'll set up on the street and call it *bleach* – staying up late, staying up having fun. You pour it on ice, and you just want to drink more and more. 'Dis taste *goood*, man!'

You bleach at night when your parents are elsewhere, out on the corner of St James and Portland Road, drinking, running jokes, *talkin' a lotta ting*. One Boxing Day, aged 13, we stay up all night – me, John Murphy, Kevin, the usuals. We have some older friends who can go to the shops on Giltress Street, Lecky's if Lenny isn't serving, and buy it there with some Dragon stout. They'll take the stout because in Kingston the gangster drinks stout, and they'll leave the lightweights with the light stuff.

We think we are men. We think we're doing what real men do. Drinking drinking, so easy with Red Label wine because it's so sweet, and very, very strong, ready to creep up on you. We even have a contest to see who can drink it the fastest. And I'm in it, fancying my chances, and I'm drinking drinking, loving the taste, so sweet, and I'm all, 'Mm-mmm! Taste good! Gimme more!'

The good times don't last. First the mouth goes, then the head, then the stomach. I can feel something running up my stomach. I know I need to lie down, so I fight my way back to the house and lie down on the bedroom floor. Which seems to flip, because I vomit all over the room. I destroy my own wicket.

My mum and dad are both disgusted and delighted: 'Yes, that's what should happen to you!' 'Yes, you're drinking dis an' dat an' you on da street . . .'

I am feeling so sick. I genuinely think it's the end. When I'm not vomiting I'm asking, 'I'm gonna die? Mum, I'm gonna die?'

And my father shakes his head: 'Yes, you drink too much, an' dis and dat . . .'

Just how families always are when you do something bad.

I vomit up the entire house. The most hurtful thing of all is that I can't even make the pavement the next day. My legs and guts and head won't allow me past the yard. And I can see everyone playing in the street, and I can't go out there because I feel so dreadful. *Man, so hurtful!* Sick in the house by myself, everybody gone to play over Lucas, everybody playing cricket, and me *mash-down proper*.

Finally my father shows some sympathy. 'Christopher? Where is hurting you? Where is hurting your body?'

I can't even speak properly. 'Hmm? Hmm?' I still think I'm going to die.

'Christopher? Where is hurting your body?'

And some of the guys can hear my father, because the street is so close to the house, and Lucas is so close to the house. So the next morning, when I'm finally back on my feet and back out at Lucas, they tease me all the day. 'Christopher? Where is hurting you? Hmm? Hmm?'

I've never drunk Red Label since. Every time I look at a bottle I remember. I don't fool around it from that day, because I remember the damage. I can't forget the damage.

★

You grow and you learn. The kid becomes a man. The man becomes World Boss.

There is so much in common between Britain and Jamaica, but culture also divides. You can't big yourself up in the UK. Sportsmen there don't like to take the credit for their skills. They just play it off in a smart way. Within themselves they know they're mighty good, but they're scared of being called a cocky person.

Not in Jamaica. Usain is not shy to celebrate it, and neither am I. I'll happily tell you with a straight face that I'm great. Look at it how you want, but I'm the best. Legend. World Boss.

It came from a dancehall artist called Vybz Kartel, a tough kid from Waterford, a place outside Kingston rough enough to get the nickname Gaza. One of the biggest artists in Jamaica but a bad man. He's currently doing life, his murder trial the longest in the country's history. In better days he had a song and gesture that everyone loved, that everyone into dancehall music in Jamaica gravitated towards: 'Why Pree (World Boss)'.

He sings it *Worl' Baass*. He is the World Boss of music. And so it spreads. Usain is the World Boss of athletics. And Chris Gayle is the World Boss of cricket. There's only three World Boss in Jamaica. It's probably enough.

The thing about nicknames is that you have to back them up. Viv Richards was the Master Blaster, and he showed you every time. Me? I've played in more places than anyone else. Sixteen teams, seven countries, six continents. I'm the boss of the world.

But it takes me time.

A year after my Test debut, I still haven't made a century. I've made some fifties, and I'm given some bowlers a taste of my bat, but I've also been schooled by some of the best. Coming up against Pakistan in my third Test, I walk out to face Wasim Akram and Waqar Younis. You're playing schoolboy cricket, you're hearing about these guys, and now you're up against them.

The air is different up here. The war is on. The challenges start now.

As a man who's played 103 Tests, let me assure you that fast bowlers back in the day were more raw and more mean. Not necessarily as consistently flat-out, but quick and nasty. Our West Indies legends were of course truly fearsome. If you watch Wes Hall, he looks wild – like an animal coming in at you and letting it go. Andy Roberts, sliding in silently. Sylvester Clarke, mean and nasty. If you want to know fear, watch the clips of Michael Holding bowling to a 42-year-old Brian Close at Old Trafford in 1976. When he spears him with a short one into the ribs it's like watching someone shooting a giraffe. Imagine the England dressing-room in that match. Nobody can move. Where's that fool who made the 'grovel' comment? You go out there and defend yourself with a bald head and sticking-plaster on your elbow!

Wasim and Waqar are just as quick and maybe more cunning. Bending them away from me outside off, tempting the drives and pushes, setting me up for the one nipping back. You're facing two of the best in the world, and you're just a youngster coming in.

You have to relish it. This is your education, and because you are an obsessive student you find it fascinating as well as thrilling. How's he doing that? Where's the next one going? How can I find a gap in his armour to strike back?

You learn and you develop, and you believe the moment will come.

We are back against Zimbabwe, this time on their home soil in Bulawayo, their attack led again by Heath Streak, 16 months after he ended my first Test match with that golden duck. The good news is that at least Sherwin Campbell isn't around to run me out. This time I'm walking out with Daren Ganga, up there for me with Leon Garrick and Wavell Hinds as my favourite opening partners. In my West Indies career I will have more than 20 different partners, a roulette wheel to contrast with the immovable and legendary pairing of Gordon Greenidge and Dessie Haynes, but Daren and I mesh beautifully. He takes his time, I go on the attack, and so it is again on this July day.

They bat first and make 155, but the wicket is flat-track. There are runs in it, and from the first swing and kiss of ball on bat I feel in control. My fifty comes up off 68 balls; after we go unbeaten to the close, we see off the fiery first hour of the second day from Streak and start to build.

For once I don't feel in a rush. My scoring rate is slowing, but the scoreboard keeps turning over. Nerves appear for the first time as the century approaches, and my Lucas schooling kicks in again: why stop at 100? Batting is an occupation as well as an assault.

Jus' breathe. Define yourself, what you want to do. Breathe an' let the stress an' anger go.

I can't remember the stroke that takes me to 100. I am thinking like a true son of Lucas: be grateful and thankful, but keep batting. There is plenty of time left in the game. Make the best use of the magic. Keep batting and batting.

It ends on 175. Streak has me again, but this time I have had him first. Not bad for a maiden Test century, even if it's not the 277 that Brian Lara made with his first or the 365 that Sir Garfield conjured up. But it sets us up for an innings victory, and we toast it until late in the night.

Even a World Boss needs to grow into his role, and age-group cricket is the perfect place to experiment. It teaches you to be creative.

At a tournament in Trinidad it rains all week. Match after match is cancelled, so night after night becomes big. We break every curfew and we beat every security man the manager puts on the hotel door. You'd think he'd learn that we're climbing through windows rather than using the door, but it's like having your grandfather fielding at slip: *him cyaan catch nobady*.

We stand outside the clubs to watch the ladies come in, nudging each other, eyes out on stalks – 'Oooh! Look at dat . . .' Inside we dance all night. Jamming, jamming.

The only problem is money. We don't have any to start with, and despite selling some of our clothes to the Guyana team (you can't get good-looking knock-off brands in Georgetown like you can in Kingston) we soon run out again. It's not that the clubs are extortionate; it's just that we're in them so often and so long. Luckily the Guyanese lads come to our rescue again and offer to buy our bats. We're not worried about crossing that particular bridge because it keeps raining and raining, right up to the point when we leave a nightclub one morning, everyone blinks and someone says, 'Isn't the sun shining?'

The organizers call a one-day tournament. We win it. Not World Boss yet but maybe deputy of a few fine lands.

The beach parties back home continue the tuition. On June weekends there are two parties in a day. Your week becomes a series of days you're ticking off until the next one. On the beaches of Negril, way out west, the parties across August are even bigger, from Emancipation Day on 1 August to Independence Day on the 6th and beyond. For the boy from Kingston it's a fresh world: clean sand and clean waves, big sound systems, DJs, bars and rum stalls, everybody dancing. The music will go high, cool down, crank up again, rumble in between, the DJs feeding off the crowd and the crowd feeding off the DJs' cuts. There are good girls, there are bad girls. There are bikinis and bodies and sights you have never seen before everywhere you look. As a shy kid finding his feet you want to dance with every girl, *wind it up 'ere an' dere*, especially after a few Hennessy. Get close, have fun. If it rains it's even better, because it takes away some of the heat, cools you down so you can go longer.

When the season changes the parties keep coming. Pool parties, house parties, club parties. The shy boy is no more, at least until the next mood sweeps in. When I'm up, I'm the life of the party. I put it out there. Once I'm in the party, you know it's a party with a capital P and a shaking sound system and bottles of rum and yo-ho-ho. So many parties, it's hard to keep track.

Those are the freedoms you have as a youngster. You think you can do it all. You think you can burn the candle at both ends and set light to the middle too. Who needs candles when the sun is shining and the waves are crashing and Beenie Man and Vybz Kartel, Capleton and Baby Cham are on the sound system?

Then you play a rash shot, and another one. You get dropped from the team. You start to think a bit deeper. You slow down a bit, and cricket comes back into focus. You look within yourself and understand that whatever else you want, whatever other fun you might have, a cricketer is what you are. There are a lot of critics out there, and the only solution to silence them is to rack up the runs. You can still get away with a few things, and you have to, because that is also an essential part of who you are. And there will still be critics, because if you score some runs they'll say you should still get more. At no stage can you satisfy everybody.

There's a balance somewhere. It's not always easy to find, and I can't always tip-toe along it. The more intense it gets on the field, the more I need to free up and let go. The tougher the ordeal at the crease, the bigger the thirst for Appleton rum and Hennessy. You might not like it or be able to do it, but then you're not me.

To this moment I love partying in England. If I'm travelling somewhere and I pass through London I'll always make a stopover for a couple of nights to hit the clubs. On my first tour with the West Indies, back in 2000, I was still searching for the balance, still overwhelmed by what lay out there in the big bad world. I became familiar with local taxi companies; not only did they bring you back from the clubs and drop you at the hotel service entrance rather than the main door, they also came in handy for overtaking the team bus on the way to the ground after you've slept in.

After the Test at Old Trafford a few of the senior guys went out with me and Wavell Hinds, the young guns. It was more of a get-together rather than a party, and though there was an 11 p.m. curfew we got back just after midnight. The next day two letters were issued – one to me, one to Wavell – and one man is going to be fined: me. Nothing was said to the senior guys, and as a kid from upfront Rollington Town I had a clatter about it with the manager. Why just me? *Yuh serious?*

As World Boss I understand how to manage it now. It's like pacing a long innings – you can still play your shots, but you have to leave a few alone as well. And when the half-volley and the gap in the field is there, you have to commit to it. Hard.

In India in the early days you can let the bat swing. Never be fooled into thinking India is too straitlaced. They love cricket, so when you ask the questions – Where's the party? Where's the girls? – they give you answers. Cricket opens doors, and when the doors open you see the girls, and the models, and the clubs that others do not see. Music? Don't worry about the music. As a Jamaican you can dance. You just fit into the beat and get into it, dancing till your clothes are wet, dancing with the cheerleaders and the DJs and everyone dancing, staggering to your room ears ringing, 4 a.m., 5 a.m., and then you go out to bat and you're still drunk.

You can still practise with big hangovers. Sometimes you get a big buzz of it, because you are sweating and there is still alcohol in your system. You get a buzz and a little energy off it, you run around all sharp sharp, you bat with freedom. And then when the heat hits you, you fall flat-out, and sleep all day like a baby. And you even can get away with it for a while, if you understand it won't last, that's it's not a long-term solution.

But trust me. Wherever you go you can find the party, and with experience you find your balance too. I've had fun pretty much everywhere. There's always a spot, no matter what city or continent. You just have to have contacts.

World Boss is fun in every way. And I've had a lot of fun, in all the areas. Because I'm the boss . . . *I'm da baass of all baass. Universe Boss!*

There are things only I can get away with. No one else would even try them. Hitting Matthew Hoggard for six fours in an over. Hitting 37 off a single over in the IPL. A century off 30 balls, another one on one leg.

If Zlatan Ibrahimović were a cricketer, it's the sort of thing he would be trying. Except the whole point about these sort of crazy deeds is that there's no trying involved – it just comes naturally. It's your personality coming through in what you do. I don't hunt these records. It might work for other people, but it would never work for me.

It comes down to confidence. Confidence enables you to relax and let the unconscious mind get to work. Confidence enables you to flourish under the sort of expectation and pressure that would see others sink back into safety first.

Confidence comes from hard work and dedication. There's Zlatan, and then there's Ronaldo. He believes he's the best, even when people doubt him or favour Leo Messi for the big awards. It doesn't stop him. Within himself he knows he's the best, and he always keeps driving. He doesn't care what they say about him. He works hard. And I fit into his style too.

That over against Hoggard at the Oval in August 2004. The West Indies were in it deep: following on, still 308 runs behind, the Wisden Trophy already lost. I had been caught behind for 12 in the first innings. Who could blame anyone for sinking back into safety first in all that? Who could possibly feel confident in the middle of such a mess?

Worl' Baass!

There is no try, only do. First ball, on middle stump from over the wicket, punch through leg. Second ball, full, smash on the drive through the covers. Third, onto the back foot, cream past mid-off. Fourth, aimed outside off, clattered straight through the fielder at cover. Fifth, pulled fine off the hips; sixth, rocking on to the back foot, thrash to the extra over fence once again. *Maximum lick.*

And I didn't even notice it was six fours. Honestly. I thought there were more deliveries to come. It was just the right shot for each ball. I remember Freddie Flintoff walking past me at the end of the over and saying, 'You enjoyed that, didn't you?' And I just smiled. I hadn't planned it.

I had no idea it was the first time anyone had done that in a Test match. I was just seeing the ball and hitting it. Doing what comes naturally, letting my character shine out.

Just as I am sometime all mouth and sometime shutters down and shy, not always is that magic there. You know within yourself how you feel, and there will be moments when, no matter how hard you search for it, it's not going to happen. It is the bowler who is the king for the day, and you have to be wise enough to accept defeat for that little window in time.

I used to struggle to dominate as I should at home. The magic was elusive. I'd scored nine international one-day hundreds before I scored one in the Caribbean. Sometime home advantage bends the other way, and all you sense is the pressure. The critics whisper, and never to your face.

As you go along, you learn, you learn, you learn. The old boys tell you. 'One likkle score give yuh big boost.' And it comes, and you can feel untouchable. From ball one that perfect feeling is back. You walk out there not knowing which foot to put first and suddenly just start timing it perfectly. It's a feeling of control; you can do what you want. I looked up one day from the crease in Bangalore to see a Royal Challengers fan holding up a home-made sign: 'When Gayle bats, fielders become spectators, and spectators become fielders.' On those sweet nights that's exactly how it feels. On those nights the critics blow fire on someone else.

As you go along you learn, you learn. When you're up you have to ride the wave as far as you can, because sometime the wave will flatten out, and there'll be no wave to surf on. When the riptide is at your back and the wind on your face, take it as far as possible. Ride the big ones.

Confidence carries you through, even if you're sometime bluffing both yourself and the opposition attack. You'd say it was like being an actor, having to convince everyone you're feeling fine, that you're the big man in control. Except if you're an actor you can fluff your lines and do another take. It's not the end of the show.

Cricket has no safety net. Yet that risk helps us. Without the jeopardy we wouldn't have the rush of joy when the impossible comes off.

Actor? You are a gladiator, fighting for your future. Mask on, chest out. Go out there and show no fear, even if the odds are stacked. Go out there and stand tall. Stare down the danger. Win over the hostile crowd.

No man wins over the crowd by standing with his back to the wall or trying to run. He does it through bravery. He does it by thrilling, by inspiring, by pulling off deeds that no one else would dare.

The Caribbean crowds will cuss you out if you fail. If you succeed, you are doing more than just smacking a bowler into the stands. You are letting your countrymen walk tall down the street. You are allowing them to point at the world and say, 'Yeah man, look at us.' There are hundreds of thousands of West Indians working in foreign lands, left as the minority, far from home. When the Caribbean kid takes on the big nations and wins, they grow too. They can walk into offices and factories with their heads held high. You want to mock me now, when my boy has just *lick yuh proper*?

People watch gladiators because they want to see man against man, but also because they want to be entertained, and you must understand your audience if you are to win their respect. All want a performance to lift them from the humdrum day, but performance means different things to different men; fire 30 off 10 balls and one man will love you but another despise you. You have to work out how you're going to win the battles on a particular ground.

You go to Barbados. You play a few shots, they love you there. You don't necessarily have to score a hundred. They love good, attacking cricket. *Yuh com' an' blaze it, dem love dat sorta ting*. You go to Trinidad, you do that and get out, you're going to get cuss.

This crowd might want a bigger but steady score, the next crowd just wants sixes for excitement. Give them four sixes and that's all they need. I calculate before an innings, particularly in the IPL. The crowd might be chanting, 'Six! Six! Six!' I am an entertainer, so I'll give them a six now, and they go berserk. You need one run to win. You know they want a six, so you give them one. And they go even more berserk.

If I can bring that joy and happiness, I've played my role. But first I had to learn.

Confidence comes from character. Character comes from being tested and coming through.

Miss Hamilton. Briggy Breese, Spike Rhoden. My brother Michael Crew blazing, the schoolings from pacemen Rambo and Lindi. You walked the streets of Rollington Town and the advice came from everywhere.

'You need to push your front foot out more.'

'Com' across more fi dat shot.'

'Youngster, you need to bat longer.'

At Excelsior High School I get lucky again. Paul McCallum is a young teacher who does lessons in the mornings and coaches cricket in the afternoons. He is another Lucas boy, playing alongside my eldest brother, Vanclive Paris, familiar with next brother Lyndon Johnson, playing too with Courtney Walsh when the two are kids at Excelsior. He feels he's known me since gestation, which may be why later, much later, he will lend me his car to practise my driving round the playground after school. I will thank him by burning out the clutch, but for now it's him driving me on.

Mr Mac is a generous man. He is always giving kids lunch money and bus money. His gift to me, aged 12, is to throw me in the school's first XI. Not my year's first XI, but the actual first XI. Against 19-year-olds.

I am terrified, particularly by the new ball. Mr Mac insists on my innate talent and technique and says I can compete. Neither will he hide me down the order. He thinks I get a bit mesmerized by the spinners if I come and face them straight away, whereas if I'm already in the groove, I'll dominate them, so he wants me to open. I sense it's more that he wants to partner his current right-handed opener with a leftie, to disrupt the opposition bowlers' line and length, and I keep refusing. He keeps insisting, even as I'm intimidated by these tall pacemen coming in, many of whom have been shaving for several years, a few of whom shave several times a day. And he must be on to something, because gradually the fear lessens, and the runs start to come – consistently 30s and 40s, men against the boy – and gradually I stop pining for the middle order and begin to think of myself as an opening batsman. When Lucas hear about my promotion they shift me up to opener too. And so a career is set, thanks to Mr Mac.

He's not a greedy man. Coaching the cricket, driving us to matches in his car, it all costs him. The school won't even cover his petrol. Neither does he care about trophies, although plenty will follow. He's about building characters for the future, preparing to send boys out into the world as men, and he sets to work studying me.

My nickname is Crampy, meaning laid-back or slow. When I'm not batting I'm lethargic; when we train without bat or ball in hand, I'm miserable. *If we running, he's always at di back.*

He works me out. Because of my natural gifts, I could miss training for two weeks, be called into a match and still make a brilliant hundred. Performing comes naturally, so why would I be motivated to train?

My energy comes from being in the middle and striking the ball. If outside that you can't get me to generate the same energy and aggression, it doesn't matter. When I'm batting or bowling or fielding, you don't get the lethargy you'd see if I was running laps or walking to class. Give me cricket and I give you everything.

So there is no finger-wagging and no forced laps. Instead I get thrown to the lions, and the lions start to get bloodied snouts.

Playing against my peers in cup matches not run by Inter-Schools, I score regular centuries. No big deal. Playing the 19-year-olds the first century comes aged 15, and then damage happens with the ball too. If we're short of a medium pacer, Mr Mac calls me up to bowl some nasty sharp stuff off five paces. When my brother Andrew leaves school, three years ahead of me, we're suddenly missing his ripping gripping leg spin, so Mr Mac asks if I can meet that need too. Give me cricket and I give you everything, so wickets follow. I've got control – I can fire it onto a penny – and I've got variation: a breaker, a top-spinner and a googly, for when you play all day every day you have time to experiment and the opportunity to fine-tune. Because of my height the bounce is another weapon; check the batsman's face when he comes forward only to be hit in the ribs, or goes back to the next one and finds his middle stump knocked back by the top-spinner. I'm even asked to keep wicket a few times, and that's a deep joy and success too.

I don' like cricket. Mi love it.

Mr Mac is a purist. He likes his batsmen playing straight, so my driving through the 'V' between mid-off and mid-on works for him, as does my preference for playing it along the turf. As my body fills out from skinny kid to muscular youth and the hitting cranks up in power and destruction, the Excelsior motto – 'Do It With Thy Might!' – becomes my own mission.

There is a 30-over competition called the Tappin Cup. We reach three consecutive finals, Kevin Murray captaining the side in one, me in the other two. I'm named man of the match in all three. Against Kingston College, one of the posh and favoured, I crash the ball all over Melbourne Park, my new muscular style carving out a big hundred. In another, also against Kingston College, I make 99 not out, playing out a maiden in the penultimate over with victory already in the bag.

There is a sign on the front wall of the school that reads, 'Be Extraordinary!' Who says I have a problem with authority, that I can't do what I'm told?

Character comes from being tested. In a big cup quarter-final, we are beaten by Jonathan Grant High School, up the road in Spanish Town, who are led by a future Jamaica captain, Tamar Lambert. Mr Mac calls the team in for a post-mortem after the final wicket goes down.

'Where is Chris?'

'Sir! Chris gone!'

I am so upset at losing that I have run off in tears. I didn't want to lose that match, to be beaten by that team. I don't think I can show any emotion, so my way of dealing with it is to run away. I can't bear the thought of Mr Mac and the team seeing me like this.

Another crushing defeat comes in the semis of the Sunlight Cup, the island's main inter-school competition, in my final year. Mr Mac sits down the entire squad and asks everyone to give their reflections on the year. As I'm captain I'm last to speak. I stand up.

'I alone is not able to do it.'

Mr Mac pulls me aside. 'Lissen. You're a future Jamaica captain. You're a future West Indies captain. So lissen.

'You made hundreds, so somebody batted with you. You took wickets, so somebody took a catch for you. You took catches, so someone found the edge for you. You are leading a team, not a solo mission.'

It hurts, but I take it in. Mr Mac never condemns. He aims instead to guide, to enhance, to bring out our best qualities. Trophies sometime come, sometime don't. This is about life after trophies: helping your brother, your mother and father; becoming a better man than you were before, having the strength and skills to get you through whatever might come next.

In ninth grade I am sitting an exam when rumours start slinging around.

'Chris, he call up by Wes' Indies' A team.'

'Christopher Gayle, he fi get a call!'

I don't believe it. I've never played a first-class game. I've never played for Jamaica in any kind of match.

It's fitting that Mr Mac is the one to confirm it, and the one to organize a happy send-off, a little celebration. Two days later I'm off, on a plane, just me alone, flying to India for the first time.

And suddenly everything is different. Instead of my old mate Kevin Murray as my captain, it's Ian Bishop – 161 wickets in 41 Tests – and instead of Mr Mac as coach, it's Roger Harper, maybe the greatest fielder in West Indies history. Instead of the familiar fields of Lucas and Excelsior, strange stadiums and ear-shaking noise and chanting. When one of their guys hits a boundary, whoah! The noise, the smells, the food. Standing on the outfield for a day and a half, guts churning, sweat pouring, knees knocking.

Confidence comes from character. Character comes from being tested. And I come through.

I score 43 in my first match, at the vast Nehru Stadium in Pune, make my first acquaintance with the M. Chinnaswamy Stadium in Bangalore, where many years later I will pepper the stands in the IPL colours of RCB, and end the one-day series with a not out 70. More valuable than any of those runs is the experience. Without being tested you can never grow. Without fighting as a boy you cannot become a man. A better player, a better person, ready for what lies ahead.

We are gladiators, here to entertain. 2004, my 100th one-day international, into the lion's den of England at Lord's.

Whoever wins gets through to the final of the NatWest series. At 280-3, Freddie Flintoff and Andrew Strauss both on unbeaten centuries with their partnership at 226, that team is England. I've gone for 52 off my first nine overs without taking a wicket as Brian Lara throws me the ball for my tenth and last. What's left to try?

There is no try, only do. Freddie, caught by Ian Bradshaw at cover off my second ball. Strauss, pouched by Darren Bravo off my fourth. Paul Collingwood, gone to my fifth.

Three wickets in four balls, England from cruising to collapse.

To the crease. It's a serious England pace bowling attack. Darren Gough, Steve Harmison, Jimmy Anderson. Devon Smith goes early, but confidence runs deep. See off the shine, look for the gaps. Hammer the bad balls. Ramnaresh Sarwan at the other end and in the stands all around the shouting and the flag-waving of the big West Indian support you can always count on in London.

I bat deep and I bat with the magic at my side. To my century with a sprinted single, just to prove I can if I need to, strolling on 132 not out, the match won by seven wickets. And we walk a lap, looking up at the black and brown faces who will be walking into offices and factories in the morning with their heads held high, and it is a happy day. Hey Mr Mac – that one's for you . . .

I entertain because I am a cricketer. As a cricketer my energy comes from being in the middle. If I can't bat, then give me the ball.

Freddie and Strauss that day at Lord's, all the big guns on others. Sachin, Ricky Ponting, in my pocket. Jacques Kallis, you're in my pocket. Kevin Pietersen – in my pocket. Brian Lara – you're in my pocket too. *Trus mi, him nuh know wah him a chat 'bout . . .*

You can stand at first slip for an entire day. That's just boring. And first slip's the lucky one – you could be at mid-on or deep midwicket, nowhere at all to be found. Out on the boundary, just making up numbers, the invisible man.

When I'm bowling I'm alive. When I'm bowling I'm like the spider luring the fly into the web. Get a good grip on the ball, give it a good rip. Think you can hit this one? Fine. This one? Okay. *Here it is, com' an' get it . . .*

It doesn't hurt me to be hit for six. You hit me for a six, then fine. It just gives me more chance to think how to get you out, and the challenge is what makes my heart beat and blood run. I would rather be hit for six than bowl to batsmen who are blocking, blocking, blocking. Yes, you hit me for a couple of sixes; in my mind I'm going to give it back to you. There can only be two endings to your story: you hit me out of the attack, or I get you out. The boring guys? You won't see me. 'Skipper, I'm not bowling any more to this guy. . . . Batsman! You're boring me! I can't take it!'

It's not all swagger. It's not all me taking this team apart. I can kill you with a slow death. I'll find pleasure in sending you off, but I'll find pleasure in tying you down too. If Skipper come to me and say, we're leaking runs, we need you to be the dam, I don't mind at all. I'm very accurate, and I can keep it super tight when the team needs call. When I play one-day matches I'll bowl every time in the Powerplay, and every time I'm guaranteed two wickets.

When you bowl, you can't just turn over the arm for argument's sake. You have to bowl off a *riddim*. And when you do you just feel a vibe, and I love that. Even if it's just two or three overs, I want to feel that vibe. Sometime in Test matches I've sent down more overs than the men who've been picked to bowl. Fire in 30 overs and then go out there and open the batting as well. But I'm involved in the game, so I'm happy.

Home sweet home for the young Chris Gayle, my mum, my dad, a sister and three brothers. Us five kids shared one bedroom and two beds

I grew up listening to the sound of balls hitting zinc fences. The front of my childhood home, with the boy become a man. Good Jamaican colours

Directly across the street from 1C St James Road.
Where that patched-up section now stands was a hole.
Beyond that was Lucas Cricket Club. A scrubby wall
to some, for me a gateway to another world

You might think us lucky to have one of the great spiritual homes of West Indian cricket on our doorstep. Well, we didn't. We had two. Lucas's arch-rivals and next-door neighbours, Kensington. Start booing now

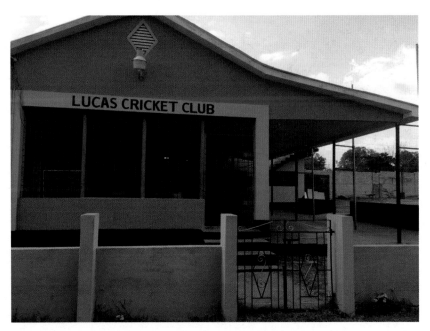

Lucas Cricket Club, 100 years old. The first club in the country where poor black men could play the ruling whites, the reason I made it in cricket. Bars on the windows to keep out the bad men

I used to love running up that rusty ladder to score the Lucas board. Through the hole in the fence, first boy to the top. I dreamed of my name hanging off those hooks

Jump a fence, steal some bottles, take them to Lecky's for the deposit, fill your hungry belly with food

They liked their rules at Rollington Town primary school. They
also loved their cricket. I'll be honest, we did do some shouting

The fantastic Miss Hamilton, my primary school teacher and first proper
cricket coach. She could bowl serious fast. I owe her so much.

A shy boy, a boy
who wouldn't say much
to anyone. You'll have to
trust me on this one

Of course I'm smiling – that's the West
Indies crest on my shirt. Plus I've just seen
the senior players going to a nightclub,
and I've invited myself along

Happy days with Lucas, winning the All-Island Rothman's Cricket Trophy.
Me moody fourth from right at back, little brother Wayne second left on
the front. Big trophy, bigger party

Do we look tired? A 435-run partnership gives a young man a lift as well as a licking. Me and Leon Garrick loved to bat together and loved to party in partnership even more

It's all about the vest and hat combo in Rollington Town. Me and childhood best mate John Murphy, boys all grown up but still united

When I was growing up the nets never had nets.
Time to put that right

Mum Hazel, dad Dudley. I'm jealous of my parents.
I'll never have a kid as cool as theirs

And when the wickets come it is pure pleasure. A Test five-for against Pakistan in Barbados, and a 5-34 against England at Edgbaston when they were a team on the mighty rise. More joyful still was in a one-dayer against England at Trent Bridge back in 2000, me just a lanky crampy 20-year-old, the West Indies on a run of 12 overseas one-day defeats on the bounce. With England only needing five off the final over, with Alec Stewart unbeaten on 100 and three wickets in hand, it should have been 13.

It comes down to confidence. I look at the scoreboard, look at the scenario and signal to our captain Jimmy Adams. 'Lemme bowl dis over.' The model is that the strike bowler gets the last one, but I'm persistent. The model is also that we have no hope, but models are for dancing with not listening to.

Time for some yorkers. Time for some darts. First ball, speared in, batsman trapped, panics for a single, gets himself run out. Second ball, yorker, leg bye. Four needed from four balls. Third ball, classic yorker, Darren Gough's stumps all over the shop. Fourth ball, Alan Mullally very lucky not to be given lbw. Fifth ball, Alan Mullally not so lucky, game over.

In some ways I miss bowling fast. As a kid I loved bowling the short nasty stuff from my 6 feet 4 inches – not necessarily to get the batsman out, but to hear the ping as the ball came off his helmet. And I hit guys. I touched a few chins. It didn't upset me; it's part of the game. As a youngster you find these things fun. It doesn't make sense bowling fast if you're not touching anybody.

I had a nice smooth action, just very simple. I could imitate Curtly Ambrose, bowling arm reaching up high, the jerk of the wrist. Dangerous, man. Steep. Good bounce. Good pace. *Blood spill on di pitch an' dem sorta tings, yeah?*

The role models were all quicks. There were a few spinners in the West Indies or Jamaica teams – Roger Harper, Carl Hooper, Nehemiah Perry with a little off spin; a little leg spin from Dinanath Ramnarine or Mahendra Nagamootoo – but they were not always in the action. And when you played on the concrete in front of the pavilion at Lucas, using a wet tennis ball so it comes at the batsman like a bullet, it's more fun making them jump than giving them non-spinning off-spinners. *Yuh cyaan bowl spin on dat – yuh get licks . . .*

I ended up doing spin because sometime I couldn't be bothered running that far. I know. Eventually it would have taken a toll on my body, because I'm doing everything then – bowling fast, opening the batting, captaining, fielding at first slip – but at the time it was just distance. There's a reason Jamaica produces sprinters rather than marathon runners.

And I took happiness in my preferred craft. I could still come in off my short run-up and bowl a quick one, but there was fresh pleasure in becoming obsessive about a new cricketing skill. You know the old pitches at Sabina Park? Cut, rolled, trimmed, rolled, shaved, rolled, wet, rolled, wet, polished. Looks like polished glass. Well, the pitches at Lucas would take a little more spin, at least after the fast bowlers had enjoyed the little moisture in it in the earlier part of the day. To begin with I was a flatter bowler, because in those early days I didn't like to give away anything. I didn't want to see my ball getting hit, so I was on a penny, just darting it in, darting it, darting it, bowling flat and fast. As I grew and played and grew and played I started to find my variations, to curve it more, to find the conjuring tricks and mind games to unsettle the unwary opponent.

And wickets came. My first victim in first-class cricket was a left-hander called Sadagoppan Ramesh, stumped off a ball that curved and spat like a snake. Sssss! *It jus' do dis an' then it do dat*. Pitch on leg and hit off, twisting him around. The first wicket for the West Indies, in that one-day tournament in Toronto, was a similar ball, another magic one, Saeed Anwar bitten by the same snake. I can take wickets with balls that spin and I can take them with those that don't; bowl five that go straight, and you only need to turn one an over to get them out.

You find your weapons and then you work out more. Some batters don't like the idea of getting out to a man they consider a part-timer. Part-timers don't send down almost 15,000 deliveries in international cricket, but them thinking like that is another weapon for me, so let them. So when they come to the crease we'll have a little talk, and I tell them I want them in my pocket. Once we're done with that, and they're thinking about something else than just hitting the ball, I'll ramp it up a little more. 'Skip! Bat-pad, silly point. Put everybody underneat' his bat!'

Now the batsman's thinking about even more. Some of them will try to blast you – fine. When Kevin Pietersen hit his first Test double century, I got him stumped when he had made just 20. Gave him the chat, showed him my web, lured him in. And the umpire looked at it and decided it was a no-ball. Kevin owes me for that one, and he knows it.

Other batsmen look at the gauntlet and refuse to touch it. That's equally good. Keep them housed. You can change the pace of the game as a spinner, finish an over in less than a minute. What a weapon! Turn round, go again, the match gone before you know it.

And it helps your batting. If as a spinner you get a guy jumping you and giving you a good hit, it takes you straight into revenge mode. It makes you aggressive, and it makes them want to hit boundaries. The challenge is on. When you think like a bowler, you expand your mind as a batsman. It's like being given the gift of mind-reading. You know exactly what the bowler is going to do, because it's exactly what you would have done yourself.

My energy comes from being in the middle. If I can't bat, if I can't bowl, let me wicket-keep. Wavell Hinds has made the call in the past – 'Lissen mi. Take off the pads. Give to Chris.' Brilliant. No sledging this time, just excited to be behind the stumps. Taking some stumpings, doing some damage. I used to study the West Indies' glovemen in case the chance come – Jeffrey Dujon, a beautiful wicket-keeper to watch, beautiful and easy; Ridley Jacobs, Mr Dependable, no technique but if he's dropped two catches in his career I can't recall them. *Yeah man. Him look ugly but him gettin' di job done.*

I've done all this in an era when fewer batsmen bowl. A few are scared to do it, because they're going to get hit and look small. Why be scared of what might happen? There's nothing at all happening at deep midwicket or mid-on. And who wants to spend their days with nothing at all?

I was always up for it, and I still am. Unfortunately these days sometime the captain doesn't give me the ball. I don't know why. I still fancy myself as the best off-spinner in the world.

We are gladiators, and gladiators always take a challenge. Even when they are wounded and other men fall.

We are on tour in South Africa in the winter of 2003/4. Just before the first Test a door slams on my finger, so I can't field at slip. I'm in the outfield, chasing all day, and this is doomsday. A ball flies past me and Wavell Hinds.

Something always has to be happening, so even though I hate running, we'll have a race to see who can reach it first. It's Wavell too, Kensington boy, so I put in a bit extra. From nowhere I hear the noise of a stick breaking. Why are there sticks on the outfield? The thought is barely popping before I'm on the deck. I grab my hamstring and scream out. It's the first time I ever experienced a tear, and I freak out a bit, and eventually they come and calm me down a bit and stretcher me off the field. I still go and bat with the one leg, strapped up and unable to move, and when Andre Nel gets me out he runs down the track, up into my face, all tongue sticking out and bad chat.

Now Andre Nel has issues. This particular South African believes there is a man living in his head, a man called Gunther, who takes over when he is angry. Gunther is angry because he is from the mountains in Germany, and when he was young he didn't get enough oxygen to his brain. Nel has said all this. He has also burst into tears on the pitch before, when he hit his childhood hero Allan Donald with a bouncer; he's been fined for smoking ganja on tour in the Caribbean, and he's been sent home from a tour of Australia after being caught drink-driving. He's also a trained accountant. And you thought I was complicated.

Anyway. *All in mi face an' dis an' dat*. And in my mind that pisses me off. I stare back at him and keep the mask on. 'Okay, no problem.' It looks like I've let it slide, but I've just placed it on ice. After the game he comes up and apologizes for what he has done, and I say, 'Okay, no problem,' knowing I'm saving it, and he will get all this back.

No man wins over the crowd by standing with his back to the wall. He does it through bravery and by thrilling.

I miss the second Test with the injury. By the third at Newlands in Cape Town I'm ready to say hello to Gunther again, even if the hamstring means I'm still batting on one leg.

Now when you're on one leg, you're going to play a few shots. When you've been simmering the revenge for almost a fortnight, it's got some serious taste to it. So that's how it all starts, playing a lot of shots, taking the attack to them, putting them under the pump.

I take some serious runs off Nel. Off Pollock, Ntini, Kallis and Adams, but particularly Nel. Where's Gunther now? All I can see is a white man with a red face, staring after his ball as it crashes into the fence.

I'm not running on that hamstring. No quick singles. I'm opening with Daren Ganga, and he's never going to be dabbing it to leg and calling me through, so let's pepper the boards.

Let's salt and pepper them and smear them in jerk seasoning. I get to 90 off 60 balls. Then I quiet myself down a little. I want this hundred. They've done some chasing, now to let them watch and enjoy.

When the hundred comes up – off 79 deliveries, 19 fours and a six, 82 of the runs in boundaries – I look over at Nel and bust a little move for him. A little Jamaican move called the Chaplin, a dancehall favourite that involves keeping one leg still and just twisting and stepping with the other one.

A little jig for Gunther, and it's all good fun. We're entertainers, after all.

6.   317

So World Boss like parties. Six Machine don't like running. But I'm a man of contradictions. I can turn it on in nightclubs across the continents and still be disciplined. I can stay out till break of dawn and sleep past midday and still be the hardest worker you'll know. I had to be disciplined or I'd never have made it out of Rollington Town. I had to be hard-working or I'd be back there now.

Another lesson from Mr Mac. My little brother Wayney was more gifted than I was. A natural talent in both bowling and batting; aged 14 he took five wickets with his fizzing leg spin for Lucas against the adults of Kingston in the Senior Cup. Wise men thought he would make it to the top, and faster than me.

He made it to captain of Lucas, but no further. Not serious enough. He loved his cricket, but not with obsession. Big brother Andrew was a regular for the Jamaica under-19 team and won the Senior Cup with Lucas, and that was enough for him.

Michael Crew, the most talented of all, up in the fast bowlers' faces all day? He'd be in their faces the day before too. One of his favourite tricks was to hunt down the opposition pacemen in the streets on the Friday before the match and tell them exactly what he was going to do to them. He would go over there to Kensington, even to fearsome Patrick Patterson, and tell them what's coming their way. 'I'm gonna kill yuh wit' licks!'

He was never going to change. That's who he was. I would be on the outfield with my friends, he would be at the rum bar on Giltress Street with his people. They still like him on our old streets and corners. He had some charm as well, the George Best of Rollington Town. But he's still doing his own thing, and that thing is drinking. When I'm playing cricket he'll come around, and he always asks for money. I give him what he asks for. It's not like he's doing drugs, so I give it to him.

I wasn't the perfect pupil. Popeye and I used to sneak through a hole in the fence to cut school. But we did it so we could go to play cricket. And we did. I would bat for hour after hour, even though I could take a couple of months off, pick up a bat and score a century, just like that. I would bat for days on that concrete, long, long, long. You don't do that if you don't have discipline. You don't do that if you can't work hard.

Michael Crew taught me other lessons. You got talent, all the bowlers on your day *gonna get perish*. On the other side, shit happens. You can be in the sweetest form, get a jaffa and you're gone. And when you're not in form, when the runs won't come, don't wait for someone else to fix it. 'Beat yuh way out of it.' Beat your way back in.

Only 24 men in almost 140 years of Test cricket have scored a triple century. But it's not just a landmark or a badge of honour, a club for the coolest cats with the mightiest bats. It's an endurance race, a strange form of mental torture, both the ultimate solo mission and a series of vital relationships, some with people you love, some with people you share nothing else with at all.

I've always done well against South Africa. I had a golden period from the start of 2004 to the end of 2007 when I averaged 68 against them in Tests and 52 in one-day internationals. Towards the end of that sweet spell I mash them too for the first international T20 century in history.

At the start of the 2005 season none of that was on my mind. I missed the first Test of their tour to the Caribbean over a contract dispute, and that was about as good as it got. In the second Test I made just six and one, the small consolation being that at least it was Makhaya Ntini who got me out both times rather than Andre Nel. And then we go to Barbados for the third Test and Nel gets me for a duck in the first innings, one of four wickets, before taking six more in the second innings. Ntini got me second time around, this time for five, but there could be no consolation, not when Nel had career-best match figures of 10 for 88. Welcome back, Gunther. It's your day in the sun.

To Antigua for the fourth Test. Nel is out injured, his back playing up, probably as a result of carrying two personalities on it. Sir Gary Sobers is around the West Indies team, and we will sit down and he and I will talk cricket, but there is something else on my mind: my mum is sick, in serious trouble with diabetes and high blood pressure, and I pack my bags to fly home. The team won't miss me, not when I've scored an aggregate of 12 runs in four innings.

Two things happen. I wake up on the morning of the match to a message that Mum is on the mend. Slowly, but there is improvement. She wants me to stay, and in that moment I feel light where there has only been darkness. Then, thinking about family, I remember Michael Crew. 'Beat yuh way out of it.'

On that compact ground it is a long first day. South Africa bat on, centuries for the openers, Graeme Smith and

A. B. de Villiers. The second day is even longer; they bat on and on again, hundreds too for Jacques Kallis and Ashwell Prince. Not until the third day do they declare, 588 runs on, a whole lot of licks.

I've bowled 31 overs, more than all but one of our proper attack. I've kept it tight with my darts and gone for only two an over, but the real job is still to come, and when you've been in the sun-baked field for two and a half days and then have to go out again and open the batting, your mind can be weary and your reactions just that little bit dulled. And so it is for my opening partner, Wavell Hinds, gone for a golden duck to that man Ntini again. Two and a half days of waiting and gone first ball.

South Africa now crank up the attack even more. The mountain for us to climb is so high you can't even see the summit. We're barely in the foothills and we're a man down, so they wind up some spicy fields and have catchers and men in close all around.

Oh-kay. Don't stand with your back to the wall or try to run away. Take them on. Beat your way back in.

I hit some balls spicy over point, down to the boundary for four. I slash some balls down to third man. And they still keep the field up and be attacking still, even as I reach my 50 off 34 balls, 42 of the runs in boundaries.

They're expecting chances. I'm a strolling wicket. They're defending a mountain. So men stay up attacking, and I keep hitting it over their heads. You play some more shots. It comes on. You start working some balls, flying off through point for four, some balls fly here, some balls fly there. They're still not changing the field or anything, still hoping I might give them the chance, and by the time they realize it's too late – I've flown past 100, 16 fours, three sixes.

And as I look up at the scoreboard, and down the other end at my partner, Sarwan, I realize my game has come back to me. From nowhere the magic is at my side. I'm dictating where I want to score, when I want to score, all around the wicket, off everything this attack can throw at me. *Big up, Michael Crew.*

I'm in command, and the aggressive part calms down a bit. I just bat naturally, cruise along and just bat and bat and bat. Lucas and the concrete strip, all over again.

South Africans don't like to back down. They don't like to be taken on. The field is kept offensive, and the ball keeps finding the gaps. 150 up, Sarwan to his own slow and steady century, the bowlers toiling toiling, the old nightmares of the preceding Tests forgotten in the dust and heat and rat-a-tat-tat of ball on boundary boards.

Mr Mac was right in so many ways. If you make hundreds, someone is batting with you. Sarwan and I are old comrades, and we love to bat together. We watch each other and give a little advice here and there; our styles mesh, and our pace and personalities complement and comfort. We get together between overs as the minutes turn into hours and the hours into sessions and days, and we plan how we will take this even further.

Batting long is as much about what you do when the ball not coming at you as when it is. The non-striker's end is your safe place, your opportunity to analyse the bowlers and the field and their body language free of heavier thought. You are in the game but not in the game, more aware of all the detail and nuance around you and able to plot it and plan it as you advance.

The 200 come. Both a wonderful feeling and a weary one. You have been batting for ever, and your body is ringing bells. Your bat feels heavy. You're not drinking enough water, you're not eating. You can't eat, not even in the dressing-room at lunch or at tea, because your appetite has gone. Your body will shut down the need for food when the battle rages on. Afterwards, when it is all done, it will come racing back in with a vengeance. You'll want to eat everything, pile more and more on your plate. *Dyamn me hungry!* And you'll sleep like a king, like a dead man king. But for now you can only pick at your food. You just want to put your feet up and shut your eyes for a while. Maybe a piece of fruit, *taste a likkle ting*, but no more.

Sarwan goes for 127. Brian Charles Lara comes in and goes for just four. There's your reminder. Nothing can be taken for granted. There is a match to be saved, there are runs that only you can score.

When you're at 230, you can feel it. A long way from the start, a long way from a landmark. On even from the 405-stand with Leon Garrick at Montego Bay. You're trying not to think about triple centuries, even though this is where Lara scored his 375. You're just batting and batting, just as you've always done. Your energy comes from being in the middle.

South Africa are weary. Their earlier hostility and conviction are long since gone. Captain Smith is at first sacrificial, bowling over after over of wobbly spin himself, and then desperate – not only do the batsmen get a bowl, but so does the wicketkeeper, Mark Boucher. You can mock it, but Boucher does enough to get rid of Dwayne Bravo. You can never relax.

250. 494 minutes I've been batting now. Aches and pains everywhere, your bat feeling like a railway sleeper. Don't think about the ice-bath, don't think about the

massage. Watch the ball and let your natural instinct take you there.

Evening on the fourth day. I've been involved in almost every over, bowling, standing at first slip, standing tall at the crease. We've climbed the mountain, and we're pushing on to a peak beyond. The total goes past 600, rattles on to 700.

When I am on 298, Smith brings on De Villiers. A part-timer, right-arm military medium, going round the wicket, the ball coming into my legs. A thought: 'Easy pickings.' A push square, and there it is.

There is nothing left in my legs but I jump high and punch the sky. Mrs Hazel G, your son sends you best wishes. This work's for you. Helmet off, bat in the other hand, raise both and let the sweet feelings rush in.

On 317 I get caught at slip. Graeme Smith and his hands there, taking some rest, only one man anywhere in the field in a catching slot now, and the nick goes straight to him and he catch it.

There are no regrets. I haven't been thinking of all the scores I have been passing, all the records that are within reach. I don't hunt records. I was just batting, doing what comes naturally, doing what I was born to do and raised doing daily. I wasn't even thinking about 375. If it comes it comes. That's how it is.

I am just grateful. There are blisters on my feet and a hunger in my belly, but there is a deep satisfaction too. Critics have said I'm not a Test player. Critics have said I'm too loose, that I'm lazy, that I don't care. Look at the board now. That's the first ever lazy loose Test triple century, is it?

You keep that feeling within yourself. You are a gladiator, and you can never show what lies behind the mask. Yet something has changed in you. You realize you have done something marvellous, that you have achieved something most have not. And it bleeds into other areas of your life. You know you've passed a brutal examination, and it establishes a deep-rooted confidence inside. When the challenge came, you were ready.

Some players do care about records.

When Brian Lara was out for four in that match, he sat in the dressing-room and read a book. Occasionally he would go out onto the balcony and check the scoreboard, then go back inside. Sarwan was watching him, because he was wondering. And every time Brian came out to see my score getting closer to his record, he looked more and more worried.

When I came in for lunch and tea he didn't say anything to me. No advice, no 'Keep it going,' no 'Do it for the team.' When I went back out he would go back to that slow shuttle: read inside on his own for a bit, come out to check my score, look worried.

There was a point in my life when Lara was the only batsman I would watch. The way he scored his runs, that attacking style, a joy to watch when he was on the go. Good hand-speed, so quick, jumping across the crease yet still balanced in every way, able to score wherever he chose. Wearing down bowlers, calculating his innings. He knew who he wanted to score off and when he wanted to score. Which particular bowler to target, which one to take more chances off, which one to avoid. And the dominance and world-beating all came from that.

But he was not my primary inspiration, and he was not my first.

Delroy Morgan. The best opening batsman I think Jamaica has seen. If you haven't heard of him, it's because you've heard of Gordon Greenidge and Desmond Haynes instead. Without that all-time legend partnership, Delroy Morgan is 50 Test matches in and everyone sees what I saw.

When I got in early to Lucas to score the board, it was Delroy and his sweet style that I was going to see. Delroy and my brother Michael Crew, the sweetness and the spice, the rapier and the wrecking-ball. I would sneak out of school early and dash across town to Sabina Park to see him laying waste for Jamaica – blagging a ticket from somewhere, finding my way in through a gap or a ruse or a friendly face on the gate. Always to the same spot, the George Headley Stand, as close as you could get to the team's dressing-room. The only place to be: a Lucas boy, watching a Lucas man, under the name of a Lucas legend.

I would sit there nervous for him, because I didn't want him to get out. I wanted him to perform. And when Delroy Morgan performs, the textbook purrs. Textbook for every single shot. High elbow, on-drive the best in the Caribbean. Best cover drive. When he cover drives, oh man! A brilliant fielder in the slips, in at bat-pad, taking catches others might just hope for and some that others could never conceive of. *Axe anyone 'bout Delroy Morgan. Unbelievable!*

There was a big, big scoreboard at Sabina Park. I used to look at Delroy Morgan's name on that board, and I'd think: one day. One day I will see my name on that.

And then the day comes when we opened the batting together for Lucas. He gave me a bat to match his – a Gray-Nicolls, a Dynadrive, one of the best bats I've ever used, two scoops out of the back, light and powerful. I'm still at school, and I'm playing with Delroy Morgan and his sweet bat. Very little that comes after can match up to that.

In 1999, just as my international career was about to start, we were part of the Lucas team that won the Senior Cup. In the final match of the season, against Leon Garrick's Middlesex team, Delroy hit 112 and I took four wickets. When they followed on, I got rid of Leon in the best way possible. Garrick, caught Morgan, bowled Gayle.

Later I would start to watch a bit of television, and I would notice Brian and his flamboyance. But only after Delroy Morgan.

There were other role models and heroes. Walter Boyd, the former Jamaica striker, a maverick and a magician. Dwight Yorke, because he was representing the Caribbean across the world. Michael Jordan and Dennis Rodman.

There was a window when basketball went big in Jamaica, and despite Kingston-born Pat Ewing being the man at the Knicks, it was the Bulls who rocked our worlds. When the NBA finals were on you would come home from school and pile to whoever's house had the TV and the access. I loved how Rodman looked and I loved how he operated on the court, totally different to anyone else. *Worm, him up in yuh face!* And I loved Jordan, not just for the success but for the way he went about playing. Taking over a game, winning it at the death, winning Game Five of the '97 finals sick as a lame dog, having the confidence in himself to deliver and the character to always come through. I watched a documentary where he said, 'Lissen man, I can shoot a free throw with my eyes closed.' And he did. Doing things only he could get away with, doing things that no one else would even try.

And so it was different with Brian Charles Lara. I'm proud that I played 52 of my 103 Test matches with him. I salute his skills. When I got the call to go to Toronto for my West Indies debut and suddenly you're in a dressing-room a few pegs down from B. C. Lara, it's another something special to lock away inside.

But he was different. He was moody. I never sat down and talked cricket with him, partly because I'm just a quiet person at times, just laid back and happy to observe, but also because you never knew what to expect from him. Sometimes you tell him good morning and you don't even get a reply. Some people put him on a pedestal. For sure he had done his thing to be recognized, and you had to give him credit. Yet I didn't believe we should accept it was just the way he was; I just thought, fine, you just don't get another good morning from me. Leave him to it. Most people don't interfere with him, and he'll just have his own way. He go left, you just go right. As simple as it is.

He got crazy amounts of attention. Everybody came to see Lara. He was the one selling tickets, and you could understand it. On the pitch he could do crazy things; when he scored his 400, I batted with him for a while, and it was fun.

I'm pleased for him. But you have to look after your own performance, so my main memory of that day was that I got out for 69. There was a century there waiting for me, trust me. I got out just before lunch, so I was scoring quickly, almost a run a ball. Caught and bowled. And that's one of the worst ways to get out.

Lara's motivation came from chasing records. Jordan's came from refusing to accept defeat. Rodman was at war with authority, Michael Crew at war with the world.

You take it where you can. Some take it from rivalries. Me against you, my strength against yours. I'm not a man who likes to get angry. I don't like to hold a grudge. *Jus' breathe. Breathe an' let the stress an' anger go.*

I'm not a man to have rivals. But I'm from Rollington Town. If you say something to me, then it's my turn to say something back. I'm not going to stop. And what I say will hurt you. Be prepared to get what you give.

The semi-final of the ICC Champions Trophy against Australia. October 2006, Mumbai. Batting first, we are in trouble at 63-4. Then in comes Runako Morton, my mad bad Morton, and his unbeaten 90 rescues us to 234.

Still, Australia are cruising in reply. Adam Gilchrist's flaying it. I come on to bowl to Michael Clarke, and suddenly he decides he wants to spark a fire.

'Lara's been speaking to me. He thinks you're an idiot. He hates having you in the team.'

Now Clarke likes his aggressive chat. Remember him to James Anderson in the Ashes of 2013/14: 'Get ready for a fuckin' broken arm.' But usually the Aussies keep their sledging for other nations. They know not to cross the West Indies' path. Because we don't take that bullshit.

They became world-beaters, so they feel high and mighty. So that's how they're going to try to come across. But they couldn't dream of coming up like we did, of going through what we've been through. South Sydney is not east Kingston. They might be rude but they ain't tough, I can tell you that. And whether us West Indians are the number one team or the lowest-ranked team, we're just not going to take your bullshit. *Nah gonna tolerate it*. Straight. It doesn't matter who. And they know it.

So I start giving it back to Clarke. *Up in his face an' every ting like dat*.

Andrew Symonds starts giving it to me too. Now that's fine, because I used to love giving it to him, give him talks and barbs. In his team he feels like the tough guy, because he's from the Queensland sticks and he fancies himself as a hunter. *Well, he ain't tougher dan me, know whatta mean?* He might chase a wild pig or a wild animal somewhere, but we chase other things. He hunts animals, we hunt something better looking.

So now the umpires come over, telling me I *cyaan* do this, I *cyaan* do that. But I'm not stopping. They started it, let me finish it then.

Now I get Andrew Symonds out, clean bowled for a slow and dull 18. Clarke's still in there. The ball goes to short extra cover off my bowling, I sprint over, pick it up and throw it at his head, and it goes over the keeper and away for four more runs. *Aaaall happenin' out dere!* He's laughing and whooping, but the aggression and the battle has totally changed the whole entire energy on the pitch. Lara has gone off the field and Sarwan taken over as skipper, and it's like we're a different team.

We're not going to take your bullshit. Wavell and I run out Adam Gilchrist, and then Dwayne Bravo gets Clarke caught and bowled, and then Jerome Taylor comes charging in with fire in his eyes and smoke coming from his ears and cleans out the three last standing, bowled, bowled, lbw. A game that was lost has been saved, and we let them know, we let them know in a way they can't miss it. *Everybody jumpin' up in dem face an' dis an' dat.*

I was the only one who got fined in the aftermath. Thirty per cent of my match fee, which was both ridiculous and harsh, because I wasn't the one who started it. But such is life, huh? I say some stuff you *cyaan* even repeat. And I won the battle, even if I lost the pocket.

So you can see why I never really get sledged. I just love to play against the top teams – South Africa, England, Australia – and when I started, those were the ones I wanted to beat ball. Sometime I would get carried away and fall in a trap because I wanted so badly to beat the best. But you have to put these boys under the pump. Put the batsmen under. Put the bowlers under. Get two batsmen going berserk, and they will crumble.

And don't mess with West Indians.

The T20 World Cup in 2014. Australia again, and this time it's James Faulkner making a fool comment. Don't say you don't like West Indians, not any time, and definitely not the day before you're meeting them on the cricket pitch. Our whole team is sparked up, our whole team breathing fire.

They bat first and make 178. Faulkner goes for a slow 13, but the bad luck hasn't started yet. I open with Dwayne Smith, and off the first 14 balls I face I mash them for 40. On to 53 before holing out to deep midwicket, and then the baton passes to Dwayne Bravo and captain Darren Sammy. Runs come but so do overs pass, until 12 are needed off the final six balls. And who's to bowl? James Faulkner . . .

Sammy on strike. First ball, dot. Second ball, dot. Twelve needed off four. Faulkner's going to be the hero.

Until he bowls a full toss, which Sammy sends over long-on for six. And then another in the slot, which Sammy slams over the same spot and way, way back.

As the ball sails I run out onto the field, punching the air, punching the sky, jumping up *an' all sort*, everybody celebrating, everybody up in their faces. Bravo and me together, rocking the Gangnam dance, but an angry Gangnam, a gangsta Gangnam.

I tweeted afterwards. 'When you come to shoot – shoot, Don't TALK!' Kieron Pollard followed up. 'Chat too much! Talk . . . nah! Faulk . . . nah!'

A few months later I was chatting about it all with their captain, George Bailey. And he said, 'When I saw you running onto the field, I thought you were going to fight us! If you could have seen the look in your eyes . . .'

A sweet victory, a sweet sweet victory. And all because Faulkner gave us that spark.

So remember. Don't play hard with men harder than you. The only hard that's going to help you is work.

And if you feel that anger, let it go. Breathe and let the stress and anger go. You can't live in the darkness.

Sometime I look at my World Boss nickname, and I like it. Other time I look at it, and I look what I have achieved in the game, and I think, how about Universe Boss?

I'm the Six Machine, and my vision is Twenty20. More runs in the world's biggest format than anyone else, one and a half thousand more and counting. The highest ever score. More centuries than any other player, by a multiple of three. The highest career average, the fastest hundred. Career sixes? Way out the back of 500, more than double anyone else.

That's a long bill. And it's not like I'm finished as well. I'm going to be building on those. I'm going to be constructing bigger milestones.

The Tsar of T20, the boss of the boundary boards. I've been called a pioneer, and I'll take that word, even though I'd put it another way: I'm a legend. Most people wouldn't call themselves that, but I think I am great. Put it more simply: I *am* great. The things I've done, *trus' mi*. Serious things I've done.

You might think I'm being big-headed. But those people just don't want to give you the full credit for what you deserve. I would ask them, what do I have to do to be great? I would wait for their answer. I just want their answer. Then I would say, is that it?

People think they understand T20. A little dash round the park. An easy hour or two for men too old or rich to care about the proper format. A slog and a bash and a mow that's ugly and ill, a rude proposition rather than a long slow seduction.

Lissen mi. T20 is the most intense experience in cricket. T20 is a crash of hormone through the brain, a blast of electricity through the heart, an old calypso classic mashed up dancehall style.

As a batsman there is no rest, and there is no recovery. On red alert at all times, your mind always racing one step ahead of the bowlers. As a bowler it's now or it's never – locked on target from ball one, no time to reassess, only four overs to strike, only four overs to fox and fool. You've got to be quick. *Yuh gotta be boom!*

And you've got to be smart. Wild swinging won't win you games. It's not Test cricket, but it's still ball onto sweet spot of bat, and that means having a look – at the pitch, at the bowler, at what the ball is doing.

Occasionally it can happen that I get a loose one first ball, and that can give you momentum as early as possible, and you can jump them. Sometime you can try to jump them in the first over anyway, but more so than often it doesn't work for me. Play what you know will actually score runs. I tear attacks to pieces, but I stalk my prey first.

You have to calculate. You analyse the bowling attack. 'Right, these two, they'll bowl two overs. Occasionally this one, he'll bowl three overs to try get me out.' You work it out, do the maths. 'You must com' bowl. *You* must com' bowl. I know I can take twelve off his over. Fifteen off his. Take him down for a big over.'

I analyse every bowler. I analyse the entire game. Who am I up against? How can they hurt me? How can I hurt them more?

You learn the game every time you go out there.

★

You learn the game from way back.

People think T20 started in 2003. At Lucas we are playing it from knee-high, just as we are playing 15-over games and 10-over games. Not to do with marketing for us, or attracting new fans to cricket, for we are all disciples and preachers already, but for a more natural reason: night is falling, and we have to squeeze in a match.

Five overs a side. Cut it and chop it as you like, three players a side, eight or 15. We will play it fast and we will play it hard, proper shots and proper bowling, on the grass under the old scoreboard or under the tin roof of the pavilion veranda. *It like we have dat vision, before it com' to perfection.*

You learn the game through youth. When we are at Excelsior, a nationwide competition called the Hotel League is established. Each of the big swish tourist hotels acts as a franchise, their team made up of seven employees, two big-name guest players and a couple of promising schoolboys. Thirty-five overs a side, four weeks of matches, and Popeye and I get the call-up from the Boscobel, an all-inclusive private resort on the north coast, a private resort with its own beach and championship golf course and waterpark and seven of its own restaurants.

The cricket is competitive and fast. The journey out there on Sunday nights after a match for Lucas is long and slow: jump in a taxi-bus from outside school out west to Spanish Town, change into another for the hour and a half drive north to Ocho Rios, change again to bounce along the coast east. Sometimes you can't even feel your legs when you get out of the taxi. You can't even walk. *Yuh legs dead!*

Oh, but when you get there . . . Popeye and me are sharing a room, but it's a room that's part of the resort. It's a room that's bigger than our house, that has a television the size of a window, and a window that looks out to the private beach. Where we can go and eat cheeseburgers for free, and then order some rum punches, and order another cheeseburger, and wash off the dust of the Rollington Town streets in the jacuzzi, and say hello to a few of the female guests who probably haven't had the chance to mix with many authentic Jamaican boys yet.

An all-inclusive hotel, and they put two schoolers in it? *Cyatch me if you can . . .*

I don't even sleep! Making sure I close the bar at night, making sure I eat enough to make up for the next five nights, feeling like a pro, feeling like any moment someone might pull the plug so let's fill our boots.

And we are professionals. We are getting paid, an amazing £14 or so per match, and we are performing, getting the job done in the middle for the Boscobel boys. The two of us open, and Popeye is the ball-beater, crashing it all over, and me, still the shy boy until I get to the middle, I play it longer. Having a look, playing it through the 'V', keeping it technically pleasing.

We reach the semi-final, win that, and then the dream accelerates again: with a week to go until the final, we get to stay at the resort all week. No more sharing a bed or a concrete floor, no more Nutribun or stealing mangoes. They bring the mangoes to your table here, and they don't slice them with ratchet knives. 'Hey waiter! Bring me two cheeseburger. T'anks!'

Franchise life. And, fuelled on the good stuff and running on good vibes, we win the final for Boscobel too, and the long taxi back with Popeye is a journey of sighs and belches and 'Dat really happen, yeah?'

So no one has ever been more ready for a so-call new format when it comes around these years later. Except the first time I play an official T20 match, it's not just underwhelming but under water. Something called the International 20:20 Championship, but don't be fooled; while there are teams from Pakistan and South Africa, there is no one from India or Australia or the West Indies or New Zealand, not least because there has yet to be a domestic T20 competition in those countries.

I'm playing for a Professional Cricketers Association select XI. Among my team-mates is a 39-year-old Phil DeFreitas, 10 years after he last played a Test match for England, and Robin Singh, the Indian all-rounder who had got me out in my very first appearance for the West Indies, but who is now 42 years old. It is mid-September, and we are in Leicester.

Because we are in Leicester and it is mid-September, it keeps raining. The tournament is only supposed to last three days, which is probably a good thing, otherwise we better start building boat.

The opposition is a club from Sri Lanka called Chilaw Marians. We start in the rain. I bowl one over, which includes two wides and goes for 16 runs. The rain forces us off, and carries on hard. After several hours of hiding in the pavilion looking for extra layers, the match is abandoned. I don't get to put my pads on, let alone bat.

Later, in some puddles, there will be a bowl-off which we lose 6-2. I'm not involved. Neither am I involved for our second fixture, against a club from South Africa called Titans, because that one is abandoned without a ball being bowled.

All glamour, dis Twenty20 ting.

So it's hardly a surprise that no one saw the revolution coming. Had you told me on that cold autumn day, in an empty Grace Road, surrounded by retired old pros and umpires in wellington boots, that this was the start of something that would not only transform my world but shake up cricket like nothing else in 140 years, that would trigger big money and huge crowds and crazy noise and posh hotels and me being called the Bradman of the times . . . I would have laughed in your face, and then asked you if there was a shop nearby that sold warm coats.

No one was taking it seriously. When they stage the first ever T20 international in February 2005, New Zealand and Australia walk out at Eden Park wearing retro kit and big 1970s moustaches. Glenn McGrath bowls a ball underarm in mock tribute to Trevor Chappell's famous dodgy deed, and umpire Billy Bowden shows him a red card.

I watched, and I thought of the Lucas games, and I thought of the Leicester lazing about, and I thought, 'Wooo, easy! Easy cricket!'

But then I played a game for real, and every ball I seemed to have to run between the wickets. Man, after two overs I was blowing. 'Whoah, is this really easy cricket?' I had thought, I don't have to practise for this, I don't have to train for this, I don't have to run for this. After that game my eyes were opened, and I changed my style. 'Oh-kay, dis see-rious. Short an' spicy but serious. An' very, very intense . . .'

I looked into it some more. 'Okay, so we got to try and score off every single delivery.' And have to run for everything, because every run counts. Going hard from ball one, swinging your arms, letting go your bat. We would just go out there and say, 'Lissen mi, it's runs for runs. Whoever score the most runs win.' No tactical thoughts, just a slug-fest. 'Beat ball, beat ball.'

Then you start to learn the game. 'Hold it, I can face a maiden over an' still win di game. I can face two maiden overs an' still score a hundred.' Give yourself a little feel, give yourself a couple of balls.

You learn what you can do, and how much damage you can do when. So now we're looking at the bigger picture. Twenty overs, 120 deliveries. How many runs you want to get off the first six? Then six to ten, 10 to 15. And you can just explode, when you want. That's the realization that is the game-changer: you can just explode.

With each month the hits and giggles became more ser-ious. The West Indies' first T20 international, my bowling now a weapon with two wickets and just 22 runs off my four overs, but New Zealand hitting a six and four off Ian Bradshaw's last over to take it to a tie, and then 20,000 boozy fans cheering Eden Park down as their boys win a bowl-off.

There was talk now among the players on the scene, but more about the pace of the game, about little ideas for tactics and tricks. The big money was still absent; you were still lucky to get US$1,000 per match. So no one was talking about new cars or new houses, or about Twitter feeds, or launching their own range of cologne, or signing up with a manufacturer of motorcycle oil so they could tap into the Indian market. We were just happy to play, to enjoy the fresh challenge and have fun. We had no idea what was in store of us.

The game matures. KP and his switch hit, M. S. Dhoni and his 'helicopter', Tillakaratne Dilshan and the 'Dilscoop'. I was chill about it – the reverse scoop was nothing new to me; we'd played it as kids, and I'd used it in Test matches and one-dayers. But I didn't need anything fancy. Occasionally I would throw something in to surprise the bowler, but I preferred to stick to my strengths. I knew my capabilities, and I knew my areas.

What blew the whole thing apart was first Allen Stanford, with his 20/20 tournament in the Caribbean, and then the first ever World T20 in 2007. More in a little while on Stanford, much more, but the main fun of that was still to come.

Down in South Africa, West Indies drawn to face the hosts in the opening game, I walk out at the Wanderers in Johannesburg to face the first ball. *Worl' Baass*, facing the first ever ball in the first ever World T20? It's a good storyline, but I'm an entertainer, so I understand this needs more.

South Africa aren't that pleased to see me. I've scored a century against them on one leg, and I've put them around for a triple century when I've batted so long their non-bowling captain has had to send down 40-something overs and even their wicketkeeper has had to swap off his pads and gloves. I can read it on their faces as I take guard and look around the field: 'Oh no, not Chris Gayle again . . .'

Some days you can just feel it. You can just feel phenomenal, hitting it from ball one. And this is one of those days and one of those nights.

Baaall one. Smash away for four. Hitting it right, just hitting it right.

It's a good wicket to bat on, and I'm taking the attack to them. I'm in a grey sleeveless sweater to go with my maroon shirt, so let's heat this up. Albie Morkel, tall and awkward, more awkward still when you lick him for 16 off his first over. His big brother Morné looking for revenge, following me with that steep bouncer of his, getting some Mama Lashie off the ones he pitches up.

I dig into Shaun Pollock. *Shaun Pollock, him get some proper stick in dere.* Hitting more down the ground, pulling and cutting square, everything coming out perfect, everything coming out perfectly smooth.

I feel unstoppable. Skipper Smith is so vexed he decides he has no option but to lean back on his spin again. Which we dig into as well, 16 off the only over he tries. We pretty much just go berserk.

You'd expect the crowd to be silenced and still. There's fewer West Indian supporters in the stadium than there are players. But in the steep triple-tier stands and among the picnics and pints on the grassy banks it's like everyone is touched by a live wire – everyone jumping and waving, the cheerleaders dancing, the fireworks fizzing and popping. The more berserk I go the more they respond. Beers guzzling, beers flying. They want to see their home team win, but being entertained like this is another story.

I should be thinking about the 100. I should be thinking about becoming the first batsman to ever hit a century in international T20 cricket – we get to 50 in 33 balls, I get to my own off 26 balls, with three fours overshadowed by four sixes. The total goes past 100 off 63 balls.

I don' hunt dese records. My personality jus' coming tru, coming tru naturally.

I don't bother with the maths. I don't bother with the what ifs. I just bother the bowlers. I'm in the magic zone and all I can see is the ball like it's lit up and luminous and the ball disappearing deep into the crowd. Up on the wave, wind in my face, riding it riding it riding it.

You get close to that milestone and for the first time you realize it's going to be possible. Now we find out what sort of man you are. Some might say, 'I'm gonna take less risk, get a hundred.' Others might shrug – 'Lissen mi, I'm still gonna cyarry on.'

From a team point of view, it requires you to keep blazing. So don't stop. Just get on with it, *blazin' it, blazin' it*.

There is one shot that makes me smile. Shaun Pollock is bowling most of his deliveries at my pads, trying to cramp me up. I'm batting with Shiv Chanderpaul, and he comes down between overs in his quiet crabby way and says, 'Chris man, jus' step away a bit.' So I do step away to leg, and Pollock still tries to follow me, but my reaction is so quick and subconscious that I flick at it like it's a fat lazy fly, and fly away it does, up and away, away out beyond the stand beyond deep midwicket.

Feel da Six Machine.

Shiv comes down for a brush of the glove. 'You see? I told you, just do that.' And the cookie is still crumbling, and a few balls later when Pollock goes full and I crash him down the ground, the history is made.

A hundred runs, off just 50 balls. Nine mighty sixes, five thrash-dash fours.

And because it is South Africa, I bust out my little Chaplin dance again. If they're sick of me, they're sick as street dogs about the moves that come with it.

I still keep that innings in my top drawer. 117 before I sky it and out, a shift in the paradigm, a number that makes no sense. In the end Smith and his men had their revenge, the night-time dew costing us catches and 23 wides and Herschelle Gibbs catching us cold, but the tournament was alight, and our worlds would never be the same again.

Yuvraj Singh would smash six sixes off one Stuart Broad over. India, powered on Dhoni and Virender Sehwag, would beat Pakistan in the final's final over.

India had fallen in love with limited-overs cricket in 1983, when they shocked our legend West Indies side of King Viv and Clive Lloyd, Malcolm Marshall and Mikey Holding, in the World Cup final at Lord's. And India fell in love with the shorter form of the shortened game when they won that first World T20, and the IPL and all its adventures and riches would soon be swallowing us all up. So maybe I need to thank my forebears in the West Indies side too.

The world change, and players change.

'Lissen, we don't know what we have here.'

'Lissen, let's work this out.'

No longer is this all about the powerhouses and the big engines. A new phrase on our ears: 360-degree cricket. Big hitting is one thing, but clipping and flicking through the unguarded gaps brings boundaries just the same. Still, normal batting can give you a strike rate of 100, a run a ball, so add in some new angles and smart calculations and you're up and away with the mighty biceps and long levers. And those shots and approaches will bleed into one-day and Test cricket, so an old slow goat is now dashing along like the flamboyant stars of old, and the older game starts looking less like the older game with every passing year.

Bowlers look at the challenge and think twice and then again. If pace just gets angled away, cut it right back. The spinners are no longer cannon fodder but the secret services, all cunning tricks and sleight of hand. Variety becomes the spice of life. An over of military medium becomes a crazy mixed bag of who can guess what – slow

bouncers, spearing yorkers, fingers run over the ball to dig
it that way, seams scrambled to send it this.

And I grow into it like an emperor exploring his latest
conquests. If other batsmen are studying it, I'm the Nobel
professor. If other batsmen are working it out, I'm coming
up with the equations.

The next World T20, and hard yards for the West Indies
team. May is a month of cold winds and minimal wins. We
lose the two Tests against England by 10 wickets and an
innings and 83 runs. Of the two one-dayers that beat the
weather we get thumped in both.

June brings warmth and life back to chilled Caribbean
bodies. In our opening group match, against those chirping
boys from Australia, we keep them down to 169. And then
the Six Machine really gets to work.

Brett Lee is an authentic rapid bowler. 310 wickets in
Tests, 380 in one-dayers. He is a gladiator too, so he is the
one who must feel the sword. Easy on his first ball, timing
it away through mid-off for four. Punchier on his third,
slashing it over point for four more.

Two more fours off his next over, and then the vio-
lence. First ball, front leg out of the way, lick him into
Archbishop Tenison's school, across Harleyford Road
from the back row of the stands. Second ball, good yorker, bowling 'Bing'. Third ball, Bing get pinged, way over
long-on and onto the roof of the Bedser Stand. Ian Chappell will later stake it as the biggest six ever hit at the Oval,
I'm not arguing. Fourth ball, good yorker, good riposte.
Fifth ball, no-ball, mash through cover. Free hit, back
where it came so fast and nasty it nearly kills my opening
partner, Andre Fletcher. Sixth ball, come on now Brett,
don't drop it short, those poor people in the stand are in
serious danger . . .

Three sixes, two fours. 27 off the over.

Lee's a good man. Figures of 1-56 off four overs don't look good on anyone, not even a pretty boy like Brett, although at least that one is my wicket. Sadly for him and his fellow golden boys, it doesn't come until I've laid down 88 off 50 balls, my side only 13 runs from the line, but at least he laughs and shakes my hand.

He won't be the last. This is a club with plenty of room to grow.

Even as the light shines and the entertainment flows there are those who look to live in the darkness. T20 is growing so fast it must be blocking the light elsewhere. The man who is doing what no one has ever done before must be to blame for why people don't want the same old same old any more.

A few weeks before that second World T20, I'm quoted as saying that I 'wouldn't be so sad' if Test cricket died out. Quickly it becomes a bigger thing than the original question: Chris Gayle hates Test cricket, Chris Gayle doesn't care, Chris Gayle is a disgrace to the maroon cap and the West Indies' captaincy.

I was saying none of those things. I wasn't bashing Test cricket; I was still playing it. To score runs in Test cricket is something beautiful. Even after the periods when injury or dispute has kept me out, I've kept coming back. I hope to come back once again. Do you play 103 Tests if you don't care about it, or make two Test triple centuries if the style and pace bore you?

Only seven men have more West Indies Test caps than me. I've played more than Sobers, more than Marshall and Holding, more than Richie Richardson or Curtly Ambrose.

I am not to blame for the way the world spins.

Cricket is a business, and businesses respond to what consumers and employees want. Players understand the toll on their body of endless long days, understand the pain of being away from home and their families on long overseas tours. If you can travel less, if you can hurt less, and still play the game you love, why wouldn't you?

Listening to dancehall doesn't mean you hate reggae. It doesn't mean you don't understand that without Bob Marley there would be no Beenie Man. And people still love reggae, but they're buying dancehall. They're filling dancehall venues and gigs and buying dancehall records, even as they're not throwing away their old dub cuts or reggae vinyl.

Test grounds used to be full. First day, second day, third day, a sold-out crowd. And yet outside of the Ashes you don't see those things any more.

Really and truly, it is only the two big teams who attention gravitates towards. Australia and England. The Ashes will always have its buzz because of its history.

But the only thing now carrying Test cricket is the Ashes. Us lower-ranked teams, we're always going to find it a struggle. We only get two or three Test series here and there. The game is not set up to develop our talents or to nurture them when they come through.

You need the names, you need the stars. England and Australia have that, and so the supporters watch it. In the other nations they are choosing to look elsewhere.

I was born into Test cricket and I have lived through Test cricket. I can bat like a true Test batsman. People in the West Indies still love cricket. They're still passionate about it. But times get a bit harder now. Everybody has to work. There are families to support, mouths to feed; to miss work for cricket is going to be a struggle.

The love lives on. It's just shown in a different way.

The World T20 in Sri Lanka, 2012. We go into it in form, we go into it with the islands unified behind us.

And we believe. Our match against New Zealand, a tie, goes to a one-over eliminator – so much better than a bowl-off, not least because I can stride out to face Tim Southee after Ross Taylor has given us a target of 17, and crash his first ball away for six, and another for three, and then Gangnam dance with Marlon Samuels when he completes the job.

Confidence enable you to flourish.

Into the semis against Australia, me and Johnson Charles opening the batting. After what happened to Brett Lee they have a plan this time: they can't stop me when I'm on strike, so instead try to stop me getting on strike. I'm still there after 10 overs, but I've faced only 18 balls, and because it's Colombo the humidity is up and I'm cramping through my core.

I've been through tougher. A scamper and a sprint when I have to, a lash and a lick when I do. David Hussey goes into the second tier of the stand. Shane Watson takes some further clatter. Xavier Doherty does get me caught, but only by a policeman standing by his motorbike, 20 metres beyond the boundary.

I can always find an extra spark against Australia. So what if they keep me down to 41 balls? When five of them go for four and six for six, the sums still stack up sweet. When Kieron Pollard adds some mighty muscle of his own, you can look in the eyes of the bowlers and fielders spread far and wide and know that their spirits are broken. Five wickets down after only six overs, they are gone long before the end, and Gangnam comes out to play once again. *World T20, Universe Boss.*

The final: Sri Lanka, home soil, immense home support.

We believe, and we are together. We have rallied around our captain, Darren Sammy, senior players giving him thoughts and tactics, young ones the energy and dash. There is hunger for this game and for each other, there is passion for what we have done and what we hope to do. Having come this far we're not going to turn back.

It's a hard start. The bowling is tight and the wicket deteriorating. It takes 17 deliveries before we score a run off the bat, and I can manage only three before Ajantha Mendis pins me lbw. After 10 overs we are a mere 32-2.

Marlon Samuels gives us life. Sammy drags us further. Mendis ends with four wickets for 12 runs off his four overs, but we do not allow defeat to enter our minds.

Confidence come from dedication.

First over, Ravi Rampaul blows Dilshan's off stump away. Now for the squeeze – for running down every push and tuck, for bowling so tight that a batsman can't breathe, for making every sliding save and skimming the bails with each flat hard return.

Eight overs gone, only 39 on the board, 99 more needed. Now to attack with your opponent's own weapon – spin.

Samuel Badree gets Sangakkara with his leg breaks. Sunil Narine gets Jayawardene with his snarling offies. Sammy strangles Angelo Mathews with three dot balls and cleans out his middle peg with the fourth.

It's not even close. With every wicket we dance and jump a little higher; when the final one goes, 37 still needed, we Gangnam on the outfield with joy fizzing through our veins, a long line of us, bouncing and skipping and spraying drinks.

We party at the hotel, we party past midnight. Two o'clock, party. Four o'clock, party. Dawn come, we're still drinking, enjoying the moment, maximizing the fun.

The West Indies' first ICC trophy since the 1979 World Cup. A proper team, all playing for each other, all in it together, getting the best out of ourselves. Back home, the Caribbean alight.

So don't tell me that T20 doesn't matter. And don't tell me we don't care.

8.   165 Not Out

I've been called lazy. I've been called irresponsible. I've also been called skipper, and those three things don't fit together.

I don't like cricket, I love it. I love it long and slow, I love it short and fast. I love to talk cricket and I love to play it. I like redefining what's possible and I like digging the small things. And that is why I love being captain.

I will always be a captain. I've been doing it from primary school. At 10 years old I was a leader. I used to lead Rollington Town in cricket, and I led them in football. I gave all my mind to it and I gave it all my energy. I felt the responsibility and I relished it. *He's a leader, on di rise, comin' tru' di ranks.*

In every scenario in every match I learned. Under every other skipper I learned more. And whether I am in charge or in the ranks, I settle on a golden rule that should never be broken: always respect your leader.

It doesn't matter whether you like them as a person or don't like them. It doesn't matter if you agree their tactics or field placings. *Yuh cyaan disrespec' yuh leader.* Disrespect them and you shouldn't be in the team.

But it is a two-way process. A captain must be dedicated to his players. You have to make the physical time and the mental effort to get to know them, and you have to know how to get the very best out of them.

You don't necessarily need a strong team to win games. If you as a captain can hold a group of players in the palms of your hands, then you have something far more powerful than a paceman with a bouncer or a number three who could hit a marble with a piece of string. If you treat your players as you would want to be treated, if you make them feel that they are appreciated and respected, if you communicate clearly with them, they will go out there and play flat-out ferocious cricket. Even when the tough scene comes to town they will dig deep for their captain.

Every captain has his different way of running the relationships. My style is to make sure the group know, if they have an issue, they should talk. Openly, and say whatever you feel, what's bothering you. So we can have a better understanding, and so we can free the air, so everybody can be clear when they go out to the middle what they should do and how they should do it. An open discussion, for all to take part in, no favourites, no cliques, no anger or snipe.

Use the wisdom and ideas all around you. Use the experience of the senior players, use the energy of the younger ones. Make your vice-captain feel a critical part of it, because no man can do it alone, and when you gone, he's the one everyone will turn to.

Teach everyone respect for the environment and each other. You do not all need to be friends, but cricket comes calling, all differences will be aside. As a captain, when I step on the field, it's one for all and all for one.

I'm an easy-going man. I don't obsess over fool little rules, over what shoes you wear or whether your shirt is tucked in or your collar up. I am a strong-minded person as well, and I will not tolerate disrespect or disunity. If you can't oblige with what I want, *it gonna be consequence.*

And you will get my total commitment. Never will I rest or take easy options.

You might have a big-name bowler who thinks he's capable of doing something special – opening the attack, coming back to go chest to chest out with their main batsman, coming back again when the game swings on an over or wicket to grab. As a captain you have to learn to read body language – not just sighs and shoulders slumped, but the tiny signs that show someone is just below their best. Then you must have the courage to act, even when he does not recognize it himself. You think you're bowling this over? If the invisible signs are telling me you're not quite right, I'm not going to give it to you. If I think you look like you're intimidated, I'm not going to put you in that position.

It's complicated, but so am I.

Playing for Excelsior over at high-and-mighty Jamaica College on Hope Road, playing well, I hit a sweet shot towards the boundary. Jogging back to the crease, thinking it has gone for four, I am run out by the fielder's long throw.

Mr Mac, who gets so stressed watching us play cricket that he has taken up smoking, loses his temper. 'How com' you run out? You so crampy!' Crampy means slow, crampy means laid back, crampy means skinny. And so a nickname is born, but don't be fooled. My commitment is total. I just don't like running.

As a captain you have to lead from the front.

I am a gladiator, and I will go out there and I will take the fight to the enemy. As early as possible I will put them on the back foot, establish the hierarchy. When your players see that, they will stamp their authority on the game too, and they will support you even more, because a true brave leader is what each player wants.

As a captain you have to perform. If you are a leader who is struggling to score runs or take wickets, players will ease off. They will think that, since you're not doing it, you can't talk to them about why they're not doing it either. When the team sees you soaking up the short stuff, surviving brutal spells, staying alive where others would fall and refusing to give in when reasons to give in are all around, then they will feel they must do the same.

The winter of 2010, Adelaide. We have lost the first Test to Australia in three days, and we have been hammered. 187 all out, following on, and the knives are out and the critics breathing fire.

There is talk not only of how poor we are but how poor our attitude is, that the maroon cap does not sit straight upon our heads. Even our own management say things that no management should say to any team. Okay. As captain, I must stand with the players and be counted. As a team we must come together and plan it out: how are we going to fight back?

You fight back first by not giving in. Expected to fold, we make 451 in our first innings, Dwayne Bravo with a strong and resolute 100. Our bowlers fight the heat and the crowd and prise them out for just a few runs less. With four overs to go in the third day, stands roaring, close fielders sniffing like jackals, I stride to the middle with Adrian Barath to lead as I understand I should lead.

Not dancehall in my head this time but Marley, singing 'Get Up, Stand Up'.

I can feel it on my lips and in my heart. Music has carried me through my life, and now is the time to summon everything you have.

If you want anything, you turn to Marley, and that will drive you on.

Stay alive where others would fall. Stand up and stand tall. We survive the darkening night and come back on bright morning, and we will not be beaten, not this time.

Early on Ricky Ponting calls for a referral on an lbw that the umpire has turned down. No sweat on my brow – he's not nicknamed Punter without reason, and this one's a gamble that's all about the dream of a prize wicket rather than the odds that surround it.

I can play wrecking-ball, and I can play brick wall.

We have a lot of time. There's nothing to chase. You are the captain, you are the one shouldering the responsibility, and you utilize your skills accordingly.

Make your calculations: what is the percentage chance of getting out to that bowler compared to that one, to that shot against this? You cannot go strokeless, for then you are not only leaning on the ropes but have your gloves down by your sides. Keep your guard up, but when they offer a little space or daylight, strike back hard and hurt them when you do. Now they hesitate a fraction when thinking about their own targets, because no one likes a bloody nose.

It's a strong bowling attack. Mitchell Johnson, all snarl and slingy left arm. The secret with him? Don't respond to the fury. It's all bluster, and will blow itself out if he can't strike early on. He struggles with long spells, and Ponting does not understand this, so stare back with your blank-eyed gladiator's mask on and wait for the loose ones that will follow.

Peter Siddle. Not only a vegan Aussie male, but a vegan Aussie fast bowler. He drinks coconut water and eats 20 bananas a day, which even in Jamaica might run a few jokes. Here you take him serious. Tight bowler, aggressive bowler. Give him no gaps.

Doug Bollinger, fast and excitable. Wears a toupee, nick-named Doug the Rug. Make him want to tear his hair out. Nathan Hauritz, Shane Watson: old stagers from the days in the Aussie academy. Bring back every memory from those days, recall and refocus on all their variations and preferences and stock balls and weak spots, use them all in the fight.

My 50 comes up off 78 balls, fast for some, steady for me. With Shiv Chanderpaul I drop a little more chain on the anchor; our 100 takes 34 overs.

Batters must try to wear down bowlers. Never let them in, never give them hope. One guy beats the edge, the whole attack takes energy from it. Tire them out, silence their shouts. A quiet field is a safer field.

Build partnerships, for two men together are stronger than one alone. Watch their body language, and build to the moment that they accept that you're not getting out.

Dictate the pace. They will try everything – bowlers with long spells, bowlers with short spells. Long, slow overs, spinners racing through others like their house is on fire. Fielders under your nose, fielders around the fence.

Don't think of the end, only the moment you are in. Don't let the mind wander to how long is left, only the ball that is fizzing towards you. Work, and graft, and grind it out.

'*Don't give up the fight . . .*'

Past lunch, past tea, the bowlers trudging off to change shirts. My century comes round almost unnoticed, and like a man in the nets I look up only at the next bowler coming in.

It is physical, hot and sticky and sweat in your eyes, gloves soaked, trousers damp under pads and over thigh guards. Your mind and memories drive you on, because you have batted like this in the past, and whether on Lucas's far side or Antigua's green field against the 11 bowlers of South Africa you have both proven you can do it and honed your skills for the next time the challenge comes.

Don't over-think it. Don't worry about failure. Talk to yourself, boost yourself, sing to yourself.

'*Get up, stand up!*'

Relish the challenge and savour your response to it. You love to bat, and you love to lead. In this fierce moment you are doing both.

Wickets fall, and my resolve stiffens. 150 to my name just before the close, 150 in over a day. From the drowning depths in Brisbane we have a lead of almost 300, and now we are the ones to fear. On the fifth morning Ponting pushes his fielders back far and wide, an unmissable admission that superiority has turned to deference, that attack has become defence.

At 317 I lose my last partner. I have batted for almost seven and a half hours. 165 not out. There for the first ball, there for the last.

Only three other West Indians have carried their bat in Tests, and only one – Frank Worrell – has scored more in doing so. Only three other overseas players have done it in Australia. One was Len Hutton, and that makes sense because he was another triple centurion. But another of them was Geoffrey Boycott, and I may have less in common with Geoffrey Boycott than any other man who has ever held a cricket bat. I'm also the only man in the history of the game to do it in T20 cricket, but that will come as surprises to no one.

We thought we might win it. We hoped Sulieman Benn's spin would bite. But the track had flattened out, and although we dug out five of them, we could get no more. Yet from where we had been to where we were, it almost felt like a win anyway: having Australia hopping in their own backyard, having them hanging on and celebrating an escape.

We were a team together again, and I had done what a captain should do. In the third Test we went hard again, and this time, attack required rather than defence, I smashed a century off just 70 balls, the fifth-fastest in history. We fell just short, but we had them on the run again, and we had respect where before there was none. And I had led from the front, just as I knew I should, just as I had always done.

You learn from every captain, and you learn the good and the bad.

From the best I played under with the West Indies, Carl Hooper, came trust and belief. He is a calm man and would not be swayed by fear. Playing in Sri Lanka, struggling badly with the late swing of Chaminda Vaas, I'm almost waiting to be dropped. Instead he come to me, no anger or recrimination: 'Lissen mi Chris, you playing every game.'

Confidence let you relax, and confidence let you flourish.

From Brian Lara came communication, although not as you might think. We won a few series under Brian, and we won the Champions Trophy, but to me Lara wasn't the best captain. You have to have the players under your wing, and only seldom did he have control of his.

Maybe he intimidated them. He was the superstar, he was the world talent. He was the big man of the team, and people might not know what to say to him sometime. But he was never really approachable, and you need to get the guys up, for them to spring how you want them to spring.

Great batsman, moody person. Lara could just flip, and no one would have any idea why. I saw it happen in the nets and I saw it happen in the dressing-room. He wasn't the sort of captain you'd want to look up to, and from that bad seeds are sown.

As a captain you have to be ahead of the game. You have to be ahead from the night before, before you come to spin that toss, and that knowledge came, like so much sweetness, from Delroy Morgan at Lucas. Alert, organized, disciplined and deep in love with tactics. I saw it too in Stephen Fleming when he led New Zealand; never captaining a superstar team, but turning them into superstars and a super unit through his tactics and motivation and understanding of what they could do rather than his disappointment at what they couldn't.

Some men are born to captain. They are born with the ability to read another man's character and the motivations that wrap around it. If you are raised in cricket and see it only as toil or pressure you will never care enough to add the rest. If you find fascination in all around you, then instead it will become instinctive; just as a musician knows what chord should follow another, so the natural captain looks at a batsman and knows the best field, looks at an over and knows what must come next.

It clicks for me. Sometime it takes deliberate thought, but often the solution just comes. *A leader, on di rise.*

Jerome Taylor, a top strike bowler. I use him upfront with the new ball, and I may use him at the death with the old. If he's bowling the last over, I will let him know as early as possible, so he can prepare and settle on the concept.

Then, in the crazy madness of the game, I might notice his little trigger movement. No one else spots it. No one else knows what it is, maybe not even Jerome Taylor, but it is there, and it means he is not comfortable. He is nervous. There is doubt when I want raw unstoppable belief.

Now your mind is alive. 'Fuck. Do I still give him that over? Who else could step in? Who else look ready?'

Next thought. 'I've told him he's my strike bowler. He need my assurance. He need me in his head.'

A jog over to him before the penultimate over.

'Lissen mi. There's reason why mi give you this. Because you da man. You da strike man. You have fi win us dis game.'

I have to get in his head, because I understand Jerome Taylor, and if you don't, if you allow him to do his own thing, shit can happen.

'Lissen man, you will win this game. If we lose with you, fine. But you can win us this game, and I know you will.'

Sometime the gentle arm, sometime the sweet nothings. Sometime the straight up. 'Lissen man, you have to get the runs today, get job done today. If it's not Chris, it's you.'

Understand that no one wants to fail, that fear can make fools of strong men.

Runako Morton, a batsman with so much going on inside. When he failed to get runs he came back to the dressing-room like a crazy man, coming back and throwing his gear and throwing his pads and rolling on the ground. 'Aaargh!'

Some want to laugh. Maybe he wants some to. From his captain he wants talk. He wants calm down.

'Morton. Is just a game an' not a life-threatening ting. So don' be too hard on yourself, you know? What is for you will be for you.'

For each batsman will fail, and fear can strike anyone.

I remember one particular limited-over series in New Zealand. I was struggling, struggling. No one helping me. No kind words, my stumps always falling, my edges always carrying. Into the Test series, first match, first over, Shane Bond coming in fast and hungry. And how I survived that over is a miracle. *Di ball jus' swinging so big . . .*

You can accept defeat and still believe in yourself and your ability. And the moment you can accept defeat and rebound and come back to war, it will be the best feeling you can know. That's what I told Morton, and that is what I have told others. Breathe, and let the stress and anger go.

Critics talk about some players who are hard to captain. For me there wasn't anyone hard to captain, because I'm not going to take bullshit from no one, and so disrespect and bad feeling could never grow. Players know the sort of person I am, and they know what I'm about as well. They know what I won't tolerate, and they know the path that cannot be crossed.

Make it personal and make it clear. When Sri Lankan hero Mahela Jayawardene joined my Jamaica Tallawahs team, I met him at the hotel, sat by the bar, and explained it all.

'Mahela, welcome. I give you a bit a where I want to go about the innings. Lissen, I'd love for you to bat early as you're used to, but since Chris Lynn, he be more attacking at the fast bowlers, I'd love to have Chris Lynn batting at three, and I'd love to have you to anchor it at four, to actually control the middle. You're a better player of spin, so I want you in that position – you control the middle and then you can know when to do what when it's required. If you feel comfortable with that, you tell me.'

I'll do the same to Chris Lynn as well. 'Chris. Trust me. I think you're an attacking player, you bat at three. You scare the fast bowlers, you continue to press gas. Play your game there. Utilize those Powerplay overs. Don't worry about saving skin or going down. You don't ease up.'

I'll always explain those things in person. And know that whichever players come in, even if I'm captaining them for the first time, I've seen how they play and I know how they operate.

Make it clear that we must all be flexible, that the team's aims come first. You want your players to feel comfortable where they're batting, first of all. But sometimes a partnership will build, and the game with it, and you must make every player aware of it before it happens.

So me as a captain now, I'll explain it. 'Guys, the batting order gonna be flexible. So I want everyone to be ready. So if, say, you're batting at three, if I see something different I might move it around. Whoever don't bat in their normal position, you have to still have the same enthusiasm to go out there and bat properly and get the job done. I don' want to see no screw-face or any attitudes saying you shoulda do this or you shouldn'ta done that. If you're not happy with it, say it now.'

And you just clear the air from there, and you'll get the best out them.

He's a leader . . .

A new kid in the team. You wouldn't say much except make him feel welcome. He might be a bit reserved, coming into a team for the first time, and sometimes I see a lot of people in his ear. So let him be himself, and don't confuse him with new ideas or thoughts on his style. 'Welcome to Test cricket, and congratulations. Jus' relax yourself and enjoy yourself. Remember what take you here, and that all you need. It maybe feel be a bit different, and most people might not know about you, but you'll get a chance to get a feel a tings.'

Know when to talk and when to fall silent.

Sometime in team meetings I wouldn't talk at all, because five people be saying the same thing over. Often on the morning of a match I'd prefer not to have one anyway, because most of the time you make your plans, and then they are all ripped up by what happens on the field. React instead to the situation in the middle. When you do speak, make it simple. One key point, maybe two. Never repeat yourself. Trust the intelligence of your players.

Be different. I used to love the five-minute meetings of Ray Jennings, the South African coach who was in charge of Royal Challengers Bangalore when I first went there. Most of the times it wasn't really about your opponents, or your tactics. It was a video clip of a kid in the stands, and a simple question: how are you going to put a smile on another's face today? A montage of us all hitting our best trademark shot or sending some stump flying or fingers around some impossible catch. 'How are you going to bring happiness to the world today?'

Every time he motivated me to go out there and deliver. Every time he made you hit the ground, running hard, running until the race was won.

A captain cannot lead alone. A captain needs a coach he can trust, just as an opening batsman needs a partner who will not leave him stranded mid-pitch.

Sometime it happens. Sometime it does not.

As West Indies captain, I had a coach in John Dyson who came from New South Wales but understood exactly what a West Indies side needs. All that is important is what happens in the middle. Don't impose rules that are for the coach's image rather than the players' happiness. Give players their freedom away from the pitch, and let them express themselves in the middle.

John Dyson doesn't give a fuck what anyone does or doesn't. As captain I respect that.

And then it all changes. One day the bowling coach, Ottis Gibson, sidles over to me.

'I'm coming in to coach the team.'

I look at him. 'You know something I don't?'

He makes a face.

I sigh. 'Lissen, I'm gonna resign as captain.'

The panic. 'No no no, don't resign, don't resign . . .'

So it happens, for whatever reason. They get rid of John Dyson, which is a big blow, and Gibson is named the coach of the team. Because I believe in respect, I give him everything. If he says jump to a player, I support it. Even when he starts behaving in a way that as a captain I normally wouldn't allow, I allow it, because I'm letting him create his environment and his team.

He's a Bajan, so you think everything will at least be relaxed. And then all of a sudden the rules start coming in. You can't wear flip-flops. Travelling from your home to the ground, you can't wear your own clothes. When you wear a West Indies shirt, it has to be a particular one on a particular day.

Now that might work in England. Not in the Caribbean. John Dyson doesn't give a fuck what anyone does or doesn't. Ottis Gibson gives a fuck about everything anyone even thinks about doing.

Players disrespected. Players talked about behind their backs. A team that was growing and succeeding is now broken and beaten. And then the captain gets it too.

I hear what he says: 'Chris Gayle is not a captain . . . Chris Gayle don't have any knowledge of the game . . . When Chris Gayle come to a team meeting, he don't come with a pen and paper and take notes . . .'

We play South Africa in Barbados. Suddenly people in the stands are full of stories about the players, because Ottis

Gibson has been telling them. Disrespecting players to total strangers.

I don't want to interfere with the match, so I wait until it is over, call a team meeting and confront him. He admits to it. Players ask him about things he has said about them. He doesn't deny it.

And so it falls apart. He would go on to keep me out of the national side for a year and a half on a personal vendetta. That's life. But he's not a head coach. Fair enough, I'll give him the green light for being a bowling coach. That I'll give to you. But he's not a head coach. That was a serious backward move, to have Ottis Gibson as head coach.

As a captain, I stand for my players at all times. I will speak on their behalf, and in return I expect them to stand with me at all times.

In late 2009 we had played four consecutive series without the West Indies Cricket Board giving us contracts. The cricket was building, building, and we were winning games, but instead of contracts there was only talk, talk, talk. The West Indies Players' Association recommended we strike; I sat down with the players and explained each and every thing to them, and everybody was willing to stand with us.

The board responded by picking a new team, a team led by a man who hadn't played for the West Indies and with another who had just turned 16. Still we stood together. Even some back-up players, guys who weren't in the original Test squad, refused the call-up.

In the crisis we found strength together. We were stuck in St Lucia, no cricket and no families, and so it became a cooking festival, Runako Morton leading the chef work, the evenings eased by a little Hennessy and team bonding.

I got called to a meeting with the board's president. They sent someone who wasn't the president, so I walked out. Still we cooked our food and carried on having a good time, regardless of the situation and the pressure, and Morton, already a top chef, developed even more skills.

Our togetherness made me proud. We had something special going: the players fought for me, did everything for me, and I gave everything back to them.

But even as the contracts were settled, something had changed in that moment for West Indies cricket at that time. Eventually they played the Bangladesh series, another meeting was called, and they came to discuss the captaincy. New terms, terms that I didn't agree to, and a threat that if I didn't agree to them I couldn't be captain any more.

I made it clear. Fine. If that's the case, I'm more than willing to be a player.

They named Darren Sammy as Test captain. I made it clear again. 'Lissen, it not a problem, you'll still get my support. Wherever. That's my policy. It don't matter who or whatever circumstance, I still play my supportive role. We move on.'

We went off on tour to Sri Lanka and in that first Test since being stripped of the captaincy, I scored my second triple century. The reaction of those who had removed me? He did it deliberately, just to prove a point. He did it out of spite.

Wow, to be able to make a Test triple century on demand! To be able to compile 300 runs, just out of spite!

I let it go. I don't like to be ruled by anger. You can't live in the darkness. *Breathe, an' let it go.*

I still love to captain. Winning the Caribbean Premier League as skipper of the Tallawahs was one of my happiest moments. Most franchises still ask me if I will lead them.

But I am older now, and while I still love the cricket, still love digging the nuances and studying the players and creating the bonds, I am tired of the rest.

A captain must be with the media every day. A captain must go to every official function, and he must always be the one to make the speech. Even after a net session there is a question and an answer, even if the question is no real question and the answer you've already given. I want my free time, I want my freedom. Someone come for interview, I'm not captain, you don't have to get it. Simple as that. Sweet liberation.

And as captain, stories spread. There is one that has spread further than almost any other – the one about me, at some formal lunch in the south of England, sitting next to an Old Etonian and former president of the MCC, who pours posh chat in my ear for hour after hour about who knows what and when's he going to stop? And when he finally does, taking his first breath for something like three hours, I'm supposed to have turned to him and asked, with deadpan face: 'You get much pussy?'

Here's the news. I remember the incident, but I don't remember saying 'pussy' to him. Maybe I did, maybe I didn't.

Yeah, a lot of people love that story. *But I cyaan concrete seal it.* I can't take credit for what I can't remember. Maybe it was the Jamaican accent, you know what I'm saying?

9.   65 Not Out

Where I come from, what I have seen, you give thanks for money and you give thanks for fame. Because they get you through – out of one life and into another, and when you've lived the experiences I have, there is no romance in staying where you were, no misty eyes and no false memories of how it used to be.

But it comes at price. A man who was once open must become a closed book. A boy who trusted all around him must now keep his mind and emotions under lock and key.

No one is out there for love. People will come around you for what they can gain or what they can get from you. Maybe things are different for you. I hope so. Personally, I can maybe count the loyal people on one hand. One hand. And not even five fingers. That's how it is.

They say more money more problem, and that is true. So, so true. If you come from where I from, you'll take those problems over your old ones. But you have to work out how you're going to deal with them, for they can chew a man up and leave him with nowhere to turn and no faith in nobody. You see something happen again and again, and you know what to expect.

And I know what life is all about and what life is like. I travel the world, and I know what to expect.

I've heard the prettiest talk. I've heard the sucker talk. You come to learn when somebody is trying to get something out of you. *Mi bin tru it all.*

In response I show no emotion or expression to let them feel any better. When they finish their talk I say,

'Okay, I'll get back to you.' I'll get back to you on that. Because so many of these talkers are just bull-shitters, and I can read that now, I can see it in eyes and hear it on lips.

It's always been like that. You live and you learn. I've seen players who have been through a lot. Who have had bad men do bad things to them, and so have appointed agents, and had agents screw them over. I'm glad I came at the right time to see those things, because I can use them as a guideline, and I can use them as experience when the same things happen to me.

Because I have been let down. I've been let down by family members. You ask them to do certain things, and they just go and do the total opposite. Within the family I've been let down for sure.

It hurts you at the time, and it hurts you for a while afterwards. How do you not get more suspicious of everyone else when that happens?

The first time I hear the name Allen Stanford, I hear only good.

A big man from Texas. A billionaire come to play in the Caribbean, but a billionaire come to play cricket, to give the game in the West Indies the love and resources it has been starved of for too long.

Antigua is his base, and Antigua becomes his pliant empire. A bank, a mansion. A private jet, a private cricket ground.

And then a private cricket tournament. The Stanford 20/20, because where Sir Allen is, his name has to be everywhere, even as the 'Sir' in front of it is another one of those strange mysteries and exaggerations that follow him around like his butlers and security guards.

Teams from across the Caribbean, cash from another world. There is excitement and there is opportunity, not only to earn money that has never shown its face elsewhere, but to let your style in the new booming format be shown around the planet.

With the private jet and the private yacht comes the image of a very very heavy man, and then follows the whispers of something bigger: a tournament between the best from the islands and the best from elsewhere. Talks come around, and now England are at the table. Whispers become leaks become concrete. A black helicopter lands on the Nursery Ground at Lord's, inside it a suitcase with enough cash to buy the old pavilion and turn it into the Stanford condo tower.

England against Stanford, one T20 match. US$20 million to the winners, a see-you-later to the losers.

Dis serious? Dis really happening?

When you see the selectors lined up for the Stanford All-Stars you put all doubt to one side. Sir Viv Richards, Sir Everton Weekes, Curtly Ambrose, Lance Gibbs, Richie Richardson, Andy Roberts and Courtney Walsh. When you look at your form in T20 you know you will be in, and when the captaincy is raised and it comes down to you and Sylvester Joseph, you know you will be nominated, because if you are looking to build a team from scratch then I am the senior man and I have that respect.

Coaches are appointed, Eldine Baptiste and Roger Harper, and a training camp is called. And it is one of the most intense camps I've ever been in, putting in serious work, putting in total focus. We're under strict rules and we're under curfews, and we are perfectly happy with that because of the prize on offer. A lot of practice game, a lot of preparation, day in, day out.

And then shit starts happening.

We are all in Antigua, on Stanford's ground, staying on Stanford turf. Long days training in the sun, long evenings for people to talk.

I am the team's leader. I am the spokesman. And the liaison Stanford puts in place, the person every request or question or report must go through, is Andrea Stoelker, his fiancée.

Like him, she's an American relocated to the Caribbean. Unlike him, she is young and a nice person.

Whatever you need, you have to go through her. The players always want this and that, and when they do, I'm the one to go down to the office. I have one-on-one meetings with her. I have discussions with her. We need this. We need less of that. What time do you want us here, and can we get that over there?

And the speculation start to float around. Antigua is a small place. *People talk an' circulating.*

My birthday comes round, and I ask her if I can break camp to go back to Jamaica and celebrate it. No go, but as we are having a team dinner at the hotel, she brings a cake to the table for me.

We all celebrate and enjoy it, but now some people feel I'm getting special treatment. Words start flying around, flying around, flying around.

More whispers. Chris man, there's photos going round of you and her talking. 'What do you mean? Dis rubbish. Bullshit.'

She's still a good lady to deal with, so on we carry. Maybe she likes me, I don't know. But nothing is happening, just as nothing happening means everyone assumes everything.

On an' on, and the shit keeps happening. I keep getting feedback. Rumours from all around – Stanford is not happy, stay out of Stanford's way. She now has his security men with her every second of the day, so even if we wanted to be alone, we couldn't be, and even if we wanted to go somewhere, we're not allowed to leave the compound.

I say to her, when we meet, let's do it outdoors. Still the stories come, still the big talk. And it reach a serious stage now where meetings start to happen and calls start to happen.

Stanford starts badgering the legends. Stanford starts pushing at captain Gayle. And then the first phone call.

'Chris. There's a problem. My fiancé thinks we're having an affair.'

'Whaaat? You serious?'

She tells me he has taken her passport away to check if she has been to Jamaica to see me. Why would she want to go to Jamaica when I was in the camp? None of it making sense, none of it making any difference.

'This is serious. He's really pissed off with you. There are some harsh things going on.'

So I say, 'Don't worry. I'll keep my cool and everyting.'

But it gets worse. The media start getting involved, asking questions about him and his girl. He laughs and tells them it's Texan horseshit, that it's nothing. But I know from what the legends are saying that he is blowing fumes. *Blowin' fumes!*

He summons the legends. I want Gayle off the team. And the legends say to him, you can't do that now. It's built up way too far to change the captain now. If Chris goes we go.

So he has to suck it up. He still has to put on a smart face and a smiley face, but inside he's bubbling and burning.

There is a practice match going on, and the players are sitting in the pavilion. All of them know what's going on, because the talk is of nothing else. I'm sitting there with Runako Morton, and out of some blue my phone rings. Unknown number. I don't answer unknown numbers. But I start wondering, and I look at Morton, and he looks at me, and eyebrows are up.

I keep watching the game. As I'm sitting there I feel something tap me on the shoulder. I turn around.

Big Stanford standing over me. Big Stanford standing over me, blowing fumes.

'Chris, can I have a word with you, please?'

'Okay . . .'

We get up to walk. The players know what is happening, so they get up too. Runako walks behind us. If anything's going to happen, he's got my back. We're walking along the boundary, and then he steers us into the car park. I'm wearing my dark glasses. And then it comes.

'Are you having an affair with my missus?'

'What? Are you serious?'

Tek off mi shades an' look him straight inna eye. 'Lissen to me. I'm the captain of the team. I have to deal with her on issues and matters.'

'Bullshit. Don't burn your bridges.'

'What bridges? There's no bridge to burn.'

He's huffing and puffing, blowing heavily. A pink steam train, struggling up a hill.

'Watch your back.'

'Whaaat?'

'Watch your back.' *Huffin an' puffin.*

'Relax yourself man. Relax. Chill.'

He strides away, all steam and elbows. Morton's on my shoulder. We walk. I'm pissed off, so we walk on. I let it go. Just breathe. Breathe. Get out in the air and breathe.

A day or two on. We're playing another practice game, and I'm batting in the middle. By the pool area overlooking the ground, where everyone can see, where I can't miss it, lackeys come in and set up a table for dinner. When the tablecloth is on and the silver cutlery out, he strides in, his fiancée behind him, sits down, and stares at me. The two of them, right there, on the boundary, his arm locked down on her shoulder, his eyes never leaving me.

She comes over to me in a flush and a rush after the game is finished and the dinner packed away and Big Stanford elsewhere. 'Boy! It's because of you that happened . . .'

Now nonsense upon nonsense. A man trying to get back at me for someone who isn't mine. A man sitting out there with someone who's not my woman, trying to make me rage for something I haven't done and don't care about.

There can be no trust now, only suspicion. I talk about the threats to our wicketkeeper, Ridley Jacobs, a native of Antigua. I'm made to understand that I can't even go to the police station. I call my lawyer back home in Jamaica to make an official record of it all, for who knows what an enraged king can call on in his realm?

Game time now. My girlfriend is here now too. She's hearing the rumours. She arrives in time to see Stanford getting some of the England players' girlfriends to sit on his knee, a man playing God, a man trying to show the world he can do what he wants, a man who is dirty and old.

Proper proper chaos. Amidst it all, the team has somehow prepared properly. Of course $20m makes a difference. Maybe some of the England players think it is going to be a walk in the park; maybe they think they can afford to lose this one, for Stanford has promised that four more of the same will follow. After all, what have the West Indies done in years and years?

We have been together a long time, and our togetherness has been sealed under Stanford pressure. Before we walk out, sat in the pavilion that he has built on the ground he owns, I look around the room.

'Lissen, nothing is guaranteed. There are no promises. So we need to be the ones to win this first game, for who knows what will happen when the dust settles from this?'

You have never seen a team more motivated.

Jerome Taylor, my beautiful strike bowler. Today there are no tell-tale trigger movements, no self-doubt. Only express pace, and the sight of Ian Bell's leg stump going all over, and Matt Prior's bent back the same way two balls later.

Now Darren Sammy to the party, Owais Shah going to the sort of slick steepling catch that only happens if you've been training flat-out for five weeks, and now the big cherry on the cake, Kevin Pietersen, stepping away to off and looking back with mouth open as another leg stump goes with a clunk and a clatter.

Freddie Flintoff, bowled by Kieron Pollard's slower one, Collingwood, slog-sweeping down deep midwicket's throat.

99 all out, not a six between them, and the serious fun stuff is still to start.

I pick up my bat, pull on my helmet and stroll to the middle with Andre Fletcher. Looking back I can see the intensity in the stands. I can see the expectant faces of our players in the dressing-room. And I can see Stanford, in the middle of it all, looking pink.

My head is fuming. I'm serious angry. Time to give it licks.

15 off the first two overs. 49 off the first five.

More licks, proper licks. Steve Harmison's third over goes for 22.

We know this wicket. We understand these conditions. We've been playing this scenario for weeks.

My 50 up off 33 balls. Flintoff taking punishment, Stuart Broad taking punishment, Graeme Swann taking punishment.

With 10 overs gone we are only 17 away. Another look into the pavilion, another sight of the pink steam train with his boiler ready to burst.

A six off Freddie over midwicket to finish it off, a millionaire's shot for a billionaire's pleasure.

The guys run onto the field. I walk straight over to the pavilion, stare at Stanford, and I hug my girl.

A 10-wicket win with 44 balls to spare. A 65 off 58 balls for me. I'm not in the mood to celebrate, even when Stanford has to put on his smart face and smiley face and hand me a giant cardboard cheque for $20m, and when the cameras are on and I'm called to the stage has to pretend to high-five me and hug me in his sweaty black polo shirt and chino slacks pulled somewhere up to his nipples.

Ridley takes me aside. The best thing to do is to leave Antigua. Immediately. I'm on the first flight.

Who could take any chances? He's a fool. But he has so much money he can do anything on that island. *Money mek di worl' go round, yuh know?* You can take nothing for granted. You are safe only when you are gone.

I did get my money, not from that photo-friendly giant cheque but wired without bells and bother into my bank account. Eleven players with $1m each, the rest of it,

$9m, split up between the reserve players and the support staff.

Months later, when the unravelling began, and the true stories emerged, we looked at ourselves again. Should we have known what was happening? He was a bad man, but he was a good actor, and those who did not instantly fall for him were blinded by the money. His power and his empire protected him. It would take the Feds to dig him out, not a bunch of cricketers with their eyes on a different prize.

Only a dirty man and a nasty man does what he did. It's really sad to know we were playing with someone else's money, and it's worse that so many lost so much, suckered in by him to bank and invest. Even our own Superstars fell foul, many of the team leaving their funds with him and losing more than they could bear when the kingdom toppled.

I spent some of mine on my house, high in the hills above Kingston's heat. Money takes you out of one life and into another. I spent another big chunk on heart surgery for my brother Andrew. More money more problems, but you take these ones over the old.

I don't have the black bat or the silver stump from that November night, but I've kept the black shirt as a reminder. Stanford? He's in jail in Florida, wearing orange overalls. He should suffer. And he is suffering.

So now I keep something back. I keep a part of myself locked away for only me, even as the world wants to take more and more.

I fly the skies, I travel the continents. I'm away from the few I am close to while surrounded by thousands who believe they know everything of me.

I don't like to say no. In an airport or hotel lobby, even if I'm late, I don't like to say no when they coming running over for a photo or a sign. Twenty cameras in your face, pushing and shoving, elbows and smartphones hitting you in the chest. You try to smile and stand your ground, everyone pushing you pushing you, up in your face, up in your face, and still you take the time to give everyone their chance. At the cricket ground, the rest of the players all gone, showered gone, showered drive home gone, and I will still be on the field signing autographs, just to give everybody the chance.

I see people dropping phones through trembling, unable to remember how their cameras work through excitement. That's weird to experience, because you're just being you, and the only way to keep that part of me locked safe away is to let the madness flow, let it flow around me.

You slow down time. You make it your time, not theirs. You might argue and push back, but what will you get out of it? I'm not going to let the chaos invade me. Just breathe. Just keep the walls steady. Walk away from it inside.

People in business like to talk about trust. There is no trust in business, only business.

That's how things happen. People try to screw you. I've invested in businesses, and they want your name and they want you to put the money in. I'm not going to trust people like that.

I invested in one sports bar in Kingston from scratch. It didn't work out, and I had to go to court to get back my money. Business, not trust.

In India there are deals everywhere. It comes with the game. Everywhere you walk come proposals and ventures and sure things.

I'm good with people. I can read them, and I can play my poker face. But I have to put up barriers. I'll let them speak to somebody else, because I'm tired of hearing these things. If we're serious about going into it, then you come up front and we take it from there. But I have to keep something back. If you come to me directly, I'll give you a number or an email. And that's it.

Most people out there want to take you for a ride, yet sometime your fame gets you through the world. It gets you a little privilege, it gets you a better service. I don't see that as a bad thing. You have put in the work, you've represented your country, you've entertained the world.

But there can be no trust.

The day came when a contract was put in front of me with the numbers US$3,000,000. The day came when even Stanford could seem small change.

$3m to play in the Indian Cricket League. Ramnaresh Sarwan had one for $2m. We looked at them together. 'Hmm. What we gonna do, Sars?'

You go around and ask. They all say, 'Chris, who's gonna tell you to turn down three million?'

I couldn't sleep. Lying there staring at the ceiling. All the time thinking, this cannot be real, this is too good to be true.

I went to bigger heads. Lalit Modi, boss of the IPL, and the view from the other side. 'I can't tell you what to do, but just know the IPL will be the bigger and better thing. And if you go and play, you won't play for the West Indies again, because the ICL will not be sanctioned by the boards.'

I still wanted to play for the West Indies, so I turned it down. Too good to be true, and in the end it was. A lot of people didn't get their money, and didn't get to play for their team.

Don't get me wrong. I've made some bad investments. Sometime you get involved and it doesn't work out. As a player I have lost a lot of money.

That's why I never sign any agreement with any agent. I'm more like a freelancer. You come to me with something on the table, then we work it out from there. That's how I do my stuff. I'm not signing anything with any particular body. Then, once a thing is whole, I have a lawyer, and sometimes even lawyers are rip-off, and sometimes you have to pay the hard price.

Know I don't shed any tears over it. I look up and smile about it. It's just a process. *Yuh cyaan have a smooth life.*

The big things I do on my own. Triple Century, my bar on Knutsford Boulevard in New Kingston. A guy came to me with the idea, and rather than going into business with him, I just bought it out.

It's a cool place. Let me recommend the CG45, a shot glass of coconut vodka, Cafe Patrón and Hennessy, dark as night, lit by flames on top. If you like it sweet try the Batter's Paradise – brandy, Bailey's, cream and a cherry.

Even there, in my chill spot, I see how some people are. You can keep a party at your house, and all parties at my house are free parties, and you'll see them come to the free parties. But at the club now, when you have to pay to come in, you wouldn't see them appear. If they appear, they won't buy a drink. If they do appear and they do buy a drink, they'll buy the cheapest drink. One beer. One beer, sipping, never another. Whereas when I'm at their places I'll buy bottles, bottles of champagne.

That's how people are. They use you to get what they want. So if I'm going to keep a party, I'll go by Triple Century. If I'm not at home, you'll find me there every night. Not necessarily drinking, just chilling, taking photos with the people, signing away the night. A lot of people gravitate to it, and a lot of people love it.

There you will find the two people I trust more than any others. Raddy Haynes, my old form teacher from Excelsior, now manager of both my foundation and my bar. Natasha, my girl, the mother of my child yet to be born.

I keep them close. Those are my right and left hand, those two. My right and my left.

I never liked maths at school. It wasn't the subject for me. The only bit I loved was the six times table.

One six is six. One six is not enough. Two sixes are 12. Three sixes is more like it. Four sixes are 24. Five sixes is proper hitting. Six sixes is World Boss.

Most times tables end at 12. That's the boundary. Not mine. I have no problem with boundaries. I actually quite like them, particularly when they're underneath my sixes.

Don't think every sporting challenge we attempted in Rollington Town was pulled off in fancy style. Popeye was once subbed off by Mr Mac in a football match after just 15 minutes. He hadn't just been playing badly, he had failed to touch the ball at all. Kevin Murray was once selected to run in the 800 metres at Champs, the annual island-wide schools athletics competition that obsesses the nation. 800 metres is never a popular distance in Jamaica; it's at least eight times further than most of us want to run. You couldn't fault Kevin's effort – he gave it everything on the second lap, and finished with a spectacular dive across the line. Sadly the rest of the field had run across it long before, but still.

The six was always different. Not always did you want to hit sixes, for we were raised as purists. Not always could you hit them, for arms were skinny and bats made of bamboo. But when biceps grew and ambitions followed, the pleasure in sending the ball way way away became an obsession.

As a Six Machine you find fascination in your chosen field, even if the field you have chosen is across the road from the one you're playing in. Not all sixes are the same. Not all boundaries feel the same to clear.

Two grounds are sweeter for sixes than any other. When you're playing well at Sabina Park, hitting sixes and entertaining people, your own people, it's a joy and a privilege to see the jumping around and waving the flag. *An' you can hear all di horns, an' it give you goose-bump* . . .

You know you're in control. You know from the crowd reaction how you're performing and how you're hitting sixes, and you know like a conductor how to raise and sway the noise.

'Lick him again! Lick him again!'

You can actually hear it out there from the middle. 'Give him another one! Give him another one!'

In Jamaica we love excitement, and if you can create excitement at Sabina Park, the cradle of our cricket, you feel the love and you bounce it back.

The Chinnaswamy, Bangalore. A long way from home, but the love has come with you. A good wicket to bat on, not a big ground and with a fast outfield as well, the bounce true and even and not too much for spin so you can play through the line. But it's what comes down from the stands that makes it, and what you send back that drives it on even more.

In Bangalore the chants reach you even when you are locked on the bowler. 'Six! Six! Six!' So you say, 'Okay, let's go fit it in with them . . .' and you just hit a six, and then all the red flags around us waving and 'Gayle Storm!' banners and chanting and chanting and everything just going off the roof.

That feeling you get, you want to grab it. You want to play cricket, you want to entertain, you want to hit sixes. And it's all because of the spectators and the fans, the joy you see operating on them when you're hitting those sixes.

Any day of my life I would be happy being in Kingston or Bangalore, hitting sixes, watching the ball fly. Just beautiful.

Not all sixes to all parts are equal. You have your favourite targets – the North Stand at Sabina Park, where the dressing-room is, where the liveliest crowd is. Your six flies in there, everybody will be jumping around, jumping to catch it. Bangalore? Not towards the dressing-room, because that's more like a VIP area, team owners, family members, and so less jumping around. Anywhere else you're going to have a lot of hands going up, a lot of hands reaching into the skies.

You bring joy but you also bring danger. A hard core of compressed cork, covered in polished leather, slammed into a bank of unprotected people. In Bangalore a six of mine flew over the waves of reaching hands, ricocheted off the back wall of the stand and hit a young girl in the face. Only afterwards did I find out, an 11-year-old taken to hospital with a broken nose.

When they told me what had happened I didn't even go back to the hotel. I went straight to see her, feeling sad and intimidated in a way, to know that my shot had broken her nose. And I went in there, and saw the blood on her shirt. Tears in my eyes.

'Tia girl, I'm so sorry about this.'

She looked at me back, big smile on her face. 'Chill!'

'I'm sorry?'

'Don't be sorry! Don't be sad. Why you sad? Just keep hitting sixes!'

'Are you serious?'

'Keep hitting sixes!'

No tears. Nothing at all. I gave her a hug, I gave her a signed shirt. And the next home game I brought her into the stadium, and she watched this time from the posh seats.

I walked out to bat. I looked up at the stands. Cardboard signs, everywhere – 'Please hit me, Chris!' Holes cut in the cardboard for their noses to poke through. 'Please break my nose!' 'Please hit my nose so you can visit me in hospital!' All the way around the stands.

Some like to see their sixes bounce off a roof; I like to see them buried in the crowd, totally disappear.

It's like watching wind go through a field of corn. Everyone swaying and ducking and a magic path opening up. You'll see 20 pairs of hands all coming together, and then the ball just goes until it pops out again, thrown back, fingerprints and sweat and love all over it. Sometimes you hit a flat one, a skimmer, and they're the dangerous ones. That ball is travelling. If you see it coming it's on you quicker than your eyes tell you. If you don't see it coming you don't see it at all. Incoming missile. Run for cover!

I've hit a lot of cricket balls. As a batter you know as soon as you've hit a ball. Big hit. This will be close. Ballboy, please duck. Lady on the top tier, please look up. And the ball goes like a rocket, and you hope that this isn't the day it happens.

Not often is the catch taken. They're not moving their feet. They can't. There's a reason why the fielder at long-on doesn't stand with his legs between the back of one plastic seat and the front of another. Neither is he trying to make a catch while being shoved or holding a beer in the other hand. People in front jumping up. People to the side jumping across. Arms coming across you. It's not a surprise so few crowd catches are taken, it's a miracle any are.

When you clear those fans, when you clear the stands they're sitting in, it can be a different kind of fun. Somerset against Kent, summer 2015, Taunton. I've hit 14 sixes, and there's another one in the barrel. Mighty six, out of the ground, into the River Tone. That's the ball gone. Bobbing around in the middle of the river.

Except this particular fan wants to lay his hands on it. Off come his shoes, off come his jeans, off comes his top. Down to the pants and in he goes, some hard-working front crawl out through the murky water, grabbing the ball, tying up on the way back to the banks but just about making it, fished out by his mates while the crowd watching cheer him on or shout, 'Shark!'

I don't know all this. I'm just signing autographs afterwards, when a man with wet hair and cold hands holds up a damp white ball.

'I jumped in the river for this.'

'No way. You're kidding me . . .'

People all around me: 'Yup, it's true.'

I sign the ball for him, thinking yeah right, and then I'm on social media later and I see all the clips of his expedition. 'Whoah, so it was true!' So I follow him on Twitter. He's enjoying that, and then comes the tweet. 'Lissen man, I'll buy you some rum. And we'll meet at a club.'

And we did. Down the club, having a rum together. You need a rum when you've been in water that's as cold as an English river. And when you've not been ploughing through it, but doggy-paddling like a hound after a stick. Good souvenir though, hey?

The adrenaline kick of a six comes from the pull shot. A bread-and-butter shot, maybe, but a rich bread and butter with fat juicy raisins and spoonfuls of rum when it goes away way way. It's a great, great scene, oh, so nice to see! Good long airtime if you get it high, low and nasty if you roll the wrists a little. A quick reaction, a harder six to send away because it can get you in trouble. Play with a cross-bat and you're playing with fire.

You can take a spinner for six when you want. Whatever. I destroy left-arm spinners. Destroy them. Coming in to you, into your groove, right where you like to hit.

It's more satisfying to hit a fast bowler for six. Hitting the new ball off a fast bowler for six – that's better still. Hitting a century is usually considered the best feeling in cricket. I can tell you that going to your century by hitting a six is the finest feeling of all.

The straight six is the most beautiful to watch, but the hook shot off the fast bowler is the most thrilling. When you pull it off your nose, the ball coming in to damage your head, you have won that battle, and you have conquered fear.

I'd like to say that it's more satisfying hitting some bowlers than others, but I've hit all of them. You name them, they've felt my hands. Everyone. I mean they get me out too, but I've had a taste of everyone. I've had a piece of them all. I make sure I've stamped my authority on the big names.

The mis-hit six? Cheap but lovely. Off the top edge, your guns and your weapon sending it sailing into the crowd all the same. Play a cross-batted shot, try a sweep, and away it can go.

The bat I use these days has got some thick edges. It's a big piece of wood. You travel back in time and give my Spartan CG Boss Force or Spartan CG Boss Thunder to an old-timer opener and he'd be dragging it out to the middle and asking for help from short leg and first slip to lift it when he gets there. You're also paying a lot of excess baggage. That's how big it is. Powerful. And it does help me a little with those top edges by getting me a bit of mileage over the boundary. Once you know you have a good willow, you're willing to take chances, because you back your weapon to fire.

You want to make sure you get good meat when you're hitting the ball. Proper meat. When you can't, you lean back on proper timing. When you can't have proper timing either, that's the time to bring out the Six Machine power. You trust your bat. Make good contact and that ball is gone. You know you want to push it sometimes – time it and it gone for six.

Try to muscle it and you will lose your shape. When you're going for maximum power your head is all over the place. Your eyes totally gone off the ball. You'll top-edge it, mis-hit it or miss it, because there's no actual balance.

It's the sound that tells you. The sound tells you it's gone.

The Chinnaswamy, May 2011. Kochi have made 125 in 20 overs, and Dilshan and I walk to the middle with the chants already in our ears. 'Six! Six! Six!'

Always have a look. Only one scoring shot off the first five balls of R. P. Singh's over, and then to the last, pop him away into the second tier beyond long-on.

The giant screens flash. 'INTER-GAYLECTIC!' It's what comes down from the stands that makes it. 'Six! Six! Six!'

Dilshan on the charge in the second, 4, 4, 2, 0, 4, 6. Okay. We're smoking, and we can finish this quickly. The bowlers are under the pump, and the crowd are ready to explode.

Prasanth Parameswaran isn't a bad bowler. He bowls pretty decent left-arm pace. But when a new bowler comes on, you're going to put him under pressure immediately, and when you're chasing a low total and the magic is with you, it cuts the risk and builds the stage.

The first one I run down the wicket, give myself a bit of room and wallop it over long-on. The second one the keeper comes up to the stumps to stop me running down the wicket, so I make them do the running in the stands beyond the point boundary instead. It's a no-ball, so I send my free hit away for four through midwicket, and then, just to show it's classical timing that drives this destruction, place the next past extra cover for four more.

Still only three balls gone, and 21 runs taken. Our total has already passed 50.

Fourth ball, mashed over cover for six more. Fifth, the keeper goes back because what's the point, so I charge that one too and watch it disappear over the sight-screen. Final ball, cheeky inside edge down fine for four more.

One over, 37 runs.

As a kid you grow up with certain solid facts in the brain. Six is the maximum you can hit off a ball. 36 is the maximum you can hit off an over.

37? That's cricket Zlatan-style. That's cricket Usain-style – new numbers, impossible numbers.

Dilshan comes down with a smile on his face and knocks gloves. I keep my gladiator's mask on. Heart can be pounding but you won't see any of it.

Nothing is said to the bowler.

I didn't destroy Parameswaran's career. Maybe I actually helped it, because I gave him such good publicity. The following year he came and joined us at RCB. We didn't discuss it much. He had a bowl to me in the nets, and he didn't start shaking.

When you get that ping off the bat, when it comes off the sweet spot – ooof! It never loses its magic. And when it comes off sweet, when you see it fly and you know it's a big one, that's a double buzz, because I know the fans are going to be happy.

Not all sixes are equal.

There's one that was hit by Albert Trott at Lord's in 1899 that cleared the new pavilion. No one has ever done that since, and when you think that the bat he was swinging could fit three times into the ones we use now, that deserves respect sent down the centuries.

Not all sixes are measured. But my favourite came in Napier on the east coast of New Zealand's North Island, penultimate day of the second Test in December 2008, with Jeetan Patel bowling to me. I hit him out of the ground. Not just over the ropes, but over the stands. And those are big boundaries. Right out of McLean Park. Anything that fly that far should come with its own drinks trolley.

I've hit a lot of sixes. A lot of balls out of a lot of parks. But if you could have seen that one go . . .

I've hit balls into stands. I've hit balls out of stands. I've hit balls that have broken bits off stands, and I've hit balls into construction sites where stands used to be. I've knocked over drinks, I've broken windows.

I would like to formally apologize to the owners of the cars I have dented. If it was your windscreen that I shattered, I'm sorry, but please remember to park further away next time Six Machine come to town. It's worth the walk.

I've never killed anything, except maybe a bowler's heart. It does happen – there's a stuffed sparrow in the MCC museum at Lord's that took a cricket ball in the beak in the 1930s, and South Africa's Jacques Rudoph killed a pigeon at Headingley a few years ago – but when I'm batting most birds take to the skies for a better view. They're not stupid. They don't mess around once I'm batting. Clear the decks. When Chris Gayle is out, they'll come back to the pitch and pick up the crumbs. To be honest, I could probably polish off something bigger than a sparrow anyway. An albatross. A hippo. *Trus' mi*.

Balls go everywhere. Rivers. Back gardens. Picnics. People will come up to you as you leave the dressing-room and accuse you of making a mess of their bonnet. *Lissen mi*. You knew I was in town. And you still brought your car, your pride and joy. That's not playing the odds.

I've never been handed a bill. One day it'll happen. For now I should maybe be careful what I autograph when it's offered to me, make sure I unfold the piece of paper so I can be certain it doesn't open out into an invoice.

'Lick him again! Lick him again!'

Still I'm pushing the six times table further and further. More than 600 times six now in T20, although now you're reading this I'll have made dust of those numbers too.

I'm alone in my world. KP can't hit sixes like me. He can't hit them as often and he can't hit them as far. He knows that already. I could even switch hands and bat right-handed and beat KP in hitting sixes. Lots of sixes, but only one Six Machine.

IPL 2012, I hit 59 sixes. KP did well. He was second. And he was still 20 sixes behind me. In IPL 2013, 51 sixes, 22 more than Kieron Pollard in number two. IPL 2015, 38 sixes, 10 more than Pollard. And that was with an injured back.

I played only three matches for Somerset in the 2015 NatWest Blast. In that time I hit 29 sixes. Luke Wright matched that total, but he batted 14 times. Ross Whiteley hit 29 sixes too, in his case in 13 innings. He ended with an average of 39. Mine was 328.

The nature of a West Indian cricketer is to play your shots, to play with aggression, to play with flair. To be the showman. Add in a gym in your own house and you build the machine even bigger.

You want to build six-hitting muscles, you do the hard work. On the pulley machine, attach a bar to the loop when it's at the bottom. Start with a light weight and work on the hand speed. Move the pulley to the top, and use the bar to play a pull shot or down the ground. Light weights, quick hands. Break out the resistance bands. Tie one end around a tree or table leg, hold the other in two hands and play natural. Tune the strokes, build the engine.

Still some critics claim hitting a six is a risky shot, as if putting the ball where no fielder can touch it is somehow dangerous. I'm not playing it as a risky shot. I've worked out the odds of the ball being in the right place and of me doing what I want with it. Don't get me wrong – if there are two guys on the boundary I'm looking to take them on for sure, because you're backing your ability. And sometimes you will get caught out there, and you'll look ridiculous. But before you fall you will have laid many low with mighty blows, and you will have entertained.

Hitting a six is a risky shot, is it? Maybe that's why, in 2,056 Tests, no one had ever hit the first ball of a Test match for six. The first ball of a Test match you look to defend. You want to survive. You never attack the first ball.

I don't hunt these records, but your personality comes through in what you do.

Dhaka, Bangladesh, towards the end of 2012. I didn't think of it the night before, or as a long-term aim. When I was walking out, the mindset was that I would be facing a fast bowler. But when I saw debutant off-spinner Sohag Gazi marking his run-up, I thought, are you kidding me?

Are you taking the piss? I'm going to put them on the back foot from the first ball.

And then in it came, floated up, and I go for it. An instinct shot, because I had set the mind for an attacking shot. I set the mind before a ball had already been bowled. It was already in the making, so I just went straight through. Watch me fly.

No one was down at long-on. So in some ways it was a risk-free shot. But even if there had been a man – two men, three men, men on ladders – I would still have done it, because he was a debutant. A fresh wicket, and giving a spinner the ball?

Most of the times when I get out fast, I know I won't last long. I'm too attacking. If I stay there some time and then think about it, I'll last longer. Sometime I remind myself, *lissen Chris*, if you keep this going you know what will happen, so I try to curb it a little, and then start back again. But in that particular moment I had to keep it going.

Four next ball to leg, then another six down the ground. To 24 before anyone had woken up, two men back on the straight boundary now, and you keep going and going and going, and then one false shot . . .

Bangladesh will have felt they won the battle, because they set the trap and I sprung it. But at the same time, within myself, I knew that was the plan, and I wasn't bothered by it. I still did my thing. I could have curbed my game and this and that, but I carried on.

I had no idea that I was the first. As a kid I couldn't have imagined it. As an adult I couldn't believe that someone hadn't done it. But then you think about it. Most opening batsmen would never even have dreamed of trying it. Most of that small percentage who did imagine it would quickly have run a mile from the idea. Which leaves you even fewer who would have considered it, and even fewer who would have had the opportunity – the right bowler, on the right day, on the right pitch, putting the ball in the right spot.

If someone matches me now, it'll have to be pre-planned. And it will have to be someone big to take the chance.

When the time comes to say goodbye, that one will give me a little smile. A little, whoah! In the moment I never looked at it like that. It was still a Test match we had to win. My opening partner, Kieran Powell, hit 117. Shiv Chanderpaul made a double ton. Denesh Ramdin made another century, and Tino Best then took five wickets in the final innings to bowl us to victory.

Those were the important numbers. But don't ever sing to me that three is the magic number. We all know what the true magic number is.

ii. 333

When he was coach of the West Indies, Ottis Gibson once told me I needed to get my eyesight checked. I had dropped a couple of catches, and Ottis Gibson decided I could no longer see the ball. I was seeing it flying off my bat and out of stadiums, but I believe in respect, so I didn't even argue with it. 'Okay, why not?'

So I went. Everything was perfect. My eyes could have been nominated for awards. The optician was beautiful too, so it was worth going for more than one reason. Amazing eyes of her own, and when opticians check your eyes they really look into yours. She was married, we're professionals, we behaved with professional respect. All that matters is that I can not only see the ball but I can make out the individual stitches as it comes in to me at 90 miles an hour and connects with my bat to go back the other way even faster.

I can see this ball going over deep midwicket, and I can see this one disappearing into that river. And I can see the fine detail on that scoreboard over there, which will be showing something special in the very next Test match I play.

My innings begins the night before. Alone in the team hotel on the south-west coast of Sri Lanka, lying on my bed, just lying there thinking about it, eyes open.

I analyse my game. I see myself doing well out there in the middle. I see each particular bowler and I see how I will play accordingly.

I visualize a particular bowler bowling a particular ball. If you know the team and you know the bowler and you know their action, you picture that action. You see the ball in their fingers and how their body shape or angle changes ever so slightly with each different delivery. I imagine the backdrop, the particular stands and sightscreen, just to get that feel before the first blow of battle is struck.

Wherever you are, whatever format, you think about the mix: four or five bowlers, their attributes, how the captain might use those against you, what damage you can lay upon them. You put those things in your mind as early as possible so you can sleep on it and cement ideas into actions. When you wake up, you refresh your mind and go back to the big thoughts. And when you go out there your mind will click back to those images and thoughts, and you will be ready.

The first Test, Galle. The first Test since I have lost the captaincy, the first Test with Darren Sammy in charge. A lot of white noise and turmoil around us, a lot of fire blown at me. Does Gayle care? Is Gayle committed? Does he support the captain?

Understand the pressures rather than letting them dictate. Make space to deal with them.

I pack my bags the night before. Sleep is more important to me than breakfast, so I shower to wash away the doubts and walk straight to the team bus. Music on my headphones to wake me and establish the rhythm of the day. You must be mentally ready before you hit the bus, because you are the opening batsman, and even if our team plan is to bowl, the coin can land either way and you can be at the crease less than half an hour later. And half an hour is not enough, never enough.

On this morning in the building heat and tension nobody really talks. I push the white noise and fire away. I prepare for what Sri Lanka will bring.

There was a time when I would make sure that every day before a Test I'd be in the nets, and always batting, always batting, against a new ball as much as possible because I'm an opening batsman. I would enjoy getting a feel of the bowlers and the ground around.

Not so much now, for sometimes the nets become a cage. I want to see the ball flying, but I am trapped. I feel as if I am suffocating.

We never had nets on our nets as kids at Lucas. Just the concrete strip, the trees on the boundary through mid-on and midwicket for the left-hander like me, the sandy outfield on the offside, the lignum tree deep at third man, the fence of the little school stretching round from deep midwicket to long leg. Surround me in netting and I can't play the Chris Gayle way. I can try to be defensive, work on my technique, feel my balance, but I need to escape.

I will move into a more open net, one not enclosed on both sides by other nets, and now I can hit balls, but it is never enough. So I will move on again, this time to the middle, to the middle of the open spaces, and get the throw-downs and start hitting with freedom, and see the ball flying.

That's my preparation. Have the bowlers bowl at you to get a feel, not looking to attack, just feel the ball on the bat. Get the hands and the eyes tuned, get your legs moving. Be explosive in another net. And then set yourself free.

Sometimes you'll challenge yourself. Take on the bowlers. Take on the bowlers and put them under the pump.

There are players who bat in the net and treat it like a series of unrelated deliveries. Every ball a different bowler. I get one man to run in for a full over, and I give myself scenarios. Four balls to get 15 runs. Give me a target and I am alive.

Freed from the trap, I do range work. A team-mate throwing the ball down, me punching the ball into the stands. Hitting sixes, hitting them in different ways – low and skimming, high and mighty, into the first tier, up into the middle, onto the roof in a mighty arc. See the ball flying, flying. Watching it go away and feeling the confidence flowing.

Sometimes you'll tell the thrower exactly where you want the ball to land. Throw it full for a couple of minutes, I want to send it straight down the ground. Drop it short and spicy for six balls, I want to pull. Onto my legs, I'm swinging these away into those executive boxes beyond deep square leg. To see the ball sailing away is a sweet feeling and a warm one.

Confidence come from hard work. Confidence enable you to flourish.

Each ground brings its own special squeeze. At Galle, the ruins of the old fort past long-on, the sea beyond, the humidity intense, you know the ball will bite and turn.

Each man finds his own way to prime for the battle. England's Ian Bell carries in his kit bag one bat that's three-quarters as wide as a normal one, and another that's only as wide as a ball. He uses it to fine-tune the eyes for the one that turns late or sizzles off the subcontinental soil.

Me? I just want a big heavy bat. Just give me my weapon and make sure it has some weight and some meat and I'm good. *Gimme my bat an' let's go an' war.*

I have struggled in Sri Lanka before. I've yet to score good runs in a Test series here. There are reasons this morning to be full of doubt and what chance do I have.

So as well as readying the body for battle you must ready the mind. Do not think of the noise from your edge as it carries through to the keeper. Do not focus on the past failures. You've got to see yourself facing the first ball, and you've got to see yourself hitting those sixes. All those years ago at Lucas, Spike Rhoden used to say it: see yourself score a hundred before it actually happen.

You have to dig deep within yourself, truly, to master it. If you can master it on your own, without using a sports psychologist, then even better. Not always will there be help around you. The man who solves his own problems can solve more when they arrive.

Confidence enable you to relax.

I don't worry if the throw-downs don't feel right. Why should they? They're only throw-downs. Where's the stress? I don't do anything superstitious. I come back into the dressing-room after the warm-up, half an hour to play, and just relax. Let the unconscious mind go to work.

The coin can land either way, but this time it lands right. I have toiled in the field in this ground before, seen three new balls come and go. It's a ground whose history is built from runs. Darren Sammy says we will bat. There is no other way.

You are never alone. My opening partner today is Adrian Barath, just 20 years old, in his first full season of Test cricket. Communication is key, so you wish each other luck. Because he is young, like so many of the openers who have been thrown in alongside me, I'm the one doing the talking. I say, don't be shy. If you want help with anything, come and tell me. Relax. Feel at home.

There are always nerves. I have been playing Test cricket for more than a decade at this point, but when you are sitting here waiting to go out, nobody wants to get in your way. You can feel your body getting ready for battle – the pulse in your ear, the sweat on your palms, the blinks in your eyes.

The bell sounds. Bat in hand, through the corridors, studs a-clatter. Onto the rolled grass and silence. You step across that white rope and it kicks in: all this is natural, and you do not fear it.

It is a beautiful ground. The red brickwork of the fort's tall tower. The blue sea and boats beyond. Grassy banks around the boundary, a pair of steep three-tiered stands. In your ears the honking of smoky old buses on the busy roads behind the pavilion.

I am aware of nothing – not the crowd, not the sunshine, not the waiting opposition. If someone was calling me I wouldn't answer. I'm thinking about the middle. I'm not looking left and right.

To the wicket. Always the same thing when I get there. Have a look at the track. Walk back to the crease. It gives me the background settings. It establishes the scene. It's like my mind is a camera, scanning what doesn't matter, then zooming in to focus on the spot where the ball will come from, locking the range, locking the range.

When I was starting out, I would feel the nerves again now. You're inexperienced. You're intimidated by some fast bowlers.

Now I have seen it, and I have survived it. This is my place.

The first ball is the most focused you will be in your life. The first ball is the most important one. When that first ball is coming, your mind is completely clear.

Nothing but you and the bowler. I slow my breathing down. I keep my head really still. Hands soft and relaxed.

People ask if you play that ball on instinct or conscious thought. It is both and neither. It is a natural thing.

It is about balance. You have to give yourself the chance to go forward, and you have to give yourself the chance to come back. Try not to get caught in two minds, even if it happens to all of us. And lean on the calculations you made on the hotel bed the night before: what has this bowler's first ball done before? If he's going to pitch it here, how am I going to play it? If it's coming at me from that angle, where is my weight?

Coaches talk about watching the ball onto the bat. It's a myth. You can't, not off a quick bowler. It's impossible. It's just a phrase. You just have to pick up the line as early as possible. And be in a good position, a comfortable position, where you can play that particular ball.

Ninety overs in a Test match day, 540 balls in all. You can tell after one delivery if the magic is there. The bowlers can know too. They experiment and assess in those first exchanges – how much bounce is there? Is there movement? Is it swinging?

When you're in form, you can sometime think that you could bat blindfolded. And that's a beautiful feeling. Sometime you go out and everything just click from ball one. Slow-motion cricket, for you if not the chasing fielders.

And sometimes nothing. You can understand why players are superstitious, because you want to control that feeling. You want to control the magic. When it's not there panic grabs at your guts. When it's not there everything feels fast. The ball is upon you before you can move.

Dhammika Prasad, coming in from the City End, right arm over, angling them across me. Pitched up just short of a length, I play and miss. Howls and growls from all around, pulse drumming harder in my ear.

Sometimes your feet might not be moving, and you get caught at the crease or you nick off. You try so many things, but sometimes the magic is not there. That does not mean that it will not return.

Viv Richards saw himself as a boxer, ducking some blows, riding others. I am a surfer, riding the wave. I tell myself to ride out the session. Survive this, and you will be good. *Tests gonna test you.* You might score 15 runs in a session. Fine. As an opener you have to ride the wave and hang on.

And it won't last for ever. Even if Prasad and Thilan Thushara are bowling a good length, you know they must get one wrong. One will definitely come in your slot. When it does, you have already thought about how you will play it.

You have to relish those calculations. It's like playing chess. Who's the smartest? Can you out-think that great bowler?

Use every skill in your mind. In Test cricket you slow it down. You've got to give yourself a chance. Be patient. Play the delivery on you now, rather than the one that beat you before.

Ajantha Mendis has come into this match with a reputation to wreck weaker minds. He has taken eight wickets in his first Test and 26 in his first series. He flicks leg breaks with his fingers, and he not only has the varieties that you know about – top-spinners, googlies, sliders and biters – but mystery ones that no batsman in the world has been able to read. There is sometime one called the carrom ball, where he bends his middle finger and snaps the ball out between knuckle and thumb. Even if you spot that one it does you little good – he can make it turn to leg, turn to off or make it go straight on. Who is wearing the blindfold now?

I have planned for it. I have studied his moods and character. What is he likely to try next? What do I want to make him do next? How can I launch into him, how can I weaken him?

I have started slowly. I am watching the wicket and what these bowlers can do on it. I can also feel the fast outfield, so I start to pick it up, pick off a few gaps, see the ball race to the boundary. From that first boundary more confidence flows. The relaxation kicks in. Now I'm in the groove. Now we can start to hit back.

Or maybe they want to hit some more. Kumar Sangakkara is an outstanding captain. He makes his own studies, and when my partner, Barath, goes to Suraj Randiv's off spin, he goes for turn from both ends and tries to tighten the vice.

A man in short on the leg side, a man under nose. First slip and keeper cackling and cajoling. In your ears, constant yap yap yap.

You cannot let them get to you, because if you let them get to you, you're in big trouble.

It's not like you're not hearing them. You're hearing them. You can't block them out when they're right under your nose. You can't pretend you can't hear them.

Instead, let the ball fill your mind. Let it push everything else back and away. Just you and the ball. Nothing else around you. The man at short leg? Waste of time. The chat coming up from the slips? Waste of time. Most batsmen who see fielders around them want to get rid of them, to force them back. They'll go attacking and they'll get out. You just play the ball and play it well.

Use your skills. A cricket ground is a large place. There will be gaps, more so with so many men in short. Push for a one. Get off strike. Get down the other end and get a little breather, so they can't bowl too many deliveries to you in a row. Rotate it round. Break the stranglehold. Give them the problem of you being a problem.

Mendis with his snap-fingered carrom. The ball skidding into my front pad. Huge appeal, screams from all around.

The pulse in the ears. The umpire shakes his head. Sangakkara refers it upstairs. The pulse beats. The decision comes back down – bat in that one too, just as I knew, just as I feared they didn't.

Getting out always hurts. Getting out when you are set makes you want to kick yourself up the ass, because you messed it up.

You talk to yourself as you walk off, curse yourself. If you're playing at home the crowd will do it too. You can hear it coming in – 'You can't bat,' and that's Jamaican style, big drawl on it, 'YUH CYAAN BAT!' 'You can't do shit . . . YUH CYAAN DO SHIT!'

You feel paranoid going back into the dressing-room. What have I done? What will they say?

You have to learn to deal with it. You have to have room for disappointment, because in every man's life it will come. Don't hit the dressing-room this way and that. Put down your stuff easily and calmly, even though you're upset. Give yourself a few minutes to catch back your breath, have a sit and hold your head down. Don't try to pick yourself back up for a couple of minutes.

It's not like you're not hurting. You're feeling bad inside. But you are a batsman, and every batsman must deal with it. I never let that anger out, not in a burst. That's the way I have set myself. I say, this is me. Disappointment must come, but nothing will last for ever.

Every day the tide turns. So it is on the rocks beyond the Galle fort, so it is in the middle.

I start to attack the spinners. Down the track to Randiv's off breaks, clouting him over the sightscreen and into one of those honking buses touting for passengers heading north to Colombo. Another dent in the side to add to its collection.

You want to score at a rate where you are dictating the game, not them. So down the track to the next delivery, on 96, and although it's high this time rather than as long, and the fielder is dashing round to catch it, the willow and the sea breeze give it enough to drop the ball over the ropes and the fielder into the advertising boards.

My 100 up, in a country where I failed to get past 50 in the preceding Test series. I take off my helmet, white bandana beneath, and lie back on the warm soil with a big smile on my face.

You never take a century for granted. No one remembers you scoring 99? That's not quite true. But a half-century, you don't even want to raise your bat. Triple figures is the only way. That's how you stamp your mark.

People ask if the feeling is better than sex. You get different sorts of sex, so . . . But when you get past that milestone, counting becomes easier. The runs tick over without you thinking about it.

No number is enough. You can't get to 100 and be satisfy. You need to be greedy. A big appetite is a good thing to have. Eventually you're going to get out, and you're going to regret it. 'Oh, if I could have stayed out there and scored another forty runs . . .'

So get to 150. Go for 200. There will be more dry days than wet days, and you have to bat for those days too. Put the cash in the bank. Go longer.

I always understood this. Just bat, and bat, and bat. At Galle as it was at Lucas. Make it big.

I had a slow start to my Test career. After four games I was averaging 13. Some of the older guys in the dressing-room said to me, 'Get one big innings and your average will look just fine.' And they were right, because my first century was a big one, 175. And that's something that has played in the back of my mind ever since.

Onwards. Never get carried away. You've got to talk to yourself. You've got to calm yourself down, for when things are flowing easily, when you've scored an easy little burst of 20 in two overs, that's when you're in trouble and the chance will come. Don't get ahead of the wave; the guy who rides the wave out will be batting for the entire day.

I tell myself that I'm playing catch-up for what I've missed out on in Sri Lanka. This has got to be a big one. Not thinking about a triple century, but batting right throughout the entire day.

On that previous tour, Chaminda Vaas got me five times out of six innings in Sri Lanka. My worst series ever in cricket. I'd just scored my first Test century, so I went there lazy. I didn't think it would be that tough. And then you're in the field for three new balls, and then you have to bat for four overs, just to survive the night. Vaas isn't that fast, the ball isn't coming on, you're pushing at the ball too early, you're nicking off.

I'm not his bunny. Mike Atherton was dismissed by Glenn McGrath 19 times in 17 matches. He was dismissed by Courtney Walsh 17 times and Curtly Ambrose the same again. That might seem full of shame, but he's the opening batsman, and they're the opening bowlers. He faced more deliveries from them than anyone else, with a new ball, when the pressure was on and the field up. That's why I take my hat off to any Test opening batsmen who averages over 40. There are no nightwatchmen for opening batsmen. Numbers three and four get one, but not us. Are they saying his wicket is more valuable than mine? I still don't get it.

It was good for me to learn the hard way, early. So now when Mendis is coming in, feeling like a world-beater, on a pitch that takes turn and with a crowd and captain at his back, I am as unyielding as the walls of the fort and as relentless as the waves beyond.

I have already made the plans. I have already worked out when to attack him and when to let him go. When he's the man doing the damage to my team-mates, see him off until the bowling change, and then get going again. Play the long game. For all that you want to dominate, he can also be on top. He can also be on good form. So you have to respect that, and you have to let it go. Let that one particular bowler go and make the rest history.

There are other ways I will take Mendis on. I will show him no fear, only my gladiator's mask. Spin brings its crafty trials, but even when a fast bowler hits me, I do not show any pain. I wear it and bear it.

I can get inside his head. I can think like a bowler, because I am a bowler.

If you're skilled at it, you can predict which delivery is coming. You hit a ball for four, you think, where is he going to come now? If I were bowling to me, what would I do?

You don't premeditate, but you influence the odds, because most times you're not going to get the same delivery again, not after finding the boundary with the last one. So you have already narrowed the range of options. For one particular bowler you might have five possible shots; that's now down to four. The sums are turning your way.

I never make notes. It's all stored in my mind. I can access that instantly in that middle, when paper would be blowing round the dressing-room or a laptop plugged in charging. And you have to think quickly, and once you think about it, you have to be in the right position to play all four of those shots.

I have accepted that Mendis will test me. I have accepted that he will create chances. If I have an escape, if someone drops a sharp catch or fumbles a run-out, I will forget it ever happened. You can't take a mistake back. Some batsmen may beat themselves up about it, get angry. But it's happened. Okay. They've given me a chance. So it's my day today. Let's make the most of it.

Randiv comes back on. Get inside his head. Give him the problem of me being a problem.

One reverse sweep, chopped away fine past a startled Jayawardene at slip. Next ball, because he won't expect it, another reverse sweep, this time harder and squarer.

Now is the time, now you're on top, to mess with the bowler. I will read his body language, how he corresponds with his captain. Because I am the batsman this gives me power.

I'm searching for weakness. Darting eyes. The bowler shaking his head. They can be bluffing, but you learn. You come to understand a particular bowler's normal mood and movements, and so then when they are under stress. Because bowlers be scared too. About being hit. About losing control. I've been batting before when a captain has

I'm a slogger, am I? My first Test triple century, against South Africa in 2005. I was used to batting all day; I'd grown up doing it on the Lucas outfield (Getty)

I faced the first ever ball in the first ever World T20. It was a good storyline, but I'm an entertainer, so I understood it needed more. The first ever international T20 century followed 50 balls later (Getty)

Only three men had ever hit two Test triple centuries. Better make that four. Galle in Sri Lanka is hot; across those two days, I was hotter (Getty)

I like to dance even on quiet nights. When the West Indies have won the World T20, I'm going to dance Gangnam, tops off and upside-down. World Boss! (Getty)

(Getty)

(Getty)

I'm the Tsar of T20, the boss of the boundary boards. I've been called a pioneer by some and a legend by others, so if someone is going to hit the first ball of a Test match for six, of course it should be me (Getty)

The secret to hitting the highest-ever score in a T20 match, to making a hundred off just 30 balls? Pancakes for breakfast. NB: I think I carry off the gold helmet rather well (BCCI)

No one had ever hit a double century in a World Cup match.
Six Machine is not no one (Getty)

Dishing out the licks for the Tallawahs at Sabina Park. I used to sneak into the stands here to watch the Jamaican greats. Now I send sixes into those same seats (Getty)

You travel back in time and give my Spartan CG Boss Thunder to an old-timer opener and he's dragging it out to the middle and asking for help from short leg and first slip to lift it when he gets there

World Boss meets Beckham Boss. A cool moment, for both of us

Usain and me go way back, on dancefloors across Kingston. Warning: when he bowls to you, his run-up is the fastest thing you've ever seen at a cricket ground (Getty)

I travel the world, but I always come home. Being born and raise Jamaican is the single best thing that has happened to me. For all the struggles, for all the pain, I wouldn't trade it to be a sheltered citizen of anywhere else

Life is about now. If you're going to do it, do it big. Do not wait for the never-comes future. Do not die worrying about the edge behind. Play your shots, and play them your way

Some people ask why I call myself World Boss. I only ask, why not Universe Boss?

From down there to up here: the dream was always to buy a house, because I know where I'm coming from, because then you've made the jump. You're not going back

I'm a complicated man. Sometimes the mood descends and I say something some people think I shouldn't. Then trouble comes my way . . . (Getty)

asked a bowler to come on, and he's refused. He doesn't want to face me.

Past my 150, six sixes and 20 fours.

You can tell when you're in charge; it's like you're in demand. The match has started revolving around you, no longer a bit part but the key role.

You can see it in the faces, on the wicketkeeper when you glance behind you, in the body language of the bloke who was fielding at short leg as he trudges back out to deep mid-wicket instead. They know they're in for a long day. They can only hope for the best. And when you're in control, it's a sweet deep feeling. We know how quickly a match can change, so when it's happening for you, you have to cash in.

175. Darren Bravo dropping anchor at the other end. Our total has gone past 300 and records are there, but more important is how I'm feeling. Is the magic there? Then the stats take care of themselves.

Sangakkara senses the battle is slipping away. A wise general, he opens a new front: mid-on and mid-off three quarters of the way back, the spinner tossing it up to tempt me, then firing one in quicker for the sucker-punch. Come into my web, said the spider to the superfly.

It's bait, but it doesn't have to be dangerous bait. I'm an aggressive batter, so I still back myself to clear those men. If you're looking to runs, and you know that's your strength, you play according to it. And you'll get them. Most times.

Heat burning me up now, sweat prickling and tickling. The humidity in Sri Lanka a rough killer.

To concentrate all day on anything is hard. Try sitting on a sofa reading a book, and an hour in you'll be thinking about lunch. I have been batting for two and a half sessions, seen 400 balls bowled.

I am a decade into my Test career, and I understand how you handle it: you break Test cricket up. In the first session of each day you get 14 overs in the first hour, then a drinks break where you can consolidate, and then 14 again. After the lunch break you have the most important session. Get through that first hour and you are in demand. You can ride it. The last session is when the most runs come. Shine off the ball, wicket flatten out, bowlers tire.

That's where we are now. Even in this moment, closing in on the double century, you can't focus on every delivery. It's like flicking a switch on and off. And then when Sangakkara turns again to his key man, Mendis, you turn up the focus. Supercharge the head.

You work together with your partner. Darren Bravo makes only 58 off 159 balls, but together we put on 196. If you're doing well you don't say so much, because you don't want to overcomplicate things. In the tough moments and overs you get involved. When it's not going your way, you need all the help you can get.

To 200. Ovations all around, but I am being greedy. Get through till the close. Get through this second new ball.

It's easy to start daydreaming. When I'm fielding at slip my mind will wander off and go somewhere. It happens to me when I'm having a long conversation. I'll be talking to someone and then it goes somewhere else. I don't know why that happens.

I don't get it when I'm batting. At the non-striker's end I'm often thinking about something else. But as soon as I'm at the business end I'm switching back on.

It's challenging, batting long. You need a lot of fluid. No batter will eat. They can't eat. You get cramps, you feel sluggish.

The sun sinks below the battlements of the fort. I think back down the years to South Africa in Antigua and the 317.

Once you experience something, you know you have the ability within yourself to do it again. Once you achieve something, you want to surpass it.

As the day ends with me on 217, I know that a second triple century is a possibility. I know too what a huge thing it would be. So many great players don't have one. You look at the legend Sachin, the man who has more Test centuries than anyone else, and he will never score a Test triple.

Never get carried away.

To the first ball of the second day, Mendis refreshed and raring, there is a screaming lbw appeal.

The umpire stays motionless. They refer it again.

Not out.

A new day, a new front. Now Sangakkara goes for death by boredom, and instructs Thushara to bowl all six balls of his over well outside off stump.

As West Indian batsmen we're not raised to be patient. We are attacking players; we want to feel the ball onto the bat. So sometimes we'll chase a wide one, just to try to score. Many times it is our downfall. I have a reputation for hanging my bat out there. It has sometimes cost me dear.

I leave all six.

I have learned patience. I know that Sangakkara can't stick with that tactic for long, because it will kill the game just bowling wide wide wide. I know I can be smarter.

No coach can convince you. It has to come from within, for if you're getting out like that you're going to lose your place in the team. Find other ways to score or else you'll find ways out of the team. What does it take to survive? Figure it out and do it.

Give it time. Never panic. When you panic, you give away your wicket. Wait for it to come round to you.

Work your odds. Bear in mind you're batting with someone else, Shiv Chanderpaul now with me in the middle. Give him a chance to move the board.

Even on 220, you can find yourself becalmed. The pitch has changed, the humidity is making the ball reverse swing. Your hands are slipping inside your wet gloves.

You're just not hitting it, not hitting it at all. You can be thinking that the magic has left you, that it's betrayed you. And then – crash – with one stroke it's back in your eyes and arms. You have to believe it's going to come back. Don't lose hope. Stay strong. As long as you're still around you have a chance to score runs.

250, lunch approaching on day two. I feel like I have been at the crease for ever. I feel part of the Galle turf. I feel as ancient as the fort.

Now is as dangerous as the first over with the new ball. Now is Sangakkara's next gambit: death by flattery.

You like that shot, yeah? Well, let me feed it. Let me bowl into exactly the slot you like, except I will also pack that scoring area with my best catchers. You relax, Chris Gayle. You play your natural game. Don't worry about us until the flattery goes to your head and you get just a fraction loose and we gobble you up and you're gone.

For some batsmen it's the short ball, sitting up and asking for it, with one man at deep midwicket, one at fine leg and one at long leg. Some batsmen are compulsive. *Cyaan resist.* Others are egotists, and won't admit they could fail.

The smart batsman plays not into the plans but calculates how he can counter them. He makes sacrifices – I'll ignore that one – and he soaks it up, maybe wearing a short one on the lid. He plays to his strengths; if he's not accustomed to ducking short stuff, don't suddenly start ducking. Do what works for you, not what might suit them.

For me it's the drive. Sangakkara puts himself in at short extra cover and another man in close to his right and gets Prasad and Thushara to pitch it up, full and juicy and winking at me. Have a drive, Christopher Henry Gayle. Everyone loves your cover drive. Here's another. Beautiful. You relax. And here comes the slower one, and here comes the same shot, and here comes the ball, straight down my open throat . . .

Stay strong. 280 now, Chanderpaul gone, Brendan Nash in his place.

Stay simple. Don't worry about technique, about what might look nice in a freeze-frame. Just focus on balance. It's all about balance.

Coaches will try to get the same effect through more complicated methods – trigger points, back-lifts, knee bends. Strip it back instead.

There is a guy called Richard Austin, long-time Jamaican cricketer, super-talented all-rounder. In later years he got lost in the struggle, falling apart after going on the rebel tour of apartheid-era South Africa, falling into drugs and homelessness. Even in the confusion he would still come up with clarity: 'Chris, yuh don' move until di bowler release di ball.'

Be still, and control your breathing. Lessons from the streets of east Kingston: when a bowler come for you, sometime it's like shooting a gun. You have to control your breathing.

Over the long years and long innings I have trained my mind for these moments. I know not to exaggerate things — *dis is a bad track, dis ting impossible.* I know to always stay comfortable in myself; you have enough men there trying to wreck you without your own thoughts trying to tangle your feet too. Be confident within yourself, whatever you're trying to do. Always. Don't hold it back. You can get it. Just know you can do it.

And take a little luck when it comes your way. A few runs later, Prasad digs one in rather than pitching it up for the drive. Surprised, I get cramped up and jam the ball off the splice, up high, down to Sangakkara at that short extra cover. He doesn't even have to move. Prasad collapses on his back, his team-mates jog over wearily and slap his heaving chest.

And then Brendan Nash, sharp-eyed Brendan Nash, puts his hand up to me and puts his little magic in the umpire's ear.

'You might just want to have a look at where that front foot landed . . .'

Upstairs to the third umpire and his replays. Slowing down Prasad's delivery stride. Watching the front foot. Watching it land fractionally over the popping crease.

Nash, you can drink for free at Triple Century whenever you want. Chris, you got a life there. Make the best of it.

And so, on 297, I see Randiv toss one up. I step out, lean my heavy bat and slap it away between those two men short in the covers, and I see the ball racing away, and I see no fielder anywhere near it and none to chase.

I kneel down on the pitch, helmet in one hand, bat in the other. I look up at the sky and I say, 'Thank you, God.'

Joy, and happiness, and relief.

I had no idea that only three other men in history had ever scored two Test triple centuries. Don Bradman, Brian

Lara, Virender Sehwag. Not a bad little posse to join. Not bad company for the kid from St James Road, Rollington Town.

Cramp biting now. My hamstring seizing and stopping. Darren Bravo back out to act as my runner.

Time to swing it some more. At some stage we have to declare in order to win the game. Your bat feel like five bats. Swinging and ducking and running for a day and a half in that heat – if you find yourself at that stage, my advice is to swap your bat for a lighter one once you past 275.

I accelerate past the 317 of Antigua. Good. Now where next will this lead? I'm targeting 350, but time is running out. Energy is running out. Body is not running at all.

On 333, Mendis has his victory at last. A flicked carrom ball that lands and fizzes through the gap between my front pad and bat.

Sangakkara and Jayawardene the first to shake hands, the rest of their team-mates following. They've kept me in the baked field for so long in the past, they can swallow this little slice of revenge.

I get asked which triple century I like most. It's like choosing between two girls who you have loved at different times of your life. They're just different.

Then again, maybe this second one is sweeter. Away from home, in a country where we've always struggled. They have just taken away the captaincy of the country from me. And I have just shown them: *lissen man*, I still can play, with captain or without captain.

The pair of them bring more respect, for sure. But when you get number two, the expectation is higher. They want number three. When I get the first one they didn't say get another one. But two? All of a sudden they're looking on.

Oh, you're going to be the first to get three. All I hear is three three three.

What I don't hear again, from anybody, is that my eyesight might be going. Which in one way is a shame, for that optician was a very, very nice lady.

12. Absent

I have cheated death.

I have heard it on wires and patches in a distant land. I have seen it pass when all alone in a hospital ward, my family far away and unaware.

But death stalk you. Death is never far away.

During the school holidays we pick up odd jobs here and there to boost the funds. George Watson at Lucas has connections, and now he's not chasing us off the square on his bicycle or looking to lock us in the changing-rooms he will often hear about a little opening here and there.

He gets a few of us in at the National Stadium, John Murphy and Garrick Grant and me, cleaning up mess. One day, boys, one day. It's north up Mountain View Road from Rollington Town, past our school gates on the left and then down Arthur Wint Drive, definitely a bus ride for us.

The job's a bad one and the pay's worse. At the weekend John Murphy and I tell Garrick we're not going back on Monday. He wants to buy his first TV, now he's got a little room of his own, so he says he's sticking with it whatever.

Garrick's a good kid, raised on Madison Avenue, the short cul-de-sac that backs on to Lucas from the east side, directly opposite my house on St James Road. The zinc fence at the bottom of his yard doubles as the boundary fence on the outfield. He's a church-going boy, no bad bone, and everyone likes him.

When we ride the buses, we do something we call *bail-off* – jumping out of the open door between stops, when we're passing the spot we want. We're skill at it, hanging out the front to let someone in, hanging out the door as the jump spot approaches.

So Garrick is going back to work on Monday morning, back to earn the dollars for his first television, and he hangs out the door of the bus, waiting for the spot, and when the spot comes, the bus swings out to overtake, and he bails off.

And the bus swings back in, and Garrick is still there, and then Garrick is under the wheels, Garrick is under the wheels, under the wheels.

And Garrick is gone.

I wanted him to stop that work. The money was small, and his friends were playing at Lucas. I wanted him to be playing cricket with us. We live without televisions. Who can die for one?

Death stalk you.

I want him to be playing with us. Instead, there is a gap in the field and a space in the batting order.

We deal with it like kids do, through fear and tears. No one can catch a bus now. We will walk, even if the hot distance takes us long, long. The memory sits on our shoulders and breathes darkness on our faces.

As we kids in the West Indies team grow into men, you settle into friendships just as at home. Me and Wavell Hinds, the Lucas boy and the Kensington kid, come together under the flag, Marlon Samuels and Ramnaresh Sarwan soon to join us too. All about fun, all about watching out for each other.

When Runako Morton joins the team he is an instant hit. He may be from Nevis and he may have that islander accent but he reminds me of my old Jamaica partner Leon Garrick, a madman to some yet a madman who is crazy for you too. The relationships build, and we bring the best out of each other. No ringleader, just come up with a plan and go. You instinctively know what to say and what not to say. You run jokes. You travel the world, bright-eyed and alive, and you find the good spots and you have good times there in them.

Morton has a reputation. A joker, a clown. He cries when he is out, except the times when he smashes all his kit instead. He is all or nothing, and when he is in the middle he is a stubborn guy. Authority does not sit easily on him.

He is also a serious warrior. You want him on your side. But it is sometimes hard to keep him in the side, because the all-or-nothing messes with his head and takes him to dark places.

In 2001 he is expelled from the St George Cricket Academy in Grenada. They call it 'disciplinary reasons'; what actually happens is that he's late arriving, on account of being at his wedding in Barbados, and is found absent without leave, on account of going back to Nevis to see his new wife.

A year on, his aggressive batting winning him a place in the West Indies squad for the Champions Trophy in Sri Lanka, he asks to be allowed to fly home because his grandmother has died. Except once he's left it turns out one of his grandmothers died 16 years ago, and the other one is still walking and talking and pleased to see you.

All that is true. So too is that sometimes we don't really know what a man is going through. He is married and passionate and all these things are happening around him. He is a troubled man.

And he is also a proper hard-core player. If he respect you and rate you he will have your back like nobody else. He is a friend and warrior and he will not let a friend fall.

When it is just me and him alone, when I become captain, we roll a lot. Just the two of us, our relationship just fantastic. I know I can trust him and I know that trust will be repaid. When Stanford is calling the heavens down during that crazy month in Antigua, Morton is at my side every step.

And yet he's all or nothing.

In the DLF Cup in Malaysia, playing against Australia, he comes in to face the second ball of the innings after Brett Lee has nailed me down lbw to the first. With 241 needed to win off the rest of the 50 overs, Morton carefully blocks his first ball, then his next, and then his next.

Morton blocks his first 30 balls. On his thirty-first he is lbw to Nathan Bracken for nought. It is the longest duck, in terms of balls faced, in the history of one-day cricket. It takes him almost an hour.

We play Australia again, this time in the Champions Trophy in Mumbai. In the match where I get a little angry at Michael Clarke. Morton saves us with a superb 90 not out, garlanded with a massive straight six back over Glenn McGrath's head. All or nothing.

He gets criticized for his technique. He gets criticized for the things he has done, and he has done some bad stuff. There is no doubt about it. Bad stuff. When he gets pissed off he can really be up in your face. But he is under a lot of stress, and everyone has their bad times. Everyone has their times when they give it away. Deep in he is a really nice guy; on the field he will do anything for you, no matter how much it hurts him. He just needs an arm and a bond.

One day he calls me, just before I go to play in the South African T20 league for the Dolphins. He calls me and you can hear the pain.

'Chris, you know if tings okay I wouldn't come to you. But tings ain't pretty at home.'

He asks me to lend him some money to see him through. I'm just sorting out a few things for the trip to Durban, give me a few days and I'll wire it to you.

I am travelling for a couple of days, and it kind of slips my mind to do that for him. And I am sleeping in the hotel, weary from the long ride, and I hear a knock on my hotel door.

Use sleep an' mark death. Sleep foreshadows death.

Fidel Edwards. And he tells me he's had a message about a car accident.

'Morton, man, Morton crash an' dead.'

'Fidel, go sleep. Go relax yourself.'

'Serious Chris.'

'What yuh mean, crash and dead and what?'

I know from his face. 'Serious man! Go on your phone . . .'

Straight away to my phone. Straight away to the news. Pictures of Runako, and the letters 'RIP'.

It's there, and yet I can't process it. Morton can't be dead and gone. I've just spoken to him.

I have just failed him.

I had made a promise to him with funds and everything, and I haven't fulfilled that. Now he passed and gone. The hurt takes over, and breathes darkness on me once again.

I flew two days west and spoke at the funeral. To let the people know he's a warrior. To tell them that I know the passion he had and the determination and guts that marked his character. To let them know that if I'm to go on the field, I will walk with 10 Runako Mortons. Any time, any day.

During the last Caribbean Premier League I went to visit him in the cemetery in Trinidad. Me, Dwayne Bravo, Sulieman Benn. To the cemetery, to his grave. *Sit an' have a few chat an' a few drink.* He loved his whisky, so I poured a few over there.

When he crashed, I learned from talking to other people, he had a lot on his mind. The way he had been living wasn't the best. He was under tremendous stress and pressure, and they said he had a few drinks.

You get warnings in life, and the wise man heeds them.

Maybe the Lord took him out of his misery. Maybe the Lord took him away from it all. He couldn't face what was ahead of him, and the Lord say, 'Com' wit' me.'

His last List 'A' match was for Trinidad and Tobago against the Leeward Islands at Port-of-Spain. He and a team-mate were arrested on the evening of day one, on charges that were later dropped. And so, next to his name, on his last scorecard in his last big game, it simply says, 'absent'.

Gone but not forgotten. You don't forget men like Runako. Absent, but always with us.

Death stalk you. But don't fear death.

When things scare me, I remember that hospital ward. Meet darkness with light. Do everything to the fullest. No waiting and wondering, no compromises, no apologies.

Planes scare me. The older I get, the more they scare, and the older I get, the more planes I have to take.

In the sky your heart just go – oh! And with the turbulence and the drops and how does this stay up, sometimes you pray, just land this plane safe. Sometimes you pray, just get me out of this, please . . .

So attack it. Come down the pitch to the fiery bowler. Attack it in different ways: early flight, stay out partying all night and go straight from club to airport, sleep on the plane. Awake on the plane, I'm having a drink for sure. Start in the lounge, take a drink up there. If I'm going down, I'm going like a king. Like a king, sipping on a glass of champagne. If the plane lands and the fear still lingers, you walk out and you kiss the ground, and the first words off your lips are, 'T'ank Gad! Before I get back on dis plane, I'm partying tonight!'

I fear my body failing.

Fate can have plans to rip yours to pieces. When John Murphy and I are 15, playing Minor Cup, playing Junior Cup, he is at his usual up an ackee tree when he slips jumping at a branch and lands on his right arm. His wrist is dislocated, and the hospital is distant, so another friend just pulls it back in. From that moment he can no longer turn his wrist.

He is a wrist spinner. He was a wrist spinner.

He is forced to switch to pace, and the same magic is not there. His chances slip too, and the dream begins to wither on that tree.

Fate and injuries you cannot control.

Sometimes you're coming back from an injury, and you get injured straight away again. It happens again, and you wonder how much more you can take. You wonder if it's the end, even if you are working as hard as you can and following every instruction. I have had sciatica, the deepest nerve pain, and sciatica doesn't go. You try so many things and so few make any difference. The rest of your body can be in amazing shape, and it doesn't matter. The sciatica wins.

Losing hurts. I might not show it. You might not see it from me, yet inside it's burning up.

Don't get me wrong. You have to lose. But sometime what the critics say after you lose can be harsh and hurt. So you stay away from those things, avoid the newspapers and television, even as my dad Dudley sits in his room in my house and reads all the ones I buy for him and watches it all on the flatscreen I have installed for him. Stay away from those things, because they're going to trigger you off, and you're going to be upset.

These days I try to clear my brain of them all. I don't keep extra baggage these days. I empty my mind.

Some people are lost in the doubt. What if I do this, what if I do that? Some people are lost in the past. Why did that happen? Why x?

It's ridiculous. There is only one way to be. Do it now. Get on it.

If I'm going down, I'm going down in style. I'm going down blazing. Going down blazing, swinging the bat, swinging the blade.

Even if I'm in the hospital, give me a shot a rum. *Gimme a shot a drink, ar-kay?* And then say goodbye.

I have to go down in style. I'm not going down blocking. I'm not going down leaving the ball. Who knows if there's another innings? Who knows if there's another match?

And when it comes, my funeral is going to be a proper party. My funeral is going to be a big dance. *Everybody is dance, everybody is having fun.* Gone, but not forgotten. Just know I'm partying with you guys. And I dance, I really dance.

Don't worry about what might happen. If the ball's there, hit it.

Don't worry about the miss. Don't worry about the edge. Play for the glory. Play for the six.

You can't die in darkness. You must come into the light.

13.   175 Not Out

My early days in India, and I'm lost.

You be in the field and you're just lost. Lost completely in the middle. Sachin and Yuvraj smashing it all round, and the noise and the heat and the humidity . . .

'Chris man, what I got myself into?'

And every day is ram-jam-pack, from the streets to the stadium, from early until past late. The ground full and noise, and every boundary they put away bringing a rolling wall of roars and whistles and drums down upon you. We can't focus, we can't hold catches. We can't work out the low turning wickets, and we can't work out the heat. Scores here and there, but every day a broken heart, out in the deep chasing and then again at the crease.

You try to ride it out, but it takes its toll. Mentally the constant stimulation drains you. Physically your immune system cannot handle it. You're going to get ill. You will get diarrhoea, you will get sick, and out here that's not a pretty feeling. You lose a lot of weight in India. You get slim. Bad slim.

Back then. Back before the Indian Premier League.

It was the moment cricket changed for ever, when the lifestyle of everyone who took part changed for ever. Doors opened up. Rewards came, at last, for many. What you make for playing seven hours of Test cricket compared to what you earn for playing seven hours of football? Cricketers were underpaid, and then suddenly some were earning $1m for just over a month. Whoah!

This is the new dawn. This is the new benchmark. And once I got to be part of it, having missed the first season through injury, it changed me and I changed it back.

It's big, it's big. It's like nothing else cricket has ever seen. You're a superstar, so many superstars, everyone there to see the stars shine and entertain them. Owners want the best players in their team, and if you're a star player you will be treated like a Bollywood hero. And that makes you want to deliver – to stand out by performing as well, to win titles, to live up to the expectations.

No more old India. Still the noise and the heat and the chaos, but now something impossible on top of it all. Still the stadiums jam-pack, but now the colour and contrast turned up again. Still the madness, but this time you're riding it, riding it. And that wave takes you to places, and those places take you to a whole new world . . .

I'm playing for Royal Challengers Bangalore, and we have a five-day break before our next match. What to do when you're footloose and fancy being free?

Team manager George Avinash strolls over with some chat. You heard of Goa? You been to Goa? The boss has a place down there, the Kingfisher villa. He'd love you to go.

I'm having a few drinks with my team-mates. There's A. B. de Villiers, Dan Vettori, Yuvraj Singh. Lots of talk, but you can tell there's some huffing and bluffing going on. 'Yeah, I'm definitely up for it, but I'll make a call in the morning.'

Brunch the next day. 'Right guys, time to go.'

And they back out. No one is going.

What to do? George pipes up again. 'Believe me, big man, you should definitely check it out.'

Oh-kay. What could possibly go wrong?

So I decide to go by myself. Fly down there, picked up in a sweet car and driven to Candolim, come down the driveway and *whaaat?*

It's bigger than most hotels. It's cooler than any house I've ever seen. It's James Bond, it's Playboy Mansion, it's the land of plenty in white concrete and glass. I'm trying not to stare, but there's so much to stare at that there's only room in my mind for one thought: 'Chris, this gonna be interesting . . .'

I've got the entire villa for myself. I'm getting a tour. Wherever I go I've got two butlers walking with me at all times. Me alone, like a king!

I go in the first pool. I go in the second pool. I walk the lawn, in my robe. I go back in the pool with a Kingfisher beer and then I stay in the pool and the Kingfisher beers keep coming, which makes sense because the one place they're not going to run out of Kingfisher beers is in the Kingfisher villa.

I take a golf cart and drive around. The cook wants to know what I'd like to eat.

'What are the options?'

'Anything you want.'

'Yeah man, but what's on the menu?'

'There is no menu, sir. You are the menu.'

This is new for World Boss. Seems there is World Boss and *Universe* Boss. Whole new worlds. Bosses of things the boy from 1C St James Road, Rollington Town, didn't even know existed. No milk and Nutribun, although if you wanted milk and Nutribun they'd bring it to you.

They drive me into town. A few bars, some drinking, some dancing. Secret stories, strangers to meet, liaisons and adventures. Walking the beaches, having some seafood, soaking it up.

I pop into a tattoo parlour, just to look around. The guy literally begs me. 'Please let me give you a tattoo. Please . . .'

'Okay, I'll send a driver.'

So we pick him up and bring him out to the villa. I'm in the gym, in the Kingfisher villa, doing some bicep curls while having a tattoo. Food is cooking, he's drawing me a dragon.

We take a break, eat some food. Tattoo Man starts to relax. He starts to kick back.

'What we eat next?'

'Hey Tattoo Man – hello? I need to work my lats. You're taking a bit too long! Come on!'

But he wants to make sure it's perfect, so he's getting the detail in and the eyes are narrowed and the focus is there.

'Yeah man, sweet work, let's order dessert. That the teeth? Fierce. Maybe no more drink for you though, yeah?'

A dragon on my hand, I'm curling, I'm burping.

Don' worry 'bout what might happen. If di ball dere, hit it . . .

Into the villa's private movie theatre. Into the garage, so many cars, a Mercedes so big I can't even work out what it is. But it's not the cars that catch my eye, it's this big bike, three-wheeler, Harley-Davidson. And I get the story about how Vijay Mallya got the bike.

He's driving through the States, and he sees a guy riding it. He tells the guy he wants the bike. And he's the boss, the Mallya Boss. What he wants, he gets. So he asks the guy how much it would take to sell it, literally climb off it right there and give it to him, and the guy names his price, and Mallya counts out the bills and buys it. Has it shipped back to India, and then down to Goa and the villa.

So straight away I jump on this bike. I've never ridden a motorbike before. I've never seen a motorbike with three wheels. But one of the butlers shows me how to drive it, and I start riding it up and down the driveway, which because this is the Kingfisher villa is the size of a racetrack. *Brrrrm!*

I feel like the Terminator, screeching around with my shirt open and my shades down and nah, no helmet, because it's warm and it's a Harley and it's the Kingfisher villa and I'm the king of the villa, the Kingfisher king, and woo-hoo, who knew this thing could go that fast?

The butler signals. 'Does sir want to take it on the open road?'

'NO WAY!'

'Sir?'

'Nah! I ain't taking the chance. I'll just take it round the driveway one more time.'

Pause.

'I will have a rum and Coke though, yeah? And the movie theatre – I can just pick any film I want, right?' *Brrrrm!*

The butlers won't leave my side. Just walk. I won't even finish my drink and the next one will be in my hand.

Every morning I wake up and they ask me what I'd like to do.

'Would sir like to ride an elephant?'

'You got an elephant here?'

Now even Vijay Mallya doesn't own his own elephant. But he's good friends with a man who does, so soon I'm riding an elephant, which has less of the speed of the Harley but all the same swagger.

I don't want to leave. I have to leave.

When I got back I told the guys all about it. Right after checking the tournament schedule for the next five-day gap.

The reaction: 'Oh shit . . .'

One of my best moments in India. A beautiful time. One of the best times. Ever since I'm in love with Goa.

'They should play cricket here. Why don't we play cricket here?'

In Rollington Town we would hustle for cents and jump fences for the dream of a dollar.

Stealing those bottles from unguarded yards and the Lucas pavilion when 'Sorro' Watson was out and away. Clinking and clanking along to Lecky's on the corner of Fernandez Avenue and Jackson Road to get back the deposit, trumping up the funds for chicken back and dumplings and time to run a boat.

In teenage years the legit stuff but never the big payday. A summer job from Sorro cleaning the empty swimming pool at the National Stadium, scrubbing under the gutters, bruising on fingers. Out in the hot sun cleaning the netball court, picking leaves and weeds out of the cracks and corners.

It paid $300 Jamaican a week, about £1.70 today. No matter how much you want to run a boat, it's hard to get motivated and moving for that kind of cash.

You wanted something in your back pocket. At Excelsior there was an old boy called Jordan, a real entrepreneur, who used to sell home-made snacks to kids after cricket training. Not being able to stretch to rice and peas, I would have to settle for his coffee strip – a lump of cake – and maybe half a suck-suck drink. Jordan had been there so long he claimed he sold the same to Courtney Walsh when he was a pupil there. 'Remember bwoy – when you made it, don' forget mi like Courtney Walsh!'

It still didn't make me want to sweat round that netball court. When no one was looking, I would climb up on the roof for a sleep or stretch out in the shade under the almond trees. I had a code for it so I could tell John Murphy or Kevin Murray without being rumbled: 'Bredren, mi off fi play an innings . . .'

On and on, and early months in the West Indies team. I didn't even ask for a pay-cheque, because as a youngster you're scared, you don't want anyone to say you're in for the money. So I was talking to Nehemiah Perry, the players I knew from Jamaica. Just quietly – 'You get your pay for the tour?'

'Yeah man.'

Quietly still – 'Mi nah get mine.'

'What yuh mean, yuh nah get your money? Pick up di phone an' call such an' such.'

So I call, and the big financial man answers. They'd had my pay for a month, just sitting there on a cheque. 'Ah, sorry about that . . .'

So when it arrived, $7,000 – 'Wooo! T'anks very!'

I was just happy to be in the team. I had no idea. This is the money you get for doing this?

I'd always said the first thing I would do when I had a little money was to buy a house. Turned out I bought a car first. A Toyota Mark II.

'Lissen, mi tek nuff buses now, maybe I'll bend a bit an' buy car, so I can move around with di practice an' games an' everyting . . .'

On and on again, and the magic kingdom of the IPL. Magic numbers are mentioned – $800,000. I'd never seen that kind of money in my life. I had barely dreamed of holding such money.

And I get injured.

We played Sri Lanka in a three-match ODI series, won the first two games and went to St Lucia for the third game, me knowing that the next day I was due to fly to India, and that night I pulled my groin.

Oh fuck. It all flashed in front of my face – the house, cars for Popeye and Kevin Murray, houses for my mum and Michelle Crew and Michael Crew and Andrew and Wayney and all of them.

I still went over there hoping something could happen, but it didn't work out. Came back home, with just a little but nothing extraordinary, and I thought the only way my head might not explode would be if my heart did first. You don't know at that stage what's going to happen in the future. You don't know there will be a second chance, and a second coming.

There is a second, and a third, and a fourth and beyond. And don't believe it's a stroll, a retirement home, a big house on easy street. That money comes with a burden.

The IPL is the hardest league to play in in the world. Reason I say that, you can go there with a dirty attitude and say, I'm getting this amount and this and that, but if I were getting that amount and not performing, I would feel bad. I would feel like I didn't deserve it. Not only is every match as intense as anything you will experience anywhere in world cricket, it genuinely hurts when you don't per-form and it hurts when you lose a game, because that price tag makes you want to be at the top at all times.

You meet the owners, you love the owners. Kolkata Knight Riders, run by Bollywood superstar Shah Rukh Khan, plus actress Juhi Chawla and her husband Jay Mehta. Playing at Eden Gardens, showbiz and dazzle and we love to have you here. Vijay Mallya at RCB, the same respect as Kolkata, the same remarkable hospitality.

Vijay Mallya and Shah Rukh are two of the coolest peo-ple I've ever met. Easy to talk to, easy-going and very, very chill. They're making you feel at home. At the same time you're making a lot of money. You don't want to go out there and not perform, so you have to be on your 'A' game. It forces you to raise your bar. The way they look after you, make sure you get everything you want, make sure everything is in order for you, you definitely want to perform. So your intensity and your game get an uplift from the IPL. This is no retirement home. It's a reach-higher zone.

And it inspires me to great things.

After the one-day World Cup in India in 2011, I pick up an injury, miss a few games and come back home. There I hear the West Indies coach, Ottis Gibson, doing an interview blaming our exit on senior players not playing their part.

I say to myself, how can he pass a remark like that? I'm a senior player. I was injured. I still tried to play with my injury. To hear such a thing like that is so wrong.

I try to clear my brain. I don't keep extra baggage. *It happen an' it pass an' gone.* A series is coming up against Pakistan. At the same time the IPL auction is due. I'm not picked up in it, and I'm somewhat surprised. 'What 'appen 'ere?'

News from India. They say they received information from the West Indies Cricket Board that I won't be available, because I would have commitments with the national side. Okay. No problem.

So I'm at home doing my rehab, getting fit, in touch with the physio, C. J. Clarke, communicating with BBM messages and letting him know how I'm progressing, because I want to make the Pakistan series. And then, all of a sudden, the communication from their end stops. Soon after, I see the squad named. No Chris.

No one has called me to explain why I wasn't selected. I was telling the physio that I was running, that I was getting better, that I'm batting, that I'm ready. I'm not even invited to the pre-series training camp, where they can assess me and say, Chris, I don't think you're fit enough, we can't select you. But nothing.

And I am pissed about that. Denied one, denied another. Stuck in Jamaica, I react as I always will – meeting darkness with light. Off to nightclubs, partying partying, out with Wavell Hinds, every night.

We're together in this club, music going, dancing, on the Hennessy, Friday night becoming Saturday morning, and my phone starts ringing with an Indian number. George Avinash, Anil Kumble, Vijay Mallya from RCB, calling.

'Are you fit?'

All of this happening in a nightclub. I look around the nightclub.

'Yeah I'm fit.'

'You're ready to play?'

I look at my Hennessy. 'Yeah I'm ready to play.'

'Right, we need you to come to India tomorrow.'

'Yeah. Tomorrow is a Saturday, I need a visa, how is that possible?'

'Don't worry, it's already been arranged. Take your passport and go to the embassy, it'll be ready for you. We'll speak in the morning.'

Whoah, is this for real? To get a call in a nightclub to come down to India right away? I finish off my night. No rush. Reach back home the next morning, sleep. I talk to my sister, to my friends. What you guys think? They all speak with one voice: go. Okay, I'm going to go. To the embassy, to the visa that is waiting, to the flight tickets prepared. Pack my bags, on a plane on Sunday.

Now, to play in the IPL, you need your national governing body to sign an NOC – a no-objection certificate. It's official clearance for you to play, part of the deal the IPL made with the game's mighty and powerful. I'm clearly not wanted by the West Indies, so there can't be a problem.

But there is. The NOC lands, and suddenly everyone is scampering around. Chris is going to the IPL? It creates a big scene, a big scene. And more is to follow.

Straight to India. I haven't picked up a cricket bat for a month. Straight to Bangalore, straight to the middle, new team, new ball, facing my old team Kolkata. And I mash a 100, off 55 balls.

I think, God, it is only you alone made this happen. Because I don't know how on earth I score a hundred in that game. *Trus' mi*. No preparation, no practice at all, man of the match, winning all the categories. One of the most spectacular things that ever happen to me.

Back home, other remarks and interviews are going on. Everybody diving in with their angry thoughts. 'Why is Chris Gayle there and not here?' *All chaos an' everyting break loose*.

I am in my hotel room in Bangalore, listening to the slander online, the anger growing and growing. There's a talk show on Jamaican radio that everyone listens to. Criticism and foolish talk against me. So I call in from India. And I go berserk.

Walking up down in the room like a crazy man, spitting fire down the phone. Like a boss speaking to a bad employee, like World Boss speaking to World Fool.

I slam the coach. I slam the system. I slam the physio and everybody. About how I have been treated, about how it makes me feel. The radio show is supposed to finish, and then they make an announcement: this radio show is not going to finish now. Extend the radio show!

I was telling the truth. And that kept me out of West Indies cricket for a year and a half. But it opened more doors for me, because I could play on in the IPL, and score how many thousands of runs around the world.

And maybe that was the best form time in my life. Scoring runs ridiculously. 107 off 49 balls against the Kings. 89 off 47 against Mumbai. Top run-scorer in IPL that season; an average of 67; a strike rate of 183, top of that table too. Man of tournament. RCB went from bottom of the table to two finals – the IPL final and the Champions League final. The coach, Ray Jennings, told me straight: 'Chris, you're a life-saver. You saved my job. You have no idea what you have done for the team, and me from a personal point of view.' *And it all very pleasant an' very good.*

And it all came from all that, all sprang from that ugly mess. From darkness came light.

The IPL is big. Being at the centre of the IPL is bigger than you can imagine.

It's difficult to leave the hotel, because you will get mobbed. It's difficult to use the hotel lobby, because they'll mob you there too. I'll go down to the bar occasionally, but even then you have to get security to lock off an area for you. Gayle coming through, storm hatches down.

Look, I'm a tall and built man in India. There's not many people who look like me. And the sunglasses don't hide you. They know your walk. Anything you will put on as a disguise – cap, funky hat, straitlaced clothes – as soon as one person spot you, you're history. 20,000 people will know in a minute.

Words fly. The first person looks at you. He turns to a stranger. 'That's Chris Gayle!' I look back at them. 'Shhh!' Too late already. Before my lips have moved that stranger has told five more strangers. As my finger comes to my lips those five have told five more each. Autographs multiplying at crazy speed. Selfies for every self.

I'd love to walk the streets, because India is such a lovely place, and there are so many sights to see. But that's something you just can't do. Going to the cricket ground is already all hustle. Everybody want to touch you, everybody want pictures with you.

When you order room service in India, three guys come in holding one tray. Battling for the handles, carrying a piece of paper and a pen. 'Sign here. And also here, and here on this T-shirt.'

Fights to bring you room service. The housecleaners will knock on your door at all times. 'Room cleaning? Bathroom checking? Minibar?' You put up the 'Do Not Disturb' sign. Still your door will be knocking. 'Everything okay sir? Sir need anything? . . . Yes sir – just making sure no one is disturbing you?'

Don't get me wrong. A man can have fun.

Ahmedabad, Bangalore, Chandigarh, Chennai, Cuttack, Delhi, Dharamsala, Jaipur, Kolkata, Mumbai, Nagpur.

All cities I have played in with the IPL, some of them I had never heard of before it. A geography education as well as an employment, a tourist visa as well as a working one. Dharamsala, with the snowy mountains as a backdrop and clear blue skies and cool crisp air, a beautiful place to play cricket.

Sometimes you get to a ground – 'Have I been here before? Yeah man, I remember these dressing-rooms.' Sometimes the ground fool you. 'Those stands weren't there before. It can't have been Cuttack I was thinking of. What, they built them last month?'

So many new team-mates to meet. At Kolkata there were David Hussey, Shoaib Akhtar and Brendon McCullum. You've been used to staring them down in international cricket, and now your eyes are meeting over the breakfast pancake stash.

You take a while to gel. And because many of the more established names would have their families there, I used to hang more with the young Indian guys, and what brought us together was poker. Lots of poker.

Ashok Dinda, Rohan Gavaskar, Manoj Tiwary, Cheteshwar Pujara. Every single night, and because I don't sleep at night, I mean the late night. Nothing else was there to do. So the routine was get the crew together, start the poker and start the new day in style.

We would decide whose room, order hot chocolate and coffee and biscuits and naan, like some Bangalore hotel version of a Lucas run a boat, and then play play play. We played for cash, for rupees, and for proper money. Proper pots. Run some jokes, ease the day.

Don't worry about it messing our body-clocks for the cricket. IPL matches start at 8 p.m. and go on late, so everything shifts later and later. Game, hotel, dinner, and then poker through to dawn and beyond, on to 7 a.m. Then I'll eat my breakfast and then I'll go to my bed.

The youngsters come around me because they know I'm the clown. I will talk a lot of crap, I will lift the moods. Come match-time and the journey from hotel to ground, I'll sit at the back of the bus. Back of the bus is the fun part of the bus, so that's my spot. Where's the teacher? Where's the coach? Exactly. Front of the bus. We're down the back.

I eased my way into the IPL. In 2009 I averaged 28, with a highest score of 44. In 2010 I averaged 32 – fine, but no blast them apart.

There were reasons. I never had a full season with Kolkata. I always had to leave early for West Indies duty, and I would be in and out of the team.

Sourav Ganguly was the captain. I opened the batting with him, and Kolkata is his town, so you don't get the strike when you're batting with Ganguly, and you can't say anything because he's Ganguly, the king of Kolkata. So sometimes you get six overs into the innings, and you've only faced 10 balls. Ups and downs. And not many quick singles.

And then the phone call from RCB while in the nightclub with Wavell, and it blew the whole thing open.

Bangalore had originally picked an Aussie journeyman, Dirk Nannes. Only when he got injured did they realize I might still be available. I owe Dirk a little thank-you. Come to Triple Century, Dirk. Settle in for the night and leave your wallet at home.

And so it was sprung open. 2011, 102 in my first match. Another century to follow, an 89 off 47 balls. The tournament's top scorer, despite missing several games, the highest strike rate, man of the tournament. *Six Machine in town*.

2012, and Six Machine gets to serious work. Even after a groin injury slows my start, I end up with 39 more sixes than KP, the man second in the table. Not even a contest.

That's a lot of sixes hit, but when you're in good form you pick up the line of the ball early. You get in position. I don't always plan to hit sixes. I don't think about it. I just let it flow, sometime more so when the game's on the boil.

Your run rate will be up there, you know you need boundaries, and when you're batting down in the death the sixes are going to come. Because you're set, and you're just going going going.

Five of them come just that way, and in something of a burst. We are playing Pune, and they have posted a spicy 182. For 12 overs they then keep me and Virat Kohli on the leash. At one stage we have scored just 30 off 35 deliveries. We need 111 more runs off just 50 balls. Kohli gets caught in the deep, and on comes Rahul Sharma – the man with one of the best economy rates in the league, a man whose previous over in this match had gone for only four.

Time to get back in the game. Time to get back in the flow.

I stroll onto strike for his second ball, right-arm leg spin coming over the wicket. Crash – six. Right into my zone – six. With some variety on the ball now – six more. With some variety of a different variety – six more.

It's not about reading the spin. Once you're in the zone as a batsman, it doesn't matter what variety or delivery a bowler come with; you're already in the holy place, so you can pick it instinctively. The magic is there. And the magic is all around me on this night.

The noise starts big and then keeps going big. You hit one six, they want another. You hit two, they demand three. They always want one more, and this day I'm going to give it to them.

After four sixes, one ball left, I'm asking myself, do I try to get a single to keep the strike? 'Nah, let's keep going with it.' Sharma around the wicket, going wide of the crease, going wide to me. So I hit another six. Maximize the over.

From 37 runs off 35 balls to 67 runs off 50. Back on the board, back on track. AB and Saurabh Tiwary lash 24 off the final over, and home we are and here we go.

2012's a good year. The first man in history to hit three centuries in the IPL, the highest run-scorer in the tournament for the second year in a row, an average of 61. And then comes 2013, the golden year in the golden helmet.

Pune come to meet us again. Pune and pain seem to go together.

The day before I am awake all night. I go to bed at 7 a.m. and sleep all day. When the eyelids flutter, a breakfast/dinner of pancakes and a hot chocolate. Usain won his first Olympic gold on chicken nuggets; I prepare my own World Boss world record on room service pancakes, with the syrup and the settings and everything.

More sleep, then a lot of water to drink, because I find that when your body hydrates it will actually let you think more too. Drain it and you become weak. So water, another snooze, down to the team room for a 10-minute meeting, then straight on the bus.

Darkness all around, brightness and big noise under the floodlights. We lose the toss and get put into bat, which you can understand, because Bangalore is always a good wicket to bat on, and so most teams want to chase there.

To the middle, boom! First over, and straight away the ball just come on nice to the bat. Cover drive, get off the mark.

After eight balls we have a rain interruption. I am already on nine, and I've only faced five deliveries. We come off the field and sit in the dressing-room, just talking. Just talking to my mate and West Indies team-mate Ravi Rampaul.

I say, 'Ravi Rampaul, lissen mi. Dat wicket out dere is so sw-eeet!'

My exact words. 'Dat wicket a one-seventy, one-eighty track. Nuttin' less.' But I am talking about the team total, not an individual's score. 'In order to win this game, Ravi, we'll need one-eighty.'

We go back out there, onto that pitch that's so sweet. And straight away – boom! I go straight back into the zone again. From ball one. A free hit, a four, and I'm going berserk, berserk – boom boom boom, quick quick quick. Two left-arm spinners in the attack, to 50 off 17 balls.

Something's happening here. Something is really happening.

The Aussie all-rounder Mitchell Marsh comes on in the Powerplay over. I take him for a couple of sixes, I take him for 28 in that single over. He bowls another over, so I get stuck into that as well.

Ishwar Pandey, on for his first over in this year's IPL. He's the leading wicket-taker in that year's Ranji Trophy, the national first-class competition. His first six balls go for 21.

Ali Murtaza, in for his first match of the season. Welcome, Ali. He gets two overs and 45 runs of punishment before getting the heave-ho too. *Beatin' it, beatin' it.*

Aaron Finch is the Pune in-pain captain. He's in the middle overs and out of options. 'Who's gonna bowl? Who's gonna bowl?'

I see him look at Yuvraj, and Yuvraj looks at him incredulous. 'I'm not going near this!'

Nobody else wants to bowl. Heads down all round the field, bowlers suddenly fascinated by their toes, or – wow, what's that in the stands? or – hmm, look at this callus here on my spinning finger, better get a close look at it.

And that's when Finch has to take the ball himself. Yuvraj will tell me afterwards: 'I told him not to bowl. I told him not to bowl. Don't do it!' But no one else wants it, so Finch has no choice. 'Don't bowl, skip!'

So I get stuck into him as well. Looping up, smashed away. Fired in, smashed away. Slower and cunning, smashed away. Faster and desperate, smashed away. Four sixes and a four. In that single over my score jumps from 67 to 95. Cheers, Aaron!

Dinda bowls me a no-ball, a low full toss, and I hit it straight back over his head, almost on the roof of the stand. Straight onto the shingles and shoot a load of them out.

That's the century, off 30 balls, with 11 sixes. I've only faced seven dot balls. I've only taken four singles.

Six Machine, he's in town . . .

Once again it's my old partner Dilshan down the other end. He has dropped anchor, but he may as well have dropped his bat. When I brought up our 50 I had scored 44 of them. When we reached 100 he had contributed just 11 of them.

I could continue going berserk. I could continue blitzing it. Instead I decide to play it properly. We still have a lot of overs to bat, so I just take my time, and make sure a set batter is there at the end. That's my thinking. I ease off the berserking.

Luke Wright comes on to bowl, so I slow things down a bit. It's all relative, but my 150 takes another 27 balls to bring up, although I'm now on 16 sixes. AB is joining the fun too. Eight balls for 30 runs. *Proper licks, serious licks.*

I could have got 200 runs, easily. Easily. Because normally you keep the set batter on strike. But everybody came in and started to play shots, and I couldn't get on strike.

So I had to settle for 175 not out. The highest score ever made in T20, the fastest ever century, 154 of those runs coming in boundaries.

You look at it and break it down and say it should always be the team, so 175 was less important than 233-5. But imagine psychologically getting the 200! I'm out there, I'm in the beautiful groove, the magic is at my side and at my back. 25 more runs? I could have made that in an over.

I didn't mind; it's only when I look back at it and analyse it that I realize the 200 was in the making easily. I had no idea of the records I was smashing. I don't know records. I've been involved in a lot of them, but someone will have to dig them out and tell me. I've never targeted a record.

But to speak the truth, it was amazing. It was spectacular. And we bowled them out cheaply, and I got two wickets for five runs, so that was my day, and I made the best of it.

It didn't hit me that night. It didn't soak in. Just another innings, just another game. I didn't sit back, but we did kick on. I was tired, but we hit the bar on the top floor of the hotel and rode that wave.

Only with the dawn did it start to sink in, dawn and looking again at my phone. It was the most messages I've ever received – those who do text you, those who seldom have, those who never even appeared on your phone.

You could see the messages piling through. BlackBerry Messenger – beep! beep! beep! Blowing off, everything blowing off. Phone shaking and vibrating, ready to burst.

It took me two days to read them. And there were so many I couldn't answer them individually – I just had to send out a broadcast, saying, 'Thank you all . . .'

Funnily enough, when I started talking after the game, and you talk to a lot of people, everybody had a story with that innings. It's like the world come to a complete stop. I've heard a lot of important meetings were halted for that innings. People were driving and had to pull over to find the nearest bar to watch it. Sometime the entire store got shut down so people could drive home to then pull over to then watch it in the nearest bar.

Everybody have a particular story. Just like when Usain ran his 9.58 seconds in Berlin. On and on, and so thrilling to listen to people telling what they were doing on that particular day. A lot of phone calls being made, a lot of plans being cancelled. A lot of mouths being left open.

Darren Bravo has a story. He was in bed at home, and normally he listens to the radio as he wakes up. And as it came on, all he could hear was shouting. 'Everybody stop what you doing! Gayle is doing dis an' dat! Gayle going crazy!'

Everybody rushed to their TV in the early morning. It went crazy all over the world that day. There was a sweet quote from the *Los Angeles Times*, which is not known for going big on its coverage of my sport: 'Gayle scored the fastest 100 in the history of pro cricket, after just 30 pitches.'

And it was like Usain's 9.58 seconds. Just as people watched him yellow-blur across the line that night, glanced at the giant infield clock and couldn't process the numbers – 9.58 for the 100 metres? Why is there a point five in there? Nine what? – so it was with the 175. How much? Sorry, I thought this was a T20. Oh fuck – it is T20!

You look at the IPL and you think all of us will keep going back to the well, year after year. Spinners in their early 40s, batsmen playing on at an age when Tests are no longer in the legs and one-dayers are one step too far.

Maybe we will. But time catches with safe hands. A back injury slowed me for a few years; other parts of your life come into focus. A new focus, a new family.

You need the same powerful energy and strong vibes, the same deep passion. It doesn't make sense going through the motions to play, and it doesn't work. You've got to want to do it, and want to do well. You have to have the same passion for the game you love as if you were just starting.

Because the IPL changes you, and it changes your attitude to the world.

Just as it has brought so much joy within cricket, it has taken away the fight between the players. It has taken away the sledging.

Unity. You become friends with your cartoon enemy. Sharing dressing-rooms, hotels and buses with men you knew only as opponents, you build a conversation. It's kind of hard to sit next to someone for dinner every night for four weeks and then go out a month later and call them all the names under the skies. The IPL has drawn that sting from the game. So if you see sledging now, those two players definitely don't like each other. That something will be personal.

You'd think it might give rivalries a new twist. Six Machine in the same team as A. B. de Villiers, Six Machine alongside Brendon McCullum. Who can shine the brightest? Who can be the wrecking-ball that demolishes the most attacks in the smallest amount of time?

There's no competition from my side. It's not the way I work. I always bat on my own capabilities, on the situation of the game we're playing. Sometimes the media will try to compare certain things we do and bring more excitement to a match, throw a little more spice things on top. But it's media hype, not personal hype. The big battle is against the bowlers, not your own.

And you forge new bonds. You form new friendships.

Muttiah Muralitharan I knew as one of the greatest bowlers in the game's long history. Now I know him as Murali, and while I respected Muralitharan, I love Murali.

One of the best cricketers I've come across: able to read the game so well, a good thinker, great game awareness. And that's just the cricket.

Murali is a man who never stops talking. Any topic at all you talk about, Murali has a solution for it. Sport, politics, the economy, social issues. He knows everything. If you're unsure or arguing about anything, Murali's the go-to man. For any scenario.

Every time I see him, always a smile on his face, always the same greeting: 'Macha!' A Sri Lankan thing, Sinhalese. 'Chrees! Macha!'

I love to be around him, because he makes me laugh. In the hotel, guys will be coming in late at night from a club. And if you whisper in the corridor, a door will fly open and Murali's head pop out with that big grin on. 'Hello macha!' Everybody will just drop and laugh. 'Murali, you should be sleeping!' Three o'clock in the morning. 'How you hear me out here?'

'Muli Muli Muli!' The best cricketer I've come across. I'll take Murali any day, anywhere.

For all the fun, for all the friendships, the IPL drives us on.

There was a time when one batsman scoring 100 in a T20 match seemed impossible. Did that. There was a time when 150 was out of reach. 175 didn't even make sense as a number to see on the scorecard.

So believe me when I say a double century is a possibility. What you need to understand is how it might come about.

I see what each innings brings once I am in it. To go out there and bat for 200 is never going to work. You won't get it like that.

It's all about the zone, the moment, the timing and magic. And that's when it comes in, and if the opportunity present itself then you try and take it. I certainly don't plan it. I wait and see. If the magic is there, take a shot at it and see where you can go.

Benchmarks have already been turned to dust. Even the fact that people are talking about a 200 goes to show what an impact you make.

You get asked if someone could score a century off the minimum number of balls theoretically possible. I take that as a compliment, but 17 consecutive sixes won't happen. That's like going to the moon and back. On Vijay Mallya's three-wheeled Harley.

There was a time when a 30-ball century seemed impossible. There was a point when a 9.58-second 100 metres seemed impossible.

But when Usain ran 9.58 he didn't plan for 9.58. It was all about the zone and the timing and the atmosphere and scenario. The magic moment. How you feel confident within yourself at the time. It just happened naturally. And when you glance back you see the record and say, wow!

If you say, 'Lissen mi, I'm gonna smash past two hundred, I'm gonna run 9.55,' you won't get it. Instead it is about quiet knowledge and deep confidence. It is about understanding when the moment is upon you and understanding what to do in that sacred storm.

Within yourself: 'I've done it already, I can do it again.' That's the thinking, really and truly.

I travel the world, but I always come home. I represent teams around the globe, but my true calling is always the West Indies, and when my heart calls, it brings me back to Jamaican sounds and shores.

They were all there for my first Test landmark at Sabina Park, where we watched as kids and learned from the skills of Delroy Morgan and Courtney Walsh and Patrick Patterson and the rest. They were all there, on the Red Stripe Mound – Popeye, Kevin Murray, John Murphy, big brother Andrew, bigger wilder brother Michael Crew.

The pact was struck among them. When I reached my half-century, they would all jump the barriers and run to the middle to celebrate with me. We got here together, we would party together. I say we – I had no idea what they had planned, and neither did Popeye, for when the shot came and the scoreboard ticked over and he hurdled the fence and sprinted for distant stumps, he first wondered why it was so quiet and then wondered where the speed had come from to leave the rest of the gang in his dust, and when he looked back over his shoulder he saw only empty outfield and a line-up of laughing faces still safely on the mound, and when he looked to his left he saw one security guard closing fast and to his right another thundering in faster.

Respect to Popeye. When you commit, you commit. 'I cyaan turn back now,' and on he came. Into my arms for a hug and a whoop, a dip of the shoulder to fool one security guard and a final burst of unexpected pace to skin the second and blow out the third who had come huff and puff in their wake.

You rule that in another part of the world as hooligan behaviour. You rule it as unseemly and childish and never come back. In Jamaica it's passion. It's loyalty. It's being who you are, and not pretending for anyone else.

I love being part of it. Being born and raise Jamaican is the single best thing that has happened to me. For all the struggles, for all the pain, I wouldn't trade it to be a free and sheltered citizen of anywhere else.

It's a tough system to come through. Never is it easy. But this is where you make your name – before all these franchises, before all the long-haul flights and sweet hotels, before the big deals and Kingfisher villas. Before World Boss, the Jamaican boy.

You start with your country, and you graduate to the West Indies, and it's a great feeling for that Jamaican boy to hold. I love franchise cricket, and no man gives more to it, but it's a different scenario and a different atmosphere. It's more powerful for the West Indies, because the people are more passionate, and you're playing for the whole region, and that's a bigger burden on your shoulders. If you're playing for a franchise and you don't get the sort of runs people expect, it's not too much a pressure. You can still feel comfortable and bounce back and get a big total another day, and everything will be okay. When the performance doesn't come for the West Indies, the abuse will. When the falling performance fails to bounce as soon as ground hits, you can get cut from the team, and it's a big struggle to come back, and a bigger one to win back your reputation.

I love the legacy before me, and I feel pride in what I have added. You come and you play your part. You reach close to some of the greats. Some people might even recognize you as one of them – one of the best big hitters, the best T20 player, one of the most dedicated. *Yuh name gonna be call up dere, no doubt.*

The Jamaican people are very passionate. Straightforward. When you do something good, they acknowledge it without reservation. No wait and see next time, no could-have-done-more. You get more love when you perform, and if you can get the job done in style you can get away with a few low scores and you won't be pressured, for they know that when you get going it's going to be big and it's going to be entertaining.

Boots on the other feet. If you come with slackness, it won't be tolerated. You'll know if you've done something foolish. The crowd will straight let you know, no doubt about that.

An early first-class game for Jamaica at Sabina Park, and Michael Crew in the stands. I get out to a poor shot. Down comes the abuse, down from my own brother's mouth. 'Get off di wicket man, yuh no good!'

We have to play for the people, not just in the Caribbean but across the world.

Jamaicans? We are everywhere. Even in the smallest nation, we are there. When the West Indies win, our brothers and sisters can walk tall into their workplace. When Jamaica powers West Indian success, we are driving them on too.

You can say it's only sport. What can sport do for a poor man in another man's land? How can far-away sport feed a man or a few runs protect him from the pressure and sticks of the cruel cold world?

To ask this question is to not be Jamaican. To ask this question is never to have known that you yourself can be the answer.

Never is it easy. And that is why sport matters more, and that is why music matters just the same. That deep culture takes you away from the darkness, and brings you to the light.

We did crazy things as youngsters. We saw things that kids shouldn't see. We lived through periods that no child should have to live through. To grow up in such a community is to understand why we take such joy in playing games.

The struggle coming up was what made you who you are. It taught me how to deal with every rough challenge that would come my way beyond. Hard-core hard times, back against a broken wall, yet with it a certain belief that you can turn it around.

You can be out there batting with the last man, still another 80 runs needed, and you still believe you can get the job done. You can be alone in a hospital room fitted to wires and pads and beeps, and you know you will pull through. Because you have been in the darkness, and you have found your way to the light.

Sport is the escape from a life that pushes you into sport. Inspiration and exodus through a single source.

Sport and music take Jamaica to the world. Calypso and Test cricket, dub-plates and one-day domination, dance-hall and T20 beats. Bob Marley and Usain Bolt, Beenie Man and Chris Gayle.

Lightning Bolt and Six Machine.

Usain and me, we're similar characters. We both love to entertain, we both love to have fun. We're lay-back. But we also love our chosen sports, and we work hard, hard, hard. Most people don't see behind the scenes. If he hiccup and lose a race, most people will say he partied too hard, just as if I don't make any runs they say I've partied too much.

He came to my opening night at Triple Century, came to show his respect. We go to Kingston clubs together. We always have, even before he shook up the world at the Beijing Olympics, way back when, a Bolt then just a growing storm in the distant clouds. Me on the Hennessy, him on the Guinness, both of us on the dancefloor. He loved to dance. You'd see him in shirt wet and eyes wide. And you'd see that raw talent, that raw talent in everything he did. One World Boss can recognize another.

One World Boss can appreciate another. In Jamaica you grow up in sport and you grow up in track and field.

I don't like to run but I love to watch it. Merlene Ottey, carrying the flag. Deon Hemmings, winning 400-metres hurdles gold at the '96 Olympics, the first Jamaican woman to stand and boss the podium. Asafa Powell breaking world records, Veronica Campbell-Brown cruising over 200 metres, Shelly-Ann Fraser-Pryce tearing up the 100 metres. Records and rivals blowing in their wake; when those Jamaicans represent, I feel good as a sportsman.

Usain changed athletics and he changed the world sporting arena. As Michael Jordan was before, so Usain is now. When he started handing out the licks – crazy times, beating records, untouchable at Olympics and Worlds – the impact was something huge on the country. Personal pride for every one of us.

In Jamaica you grow up in sport and you grow up in cricket. Usain always had that passion for the game. A fast bowler, of course, a big-swinging batsman who loved to charge bowlers. His brother played cricket for Melbourne, one of Lucas's big cross-Kingston rivals; his training partner

Yohan Blake bats punchy, with a bowling machine at home and a boast that he can out-pace it with ball in hand.

Two worlds come together. When Usain returns from the London Olympics with his titles retained, I have a little charity match going on up at the Kaiser Sports Ground in Discovery Bay, up on the north coast. He is coming off his sprinting high, I'm captaining one side, I ask him to captain the other.

He doesn't hesitate. He also brings Yohan to open the bowling and his brother Sadiki to open the batting with him. No hiding in the middle order, and no waiting for the tailenders later on – I walk out for the first over, and Usain is pawing ground at the end of the longest run-up I've seen since Shoaib Akhtar.

There's been a lot of chat off him in the pavilion. 'I study these guys' technique, I know how to out Chris, I know where to bowl him. It should be easy enough, I'm a very smart man . . .'

Coming in off that long run, like Mikey Holding, and it's the fastest approach a cricket ground has ever witnessed. Although I recognize that long stride and smooth style I've never seen him bowl before, and honestly, I swear to God, the first ball he bowls is one of the best bouncers I've ever received. Proper bouncer – lines me up, follows me back, forces me to duck underneath it with a whoosh and a whoah. 'Yow! This is serious!'

Then I think about it. 'Lissen Chris, you don' wan' get out to Usain.' And then after a while, 'Come on Chris, this a charity game.' So I start to play some shots off him. I pull him through midwicket for a six, hit a few fours through cover, hit a few through point. Then he bowls another short one, and I'm cutting again, and it shoots through a little, and I drag it on, and over go the timbers. 'Oh shit . . .'

Usain celebrates like it's the 100-metres final in London all over again. The big 'To Di World' move, leaning back and pointing that long left arm and long finger on his right hand, over to the slips for the hugs and high-five and then back to me, making to slice his throat, pointing me off to the pavilion with the big send-off.

He comes out to open the batting. Let's calm this down. Let's right the natural order. On I come with my off spin, and off goes my off spin, back over my head for six. My story is that I was trying to buy his wicket. But it's his day, and the charity game becomes the Bolt show.

He puts it in his book – that Usain Bolt owes me a 100-metre race, to give me a chance to redeem myself for my beating. So one day I will take him up on a charity run. Get in shape and bring him down, get in shape and get back my title. Doesn't matter that I like to watch others run rather than do it myself. Doesn't matter that sprinting is for emergencies, not good times. He owes me. World Boss coming to bring World Boss down. *Worlds gonna shake.*

Usain feels the same critics' fire as me. Too much mouth. Too much boasting. Too much flash, in those gold spikes, and too much mess around, in the clowning behind the blocks and when the stadium is supposed to fall silent.

You have to understand Jamaica to understand Jamaicans. We say what we think. We don't hide it all bashful. We come from little so we like to live big.

We like to look good. When you have no money, you work with what you have. If it comes, you spend it while it lasts. It was absent before, so enjoy it before it goes absent again.

Fashion over style. Fashion over funds. Even if it's only a T-shirt and jeans, it must look neat and match.

It starts from school. Boys walk around with a bar of soap, to make sure they can wash their face and look cool. You can't even touch their uniform. They don't want to sweat. They want to be tucked in properly and neat, with a comb in the back pocket and the hair just so.

Yuh don't wan' any dust brush on yuh shoes. If their shoes do get dirty, they will have an old toothbrush in another pocket and tap tap tap, they dust that dirt away.

Jamaicans will spend their last money on clothes, just to make sure they look fine, just to be looking fine for others to see. You see men on the street looking really bazzle, meaning really sharp – *byazzle!* – and not even a dollar in their pocket. And they'll come over and ask me to buy them a drink, and they'll be better dressed than me. That's Jamaica. All the cash gone on clothes, hitting up the big star for funds to put a matching bottle alongside it. That's Jamaican style. That's our culture. We have to look good. *We cyaan look pop-down! We cyaan look shabby.*

The brand is the thing. And once there is a brand, a Jamaican is going to let you see the brand. Nothing is allowed to cover up the logo. No one is allowed to stand in the way. You will know what they're wearing. If it's Gucci, Prada, you know. If it's Louis V, you're seeing it.

Even if the brand is shoes and the logo is on the foot bottom they're marching like a Russian solider so all can see. Marching round a crowded bar, swinging legs high, soles to your nose. All to show you it's Louis V. Step. Louis V! Step. Louis V! That's Jamaica. *Boasie!*

A lot of those brands will be fakes. Of course, because people can't afford the real thing. You live in the UK, you go into a Louis Vuitton store, even a belt can be £1,000. So in Jamaica don't expect the real deal on streets that are meaner.

It might look like it is, but that's because they're making it look good. When it is fake, when everyone knows it's fake, no one will show it. You won't be allowed close enough to see the knock-off. They're bold with it. And you don't challenge on it, because you came through the struggle and you lived the same. You give and take and understand.

'Chris, yuh wearing Gucci – I'm wearing Gucci too!'

'Yo Worl' Baass, mi see yuh wearin' Prada, mi be wearin' Prada too!'

You see the knock-offs in the markets. You see the knock-offs everywhere. *Everybody 'ustlin'*. That's customary. You have to know what you're buying, or you will get your fingers burnt and the rings on them stolen away. There is scamming out there, and they're good at it.Professional. Trust me.

In South Africa, for the under-19 World Cup. A guy came to the hotel selling nice jewellery, nice watches, at a very nice price. But we're Jamaican. 'Those ain't real!' He showed us the chains, which he said were gold and to be fair to the man looked like gold.

Now us Jamaicans have a tendency. We know how to check real gold. If you're buying, we'll say take a hair out of your head, lay it on the gold. If it sticks it's real. And if you rub it on the ground without seeing too much change of colour or damage, it's definitely real.

This man. This deal. *We say nuh. This guy price cyaan be real.*

'Where you get these nice gold chains?' He took us to the jeweller's shop and showed us. The jeweller backed him. We did the hair trick. Sticky. We did the rub-the-ground trick. No damage.

I was convinced. We were all convinced. So I bought three of them and came back home with pockets full and wallet empty. I told a friend, and she was actually vexed with me. 'Whaaat? You shoulda buy ten!'

Honestly, in the space of two days, those chains were looking as gold as my skin. I put one in a jar, kept the air out and checked it again in the morning. It was literally black. 'Naaa, knock-aaf! Proper brassed yuh!'

My personal style you might have seen. You might have seen my look on Instagram. Maybe it's you, maybe it's only for me. But Jamaicans like to look different. We don't like to see other people in the same clothes as us. At a party we want to stand out.

I don't have disasters. I don't have gambles that don't look good. If you check my dressing, I feel whatever I pull on I can pull off. It's the confidence I have in myself. You just give me whatever, I'll make it look good.

I wear some serious colours to some beach parties sometimes. Some unbelievable cuts. But the world knows I'm a man who has the dressing thing covered. It doesn't matter what I wear. I can wear slippers on a red carpet and look good. I got the swagger!

So I have spent money on some cheeky items. A black velvet jacket from Harrods. Some trainer boots with gold studs along the tongue and tops. The most I've ever spent was a couple of thousand euros on a pair of gold shoes in Munich. Not real gold – but they looked good and I knew no other man in Jamaica would be sporting them.

I wore them less than five times. Because once the thrill of spending money you never had on things you could never dream of wears off – and it takes some time, it takes some time – you realize that much as you want to escape from the past, you are also formed by it.

I have jackets in my closet. I have suits bought on a whim and a dream and a desire to be different not only from others but from how I was before. And they don't get worn. They sit there *untouch*. Because most of the time I want a T-shirt and jeans, and that's me. Or I want a vest and some shorts and that's all of it. Just simple, just the way it was for so long. We move on but our baggage comes with us.

The hair? The hair must look *bazzle* too. The hair must look cool and extravagant, slick and sexy. Jamaican women go for extensions, because the stars like Rihanna and Beyoncé wear extensions, and because this is Jamaica, they take it further and bigger and louder. Shelly-Ann with her red or green from her own salon, girls on the street spending their last dollars on a little more. If you see hair that's natural you may be looking in the mirror.

Us boys, we cut the look for the occasion. Most time we used to be on tour with the West Indies, Wavell and me would agree that we weren't going to trim, we weren't going to shave. We just wanted to have that rough tough look. The thinking was simple: you see the beards on TV, back home they'll be saying, 'Ya man, dem guys dem look mean! Like some animal!'

So now I wear my hair in braids, because I came back from one tour where I had let it grow, and I decided to twist it a bit, because I'd always wanted to try that look, and it worked for me in that moment. When it gets too regular, when it gets too popular a look, I'll cut them off. It just depend when that mood come. *Jus' slice it like a bread.*

All this I love about Jamaica. All this culture runs through who I am and what I have become, and all that I am and that is around me explains why winning for Jamaica feels like nothing else there is.

2013, and the first season of the Caribbean Premier League. The Jamaica Tallawahs into the final, up against the only team who had beaten us all season, the Guyana Amazon Warriors.

They had the best bowling attack – Lasith Malinga, Sunil Narine, Krishmar Santokie, the leading wicket-taker in the tournament. We had the best late arrival, Murali and me hatching and pulling off a plan to get Kumar Sangakkara in for the semi-final and beyond.

We had a captain who cared more than any other, a team who wanted to win and a nation to roar us home. 129 needed to win, and I just knew I had to stay there until the end. No fireworks until the trophy was in the bag, no risks and no losing thoughts or letting thoughts get ahead. Santokie crumbling, Andre Russell beating it, the captain taking us home.

It was glorious to win that tournament for Jamaica, glorious to do it with a young team. A weight felt like it had slipped from my shoulders. Jamaica had given me so much, and now I had given something back.

Ask any cricketer in the world where he most likes to play, and he'll say the Caribbean. Ask any cricketer in the Caribbean where he most wants to be, and he'll say Jamaica. The food, the nightlife, the people.

The gun culture? I've seen it. But every place has its own problem, its own bad areas. Guns are everywhere in the world. Talk to someone outside and they might say, isn't Jamaica dangerous? And I say, is your country not dangerous? Where in the world is not dangerous? Jamaica has had it bad, but it is a better country now.

Neither is it all in the past. Just as music keeps reinventing itself, so does sport. Just as Shelly-Ann succeeded Merlene Ottey, so men will come to take my place.

We had calypso, we had ska. We had reggae, we had dub. We have Beenie Man and Bounty Killer, then along come Baby Cham, Capleton and Gage. Jamaican women representing themselves: Lady Saw, the Queen of the Dancehall to Beenie Man's King; you have Tifa, you have Spice. They know when to hit the note – the high ones and the low ones, the ruff and the tuff and the easy ones. Even I'm recording tracks, laying vocals on tunes. First time in the studio, absolutely nailed it. Culture.

But there is darkness too. People will be pleased for your success, but there will be jealousy. Once you buy a fancy car, you build a house, some people think you shouldn't have raised your head. They think you should always be where you started out, even when you have worked for it.

You have shed tears, you have thrown cuss words. You have shed blood for what you have achieved, and you have excelled. Still that is sometimes not enough.

A lot of open hands are going to come to you. People look at you different now.

I give back, but people don't see that because I don't highlight what I've done. I don't talk about what I've done for a school, or for a heart foundation. So people don't see those things. They just see you having fun, and they think, this guy's always partying. Always partying, and nothing more to him. In Jamaica they see the negative side, and they talk negative.

I've been partying since I started, since before I played for the West Indies, since I escaped with a rewire heart when death came stalking. I party to be free and I party to celebrate each day and being alive within it. That's the thing most people don't understand.

Jealousy is there even within the cricketing arena. Guys are competing with you. Guys want to make you look small so they can look big.

I will try to ignore it, because I walk away from darkness. *Breathe an' let the stress an' anger go.*

Eventually it will prove itself. It will be real. But I don't make them feel any wiser by saying anything. I just leave it where it is. Carry on doing my business, letting my smile kill them with success.

From the government has come very little. Sport and music are the most powerful forces for Jamaica in the world, yet while Courtney Walsh and Jimmy Adams have been recognized for what they have achieved, the same light has not shone on the younger group. I keep the flag flying. I bring people in the country. I've done something to uplift.

In 2015 I was given a diplomatic passport, which I'm grateful and thankful for. But for a long time there was nothing, and for long afterward there may be no more. I breathe, and I let it go. I use these things to drive me more, to excel in what I'm doing, to keep knocking down barriers, to keep doing good things for my country. I keep doing good things for my country, and I will never stop, because my love affair with Jamaica is long-term.

Kingston has Norman Manley Airport, it has Marcus Garvey Drive. Usain Bolt National Stadium should have followed already. They wait till you're retired, but I would rather it happened now, while we're still doing it. There's no guarantee you're going to live to see it.

I will keep giving back, for everything I want is in Jamaica. The people, the passion, the colours, the culture. We are it and it is we.

And that is why I have my foundation.

I understand that some kids have it hard. It is tough out there. Some parents find it hard to even help their own kids, just like growing up for me wasn't easy as well. Sometimes you have to hustle yourself to get your own money. I've been there, and I know what it's like. I know how it feels to beg for money. I know how it feels.

Eight kids every year, aged between 16 and 22. To Lucas every Wednesday afternoon and again every Saturday, bus fare and lunch paid for. Cricket coaching and academic assistance; guest speakers and public speaking, help with etiquette and confidence for the younger ones, help with job hunting for the older. When they graduate, they come back into the academy to talk to those still there.

The boys have lived a life. One about to be kicked out of school for running in gangs and fighting wherever. Another kid who barely spoke for the first two months, us trying to gradually coax the fears and the laughter out of him. We mentor and we mend. There is so much to do, but we do what we can.

We don't pretend it will be easy. I hope the upcoming youngsters can look at me and think, if he can do it, I can do it. Men have done it before me and there's no doubt they'll do it after me. I'm just one lucky enough to excel. I utilize and take the chance.

I put in my work to be where I am today, and I send that message. If they're willing to make the sacrifices and put in the hard work, then one day they can be as Chris Gayle, or even better than Chris Gayle.

It's not going to be that it will all come to you tomorrow. Since the day I was born the work has been put in. Climb the ladder, take the step one by one.

Everywhere I have been, I have made sure I leave a mark. From a young age, always leave a mark. Always an innings, in whatever tournament, and I will be remembered for that. Wherever I go in the world for franchise cricket, I leave a mark still. That's how I portray it to the boys. Take control. Leave your mark.

A lot of kids are out there, not getting the opportunities, not getting an education, getting in trouble. We run one small programme, even if we want to spread it to Dubai and India and beyond. But even if you help one boy then that is one life more to celebrate. It is one more life in the light.

And celebrate we will.

I had scored a century in a Test match in my home stadium of Sabina Park, getting there against England in 2009 as captain in a match and series we won against the odds. I had done it three times in one-dayers – 123 against India in 2006, 125 v New Zealand in 2012, 109 against Sri Lanka the year after. But the Six Machine had never done it in a T20, and the Six Machine does not like to be stopped.

The Tallawahs against Trinidad and Tobago, Caribbean Premier League, July 2015. Under the lights, in front of my dad.

Jacques Kallis with the first over, his fourth ball beaten over long-on for six. Johan Botha with the opening over from the other end, two more sixes taken off him. Dwayne Bravo into the attack, three fours off his first dart.

After seven overs we were 70 for no wicket. My opening partner, Chadwick Walton, had just 13 of them.

I wasn't going to be stopped. Not now. Not here.

Six after six. Some were going in the George Headley Stand, where I used to sit; some into the North Stand, where my father sat watching.

Once you're on the go in Sabina Park, it is the match for even India's noise. Horns blaring, people shouting. 'Lick 'im Chris! . . . Lick 'im proper!'

Jamaicans like to be entertained. I entertained them. 105 out of a total of 180, nine sixes, six fours.

From Rollington Town to here. It's a mighty ladder to climb, even if most people wouldn't even understand.

Me, a Jamaican man, I understand. I'll always keep the flag flying. I travel the world, but I always come home.

I don't like cricket. I love it.

Sometimes in a love affair you have to be tested to realize what you have. Sometimes you have to face a future without that love to cherish the present.

A few years into my West Indies career I am dropped, and the funds dry up just as the runs had before. Back in Kingston, back from the spotlight, back on the hustle and the worry.

Lucas is a family, and a family looks after its own. A beautiful lady named Miss Cook sees that a youngster needs help, and she finds me a job with the Port Authority down by the docks. She's passed away now, and I'm sorry every day, because a woman like Miss Cook makes a heartless world a softer place, and a woman like Miss Cook changes a young man in ways she'll never know.

So I have this job, and to get through downtown Kingston in rush-hour traffic means you have to ride the bus extra early. When I reach the office I am still half-asleep, bag in hand with kit in to practise afterwards, but no chance to practise until the real day is done.

I sit there on my first day, quiet office rather than warm and noisy streets outside, a computer screen and keyboard in front of me. As I look around and wonder a trolley arrives with some big, big files. You hope they're not for you. They are for you. My job is to go through each one and input page after page of data. No thrills, no spills, no changes of pace and no chat from anyone about anything.

I'm a sleepy man even after a long lie-in. Getting up before dawn I'm barely awake enough to move my data fingers. The head starts to nod. The eyelids are dropping like the shutters on Mr Lecky's store. The pile of files stays the same.

I ask where the bathroom is, go into the stuffy smelly cubicle and have to take five on the toilet seat. 'I jus' wan' a likkle five . . .'

Morning blurs into afternoon. Day turns into day. No batting, no off spin, no catching, no competition. Just those files, never getting smaller, going only to be replaced by identical ones with all the same numbers in a slightly different order.

I begin to obsess about my lunch break. Kevin Murray works at the nearby sports shop, Sports and Games, walking distance two minutes. Lunchtime I am straight over there. I won't even eat lunch in the cafeteria, because I'm a youngster surrounded by some big women, and the men are even bigger and even more intimidating. I'm the only youngster in the office, and stern looks and words are all around. To kill an hour at Sports and Games, to talk cricket with Kevin Murray, to just chill and relax, is all I have to look forward to. Occasionally they will let me off work a little earlier to get to cricket practice. It becomes the light that I must gravitate towards, the porthole in a ship that's going down.

The mornings are the hardest. Giving yourself an hour to get there. The bus ram and jam-pack. Travelling with your little bag of kit in case training can be squeezed in afterwards. Dreading the day before you.

I'll never forget the moment. There is a tour to Australia going on, and the chat on the bus is all about it. I'm not on the tour but I am on the bus. The promise comes naturally:

'Whenever I get the chance to get back on the team, I'm going to take it. If the chance doesn't come, I will make it. When I walk out of this office, I'm never walking back in.'

And so it begins. Climbing back up the hills. Scoring the runs in first-class cricket. Making my selection a must-do decision rather than an option.

There will be no turning back. The love affair burn afresh, and the passion is rising.

People call me a gun for hire. Sixteen franchises in nine different countries across five continents.

People call me a mercenary. A year that goes Pakistan Super League in February, Indian Premier League in April and May, Caribbean Premier League from June to July, NatWest Blast in England in August, maybe some Ram Slam in South Africa or Bangladesh Premier League in November and into the Big Bash in Australia to end it all.

If I'm a gun for hire, I'm a man who loves each assignment. If I'm a mercenary I grew up amid sporting conflict and I take pleasure in every fresh battle I spark.

People think it's all about the cold cash. When you're on the road for 10 months, jumping from team to team, it's more about the confusion.

You step into a new franchise, the first thing you try to do is to get the names of your new team-mates right. And more often than not, I don't get the names right. I have to wait until the players put their shirts on, then I can take a sneaky look and get it. Trouble is, only their surname appears across the shoulders. So it makes me a very formal man – 'Good to meet you, Badrinath.' Whispers from my right: 'His first name is Subramaniam.' Gayle: 'Er . . .'

Forget that first name. Even the surname can be hard to pronounce in the IPL or Bangladesh Premier League, and

I'm not good at names in the first place. Never was. I will let everyone know at the start so no one gets offended. 'So just bear wit' me, yeah? Don' take it personal. I might give you a nickname instead, oh-kay?'

But nicknames. I might give them one, but they'll already have another. So just when I've worked out they're called James, I find out they're never called James. They're called Sniffer or Trigger or Rhino or something just so impossible to guess.

Some people rely on a fall-back. 'Hello mate.' I'm more of a bro man. I'll call everyone bro. Ten bros in a room. 'What's up bro?' Fifteen bros in a room. So now you know; if I call you bro, I've probably forgotten your name, or failed to ever hold it in the first place. That's how I'll do it.

One country one day, another the next. From hotel to hotel, never under your own steam. Go out at night and you can forget the name of the hotel you're staying in, so you become reliant on the driver of the car laid on to take you places. His name you don't forget. You go down to breakfast and give the room number from your last hotel. Sign a bill at reception and give another number again. 'Jus' check the name. Only one Chris Gayle.'

You travel light. You have to, because every team has a different kit. For a Jamaican man who likes to look different it is the one time to accept that you will look as someone else chooses. The RCB kit works for me. What's not to like about a gold helmet for the gold standard? If it doesn't, you take it for the team. You alone cannot say, 'Lissen mi, change this. It's not my colour.' Don't stress about the colour scheme and don't stress about the accessories. A word to your sponsor and they will make sure a set of pads arrives in time with the right shade at the right hotel.

World Boss travel business class or first class. World Boss travel easy: two bags, one with bats, one with clothes. No iPad or laptop, sometimes not even a belt in the trousers. When so many days are airports, too many hours are lost to queues. A phone for chat and Twitter and Instagram, a head for the simple things.

Arrive in a new hotel room. Jump the bed first. Is it a comfy one? Check your bathroom. TV on. Check your view.

Check your menu. With the attention I get even in the lobby I am king of the T20 regime and I am also king of the room service scene. I've eaten more club sandwiches than any other living man. I've signed more chits than an Indian government clerk. I can tip a man in 12 different currencies.

I'll do a lot of sleeping, especially during the day. If you want to hit the nightclubs, you need your sleep. And everyone knows not to call me early mornings. Never wake me up.

Down come the blinds. No light can come in. This is my comfortable cave, this is my safe retreat. Under the floodlights at night I dazzle. In the daylight I sleep it off and wait for the next surge to arrive.

Club sandwiches and water, pancakes and hot chocolate. Six Machine runs on simple fuel. When runs are scored Hennessy adds fire to the sparks.

I'm not a caffeine man, but in franchise cricket I sink an energy drink before I bat. Make sure there is always a drink for me ready to go. All the time. It will give you a buzz, really. That aggressive mood, put you on red alert. You might think it a problem if your wicket falls early and you have all that energy to burn. So put it back into supporting the guys. Put it into the watching and the working the nuances.

Because I am playing cricket rather than riding buses. I'm talking to team-mates rather than scary older ladies in a cruel canteen. I'm seeing the wide wide world rather than the inside of a toilet cubicle door.

I have my memories of the affair and I have my keep-sakes, a shirt from every team I've played for, in every season. It's quite a collection, even if sometimes when I have guests they'll borrow one, take it and be gone, or people will ask for one to raise funds, so I'll give one away for their charity.

World Boss loves to see his world. Bangladesh, great people. South Africa, much love back. Every franchise I represent, I've never had a hiccup with anyone. Whatever you want they will try to get. If they can't get it they will try again. I have to thank each and every one, and because you get taken care of, you want to deliver for them as well.

I'm looking forward to playing on around the world, however long until I say when. Keep touring the T20 universe. Keep building franchises. Keep shining, and keep entertaining. And have fun at the same time.

Call me a mercenary if you like. But that's a lot of love for a man supposed not to care.

You take special times in unexpected places. You celebrate the cricket and you let the cricket carry you to experiences that the kid from Rollington Town never knew were out there, let alone ever within reach.

I was supposed to play for Somerset a few years ago, only for a situation with the West Indies Cricket Board to intervene. A contract had to be cancelled, but the personal commitment remained even as the legal one had to be torn up. 'Lissen mi, I owe you guys, so whenever I get the chance to play for Somerset again, I'll just be ready.'

So when after the IPL 2015 I had a slot for a few matches, it was an easy choice. Not even any big negotiations, just, 'I owe you, I'll come and play for you.'

Four games in the NatWest Blast lined up. I told them I would be in London, and they said that's fine, just find your way to the ground. So straight to London, straight to parties. Let them know the World Boss is in town. When's the game? No problem, no time for net sessions, still no problem. Where is it? Essex? Cool, I won't come to Taunton, I'll meet you there.

Except there's a lot of sex around London. Essex. Middlesex. Sussex.

I called on my friend Donovan Miller, who knows about a town called Chelmsford. He took me out there to avoid all the other 'sex on offer. We reached it a little early, but that gave me time to see my new team-mates come in and meet and greet each and every one. 'Hey bro . . . All good bro? . . . 'Scuse me bro – what's that bro called? Cheers bro.'

Into the field for a few throw-downs, and a bat in my hand for the first time since wheels landed at Heathrow. I started hitting a few balls, hitting a few balls, trusting the Six Machine magic had come with me in the single kit bag.

Into the field, me into the slots at first slip, Marcus Trescothick keeping wicket. West Country born, raised in the chill winds of the English summertime. He looked at me and shook his head. 'Cold, isn't it?'

Gloves and pads on him, thick sweater. Thoughts – 'Is he serious? This is my first game, and he's telling the man from Jamaica that he's cold? How would I feel at first slip here?' Words under my breath, 'Lissen mi, batsman, just don't nick anything, okay? If you nick anything to me it's a waste of time. So nick it to the man wearing two pairs of gloves, yeah?'

They set us 176. Back out there with Trescothick, both with gloves on this time. The usual look-and-see start, ignoring the first five deliveries, dabbing a single off the sixth, yet I couldn't middle the ball. Just couldn't get my timing right. Two overs, three overs, and it still wasn't there. Eighteen deliveries and I was only on six. Trescothick then got out for 20. Okay. Time for World Boss to conquer new kingdoms.

'Lissen, you been in this situation before. Don' panic Chris, jus' keep batting on, an' you can mek it up back down at the end.'

And then one over, I hit one through the covers and it went for four. Hit another one, and then things started to flow. Getting a feel for the wicket, getting a feel for the bowling. Shaun Tait bowling flat-out fast, Graham Napier more cunning, but everything suddenly boom boom.

I started to hit a few balls out of the park. Three sixes, four sixes, five. Six sixes for the Six Machine, a little poetry for the opening-night crowd. Closing in on the total, closing the door on them. I tried to finish with another six, only to be caught for 92, but with only 13 needed off 10 balls the bros squeezed us home.

The mood had been established. The rhythm was in place.

Back to London, out to party again. 'Guys, I know it's a long drive, so I'll come down to Somerset the day before the game.' The coach, Matthew Maynard, understood my thoughts and what works for me. 'Okay, whatever you say big man. Just keep us posted.'

Out west the night before. Finding my feet, finding out what time the game started. Finding the ground.

Meeting some executives, meeting the CEO, meeting the fans.

And the fans were something special. Autographs, photographs, fist-bumps. It was just unbelievable – I signed for an hour, then more, then kept signing. Into the dressing-room with the players, forming those bonds, learning those names. 'Your name Tregs? You tell me what this guy Peter Trego looks like? What you say? That's you one and same? Apologies, bro . . .'

New friends, new surroundings, new words on the lips. Scrumpy pumpy, a bar order and a vibe and an education roll into one.

Kent up next. They batted beautifully under West Country rays, the opener Daniel Bell-Drummond 51, the finisher Sam Northeast 114, hammering us all over the park, *beatin' it, beatin' it*. 227 to chase down, a serious task ahead of us.

I opened out a little slow again. The team started slower. 22 for two and going down the gurgler.

Then the magic began to flow. Three long and handsome sixes in eight balls, up with the run rate, up to a half-century off 29 balls.

Time to get to know my surroundings. A six into the River Tone, and another, and another with my new friend the swimmer stripping off to fetch it. Over in that direction, St James's churchyard, and a peppering of the gravestones with some more high and mighty blows. Ghosts and duppies, graves and marble, white leather and rebounds. So that's the Sir Ian Botham Stand that one bounced out of, and those flats with windows in danger are Pegasus Court, and those hills in the distance that the next one nearly reached are the Quantocks, or are they the Blackdowns, or are they the Brendons?

To my century off 45 balls. But wickets kept falling even as we were chasing chasing, and I couldn't get on strike, and with two balls to go we needed 10, and the bowler came up with a brilliant delivery right on my toes. A six to finish it and take me to 151, but in a losing cause. Those supporters singing on the scrumpy and cheering every ball gone over the stands left to applaud and wonder at the numbers – 150 off 62 balls, 10 fours and 15 sixes. And even Kent could enjoy the entertainment, their coach, Jimmy Adams, inviting me into the dressing-room. Everybody taking selfies, a photograph with the entire team, laughing, 'Well done big man . . .' Pretty cool, pretty cool.

And it continued. 89 not out from 45 balls against Hampshire, eight sixes sent sailing, a win sealed from the last of them with two and a half overs still to run.

Not everything came off. Spinner Danny Briggs was bowling, and the guy bowled a good over, so as he came on for his next one, I said to the wicketkeeper, 'Yeah man, this over gonna go for runs.'

'You want a bet, big man?'

'Yeah, and if I don't do it, I give you a bat.'

'How many you taking me for?'

'Three sixes. Maybe more.'

And I didn't get the job done. I got one. So I gave him a bat after the game, because I am a man who fulfils his bets.

'Thanks man. I'm going to frame this one . . .'

One more game to go, and the English summer rain washed it out. Left high and dry on 328 runs from three innings, two not outs, so an average to match my total. And a strike rate of 192, meaning off every ball I faced, I scored an average of almost two runs.

All pleasure, all part of a job that can never feel like a job.

The hospitality in Somerset, the fans, the nights in Taunton's bars and clubs. This is why a man plays cricket, this is why a World Boss travels the world.

Everywhere I go, the high fives and tall drinks. When I first heard about scrumpy I imagined it as the Somerset version of a Jamaican fruit punch. Then all I heard was how dangerous it was, followed by how many someone had ordered for me. All smiles and winks – 'I'd love to see you try two of these, mate!'

Then the quieter times and the bigger compliments. An old boy coming over for a pat on the arm and a shake his head. 'Now sir, I've seen Viv Richards, but I'd never seen you. I'd seen Viv, but Chris, you're different. Just unbelievable. Watching cricket for fifty years, I've ever seen anything like this.'

On an' on. I get to know my team-mates and I grow to love their company. Tregs is Peter Trego and then when I'm in the groove he's Tregs once again, and it's his benefit year and he's got a benefit match going on against South Devon, would I fancy coming along? Not to play, just to be around and have some fun and sign some bats and glad some hands.

Of course! On the sideline, a little watery sun, drinking some rum and Coke. Toasting the Port Authority office, tweeting the rum, tweeting the good times. Chatting with the fans, them buying me rum and Cokes, me buying them beers.

And then for some reason, against the promises and the logic, with the mood and atmosphere, they say they want me to put on the pads and go out to bat.

'What? A lot of rum go down . . .'

They insist. So I borrow some pads, put them over my jeans, leather jacket, black cap turned backwards.

Out I go, and I can't even see the ball. I'm trying to hit a six for the crowd, and it's like playing with the cap pulled over my eyes, or with an invisible ball. Swing, edge. Swing, miss. Swing – what's that, I'm at the non-striker's end?

I drop my phone going for a quick single which is a very slow single. I drop my guard and trust my new friends and new surroundings entirely.

Yuh cyaan keep a good man down.

I call a kid on and ask for a different bat. Maybe it's the bat. It must be the bat, because eventually I do hit a six, over the rope, over the fence, into the road. Junior Senior playing on the PA, arms in the air like it's my triple century. 'Everybody, move your feet and feel united . . .'

Another, all muscle and fumes on the rum. Bowing to the crowd. Snatches of shocked conversations blowing in from the crowd in front of the Portaloos at long leg: 'Is that really Chris Gayle playing for South Devon?'

Eventually I have to come to my own rescue and come off, yet the night goes on. At some point I even sign for the season. South Devon's club secretary, Ian Shepherd, comes up to me and hands me a pen and a piece of paper. 'World Boss, you've got to sign for us. Now.' So I scribble on the paper, which turns out to be a Devon League registration form, and suddenly there's another franchise to add to the list, this time one in the Devon Cricket League 'B' Division side.

For the record, my new team finished that season seventh in that league. Let me tell you, we're not finished. Chudleigh CC, we're coming for you. Ipplepen, watch your back. *Plymstock, Gaylestock com' fi blow yuh away!*

You don't need a noisy nightclub to find fun. My life has been measured out in cricket pavilions, and in this one I'm even serving behind the bar, even serving their real ales once the barman shows me the pull. A great day and great night, a lot of happy people. 'Hey Chris, you can stay down here if you want . . .'

New lands, new experiences. A spot of golf, Tregs bringing the outfits Jamaican-style − black plus-fours with yellow, black and red flashes, matching cap, knee-high white socks. I lean on the same line as Muhammad Ali when he was once asked if he was any good at the game. 'I'm the best. I just haven't played yet.' Although there seems to be a lot of walking in golf, and that may be a flaw they want to look at.

A spot of shopping in Selfridges, a bumping-into with David Beckham. 'Yo Becks!' We take a picture together, just strolling without any harassment, just walking cool and collected. Easy-going, the big man Beckham. A very cool five minutes. For both of us.

A man travels and a man learns. A man says something and he learns from the reaction who he can trust and who he cannot.

So it is at the Big Bash in January 2016, when I'm playing for Melbourne Renegades against Hobart Hurricanes. I'm out and Channel 10's reporter Mel McLaughlin comes over to ask me about my dismissal.

Now T20 is different. It's not Test cricket. It's chilled and fun and let's do things different. So when Mel asks me that question I stay in the T20 mind, and answer informal and fun . . . and this is certainly different.

'I wanted to come and have an interview with you as well − that's the reason I'm here, to see your eyes for the first time. Hopefully we win this game and we can have a drink after.' A pause and a grin. 'Don't blush, baby . . .'

I meant it as a joke. I meant it as a little fun. I didn't mean to be disrespectful and I didn't mean it to be taken serious. Channel 10's commentary team could be heard laughing in the background, and even their own official Twitter account joined in: 'Gayle to Mel: "Hopefully we can win this and have a drink after. Don't blush baby" #smooth.'

But someone up above them clearly decided to step in, and a throwaway comment in a fun format escalates and blows up and within hours it has turned into a major international incident.

Suddenly I'm the number one thing trending on Twitter worldwide. Kim Kardashian is nowhere. Headlines and news reports and outrage and uh-oh . . .

I tried to phone Mel that same day. Because of everything that was going on, I wanted to apologize in person. It didn't happen; I couldn't get hold of her. But when we had been at the ground I got the impression it was no big deal for her. No one in the stadium complained. No one at the franchise complained. Mel then asked everyone to move on. Except some wouldn't.

It all came down upon me. Ex-cricketers and former team-mates bringing things up, making comments to the media, saying things they had never said to my face. Some parts of the media throwing petrol on the flames, chasing me round airports, accusing me of things I've never done and would never do. *Everyting all outburst.*

People I thought I could trust, suddenly turning into cartoon characters. Andrew Flintoff, tweeting it out: 'Big fan of @henrygayle but made himself look a bit of a chop there.' This coming from a man who admitted he took Viagra during a Test match. Freddie Flintstone, a young boy like you taking Viagra? Don't lecture *me*. The only chop Freddie knows is when he used to bowl short to me and I would chop him past backward point for four.

Then it was former Aussie opener Chris Rogers, acting more like Roger Rabbit, claiming I'd led young players astray when we'd played together at Sydney Thunder. Chris Rogers, how can you claim that when it was you and me at the bar most nights? I'm not a snitch, but I've heard from your own mouth what you've done. Next time you want to open your mouth, maybe chew on a carrot instead.

Ian Chappell, calling for me to be banned worldwide. Ian Chappell, a man who was once convicted of unlawful assault in the West Indies for punching a cricket official. Ian Chappell, how can you ban the Universe Boss? You'd have to ban cricket itself.

I was just being my usual joyful self, giving a compliment. I've given bigger compliments to other reporters many times, and no one complained and no one used me for a punchbag.

So I learned from it. I learned when big players in the Big Bash were happy to back me in private but not in public, while a real friend supports you both ways. I learned when players who claimed they had my back said they had no opportunity to go public with their support, even as their Twitter and Instagram accounts sat quiet and cold. I learned when accusations started flying and suddenly those same friends were nowhere to be seen. I learned that some commentators could be fakes to my face, and I learned how my name could be hijacked by people to get their story highlighted, to bang their drum, to sell newspapers and to build their audience figures. I learned all right.

Don't hate me just because I'm not what you want me to be. Don't hate me because I'm not who you are. I am me and I am honest. I stand by my friends and my friends stand by me.

Too many people were scared to speak out. Too many people were happy to see these things happen to me. But it didn't break me, only built me. I've spent my life fighting through tough situations, and I will always pull through, whether you help me or not.

Breathe, an' let the stress an' anger go. Sometimes it's hard to take your own advice. Sometime it's hard to stay with your philosophy, when the stress and anger swirl around your head and you feel like you can't escape.

And so. If you're the man making money out of your Don't Blush Baby T-shirts and merchandise and everything else you can rattle off to feed the fans, don't forget to pay a percentage to the Chris Gayle Foundation, so some good can come out of all this.

Just don't stand around waiting for me to blush. It hasn't happened since the shy boy became a man. Baby.

This office is not a quiet one. This working environment hum and come alive all hours, all days.

500,000 followers on Instagram. Climbing towards three million on Twitter.

You share the love, you share the pleasure. Sometimes something just pops up in my head, and I have to communicate. It gets me in trouble, but that's the thinking in the moment – just blast it out, just talk what is on my mind at that particular time.

I'm a weirdo. *You cyaan know me.* The moods come down and I'm a different person, and when I get in those moods I can be on Twitter for a couple of hours, talking to fans, speaking my weirdo mind.

If some of them are out of place you put them back in their place. If they're rude I'll be rude. It doesn't matter who, I'll say what I feel. Whoever or wherever, at any particular time. That's the person I am, and you just have to accept it.

And yet. As a man grow older he learns to curb certain things, let other things slide other days. They used to say don't drink and dial. Now they should say don't sip and social media. When you're drinking, put the smartphone down, because that's when you're going to get yourself in trouble.

But oh! When I'm on it, when I'm on the booze, I'll blast out Twitter even more. *Blast it out, some more cheeky ways.*

Sometime you're trying to tweet and you can't even spell the word. Why are my fingers not working? Phone up close to your nose. They will know what I'm talking about. They will get the point still. Now the autocorrect messes you up. Why is it talking about ducking? Oh yeah . . .

Now what? I've never seen this word before. Can I argue with autocorrect? Maybe it knows what word I actually want. Why are the letters in the wrong order?

I'm aware of what I'm doing, but I still feel like doing it. It's a release for that side of my personality, and without a release a man explodes. And there are worse ways of checking that pressure than popping out a tweet.

Sometimes it's a little something you can give back. Most people you tweet, you make their day. You give them a tweet, they'll cherish that tweet for the rest of their year. 'Oh, Chris Gayle tweet me!'

I like a picture on Instagram. 'Oh my God! I cyaan believe it!' Just a tweet to someone. Coming from you it's just a little chat, like being back in the George Headley Stand at Sabina Park, running jokes, a little tease. And then you retweet somebody, and they tell the entire country. 'Chris Gayle liked my picture!'

On Instagram I will 'like' a lot of pictures. I will 'like' pictures of different women, because sometimes you will get a reply that says, 'You make my day, you make my day.' Everybody has feelings. And when those likes are coming from a superstar, maybe it does something different. Maybe one or two will feel good within themselves, more confident inside, more confident with how they look outside.

Maybe not. But if it works for one or two in three million, at least I'm not being those big men and big women in the Port Authority canteen. At least I'm talking to all, and I'm talking on each and everyone's level.

Because the love is still there. And with the passion comes the performance.

The 2015 World Cup, Canberra, Australia. Thunderclouds around the Manuka Oval, and question marks about my commitment and class.

It is 20 innings since my last one-day century, with only one score of 50 or more in that time. Across my seven previous ODI innings this year I am averaging 15. A Six Machine is not a machine that produces only one or two batches at a time. A score is needed, and the clouds must clear.

Drizzle in the air, bright colour on my bat; stripes of red, green and yellow on my grip to bring a little Jamaican rhythm to the middle of the Aussie nowhere. With defeat to Ireland in our first match and a little pride won back against Pakistan we need another win against Zimbabwe to kick on, except Dwayne Smith is bowled second ball for a duck, and then to my first there is a huge appeal for lbw, and everything stops except the thud, thud, thud of my revamp heart.

Umpire Davis. Not out. Maybe he heard an inside edge. I didn't.

Zimbabwe refer it. Now we'll see.

No inside edge.

'Oh, you gotta be kidding me – not now, not first over . . .'

Hawkeye replays on the big screen. I watch. Thud, thud, thud.

The ball is hitting, but only the top half of the bails. Umpire's call. Not out.

If it had been given first and I'd referred it, I would have been gone. Still gone. And so I say, 'Oh-kay, I'm riding this luck today, I'm gonna make the best use of it.'

A slow wicket, and it's a huge outfield. Bigger than Lord's, bigger than the Gabba, bigger than Newlands in Cape Town and bigger than Sabina Park. I take my time and make the adjustments. My first six doesn't come until the 11th over, but that time has not been wasted. I have worked out the bowlers, how they're using it, how they're being used.

And once they're in my half I decide I'm going to go. Start getting it, getting it, start clearing the boundary. Except the boundary is so big, I'm having to time it so sweet and add a little muscle. Most of the sixes look like they're going out of the ground, only to drop into the red plastic seats or scatter the boozers and dancers on the aisles.

Still it is tactical. The off-spinner Sikandar Raza is bowling well, and will go for just 45 runs off his 10 overs, so I don't bother with him, just a little milking, only the occasional boundary. I know they have a left-arm spinner, Sean

Williams, to work through, and the way they calculate their bowling attack is to load more spinners coming up in the back end, so I say I'll stick around, but still be attacking at the right time.

And so it is. Forty per cent of the deliveries I face will end as dot balls. It will still be the fastest ever landmark score in World Cup history. Never a slogger, always a thinker. *Yuh cyaan read me.*

100 off 105 balls. Steady.

35 to 40 overs, and now I'm really picking it. Six Machine is firing. Balls are flying all over the park.

150 off 126. Now we're cooking. Bowlers wearing scars, bowlers not meeting captain's eyes.

Two of the spinners, Williams and Tafadzwa Kamungozi, are turning the ball into me. In the 44th and 45th overs, I send them for 21 apiece. In that time I move from 151 to 193, our total from 258 to 300.

I knew that no one had ever hit a double century in the World Cup. I knew that because there had only been four double centuries in 50-over cricket, and I knew that because I don't like cricket, I love it.

I got to the 200 with a big drive through cover for four. A big smile on my face, helmet off, down onto my knees, arms out wide, helmet in my right hand, big old bat hanging out of my left. Not over-celebrated, but enjoyable.

200, off 138 deliveries. So the second 100 off 33 balls. Commentators yelling it. 'He went berserk!'

Sixteen sixes, 215 runs. I got out on the last delivery, trying to make it 17. I could live with it, only grins on my face. For once the mask had slipped. That's the thing about love. Sometime you've got to let it show.

Wisdom took me there. Wisdom from experience. When you have a run of low scores like that, there's always one big innings coming. The magic will return, and when it does, you have to make it big. Cash those chips in. Make it count. Make up for what you've missed in all those other innings.

Not all are so wise. The president of the West Indies Cricket Board had retweeted something during that previous match against Pakistan.

'Gayle goes . . . Can't buy a run. Let's give him a retirement package!'

That goes to show what you have to deal with as a cricketer for the West Indies. That goes to show that a man needs a philosophy. *Breathe, an' let the anger go.*

At 138 balls, it was the fastest ever ODI 200. Twenty-eight times someone has hit a Test triple century. That one I know first-hand too. At this point now, only six times has someone hit a one-day double hundred.

Only two men have a Test triple century and an ODI double century. Only one man has a Test triple century, an ODI double century and a T20 international century.

Six Machine. World Boss. *Universe* Boss.

Afterword

C. H. Gayle Not Out 36

Stray dogs bark at night far away. Cars and buses huff-puff round the city streets but the noise and smoke do not reach me. Hot and sticky in the dusty concrete down there, cool breezes and tall trees up here in the hills.

From the balcony of the house that cricket built, Kingston becomes a twinkling panorama, a map of the past as well as the present. Out to my right, out to the west, the headland curving round to Hellshire Beach. Moving my gaze across the city, the lights of Tinson Pen aerodrome, the cranes at the wharf, where the container ships come in off the Caribbean, where I once worked that job for the Port Authority. Big jumbos coming into Norman Manley airport on the peninsula beyond, then downtown, dark sea in the distance, and the Coronation Market, where I used to go as a kid and sell bag juice to hustle some funds. Keep coming around, to Cross Roads, where Half Way Tree Road meets Old Hope Road and traffic crawls, and then to the high rises of New Kingston and the Pegasus Hotel, where touring teams stay; leading away from it Knutsford Boulevard, with Triple Century at one end and Emancipation Park at the other. On and on, moving east, floodlights beam at the National Stadium, Rollington Town hidden a mile or two on and Sabina Park just over there. The big houses on the slopes of Beverley Hills, Usain's neighbourhood of Norbrook further east, Smoky Vale closing it out. Lucas is flat and dark, invisible from this distance, yet I know exactly where it is. I can see Lucas from the other side of the world.

The instinct was always there: when I get the right money, I'm going to buy a house. That was always the dream. Because I know where I'm coming from. Because they can't take away from me a house I've bought and paid for. Because then you've made the jump. You're not going back.

The view holds me still and silent. Sometimes it makes me pinch myself – 'Wow, this is you up here?' Sometime it makes me shake my head. You can never forget the down there, and all that comes with it. Down there, looking up; down there, walking streets, chasing runs, toiling for more.

It fills my mind, and clears it. If you're in the darkness and you feel a sluggish day, you come out here and the breeze start to blow and your vision clears and your belief comes back. Listen to the water running into the pool, listen to the wind through the branches. No factory next door, no battling for a single bed. A kitchen inside with cupboards full and sinks that fill.

You look down, and you look back. How you came through. What you had to survive. The things you did to break out.

Sometimes I sit here, and it's too much to take in. I dreamed of a house, but never a house like this. I dreamed of escaping, but I never dreamed I could take so many with me.

For they are all here. My mum has the best bedroom in the house, and a house of her own nearby, where she lives with my sister Michelle when she wishes for that. My dad Dudley has the first bedroom you come to, his flatscreen and newspapers so he can follow the world; 85 years old, and nothing now to worry about. My brother Vanclive's son in another room, space for all my friends when they come back from trying to earn around the distant world. I bought Popeye his first car, a Nissan Maxima. Now he has a roof when he needs one too.

Sometimes I sit here and I think of Noah building an ark. I escaped, and I brought them all with me.

You alone cannot enjoy it. An escape on your own is into a prison of a different making. You bring your family, you bring your friends, you look after all. Trust me, I do. If they have kids, I school their kids. All the books, all the fees. I pay for everything. *Mi alone cyaan enjoy it.*

You might see that as a burden. Sometimes they take it for granted. There are nieces and nephews, and you have to care for them like a parent. You do those things, but you want them to be responsible as well. 'You can bring in food for the table too.' That's important, so they don't just rely on Uncle Chris. But I still give them what they want, and I still give them what I never had.

Roots hold you back as well as sustaining you. My dad leaves the house some mornings and goes back to Rollington Town. He still walk around the neighbourhood.

Sometimes you want to stay where you are. My brother Michael Crew, in a smart house in a smart area that I bought for him, and every day he's still there where he grew up. The same streets, the same rum shack on Giltress, the same story played out over and over again.

I go back too, and I go back with time on my hands so I can sit and talk and take a drink. I go back and walk down St James Road and look at the old zinc fences, and I walk round the corner onto Preston Road, past the gates to Kensington Cricket Club and on to Lucas, and I walk out to the middle once again and take guard on the unmarked wicket, and I walk back to rattle the bars around the old pavilion and Briggy comes out and we talk old times and new nets and Chris, could you fund a little academy here so the nets can actually have nets now?

When the cricket comes to an end, I'll be here. My family will be here. Helping out whenever I can. When you're gone, someone else will be spending your money, and I want to spend my money, how I want. I came from nothing, I will leave with nothing.

My heart is strong now, and my vow is unbroken with it.

Life is about now. If you're going to do it, do it big. Do not wait for the never-comes future. Do not do it apologizing to a man you never met. Do not die worrying about the edge behind. Play your shots, and play them your way.

When you go to party, do it big. I don't want to go to a party and just stand up. Fuck, I look good already.

I want to dance. Whether I'm going to dance by myself or dance with someone else. Whether it's my friends I'm with or on my own. You dance, you drink, you come back home, you sleep. Then you wake up in your clothes and find a piece of jerk chicken in your pocket, and you know then you have had a good night.

Lissen mi. Listen to Chris. Nothing can protect you from the ball you never saw coming. *Death stalk you.* Garrick, gone to the swerve of a bus, Runako, lost to the darkness.

Those are the things you have to live with. When you have good health and life, make the best of it. Make it count. If you can't make it count for you, make it count for someone else. Make fun for someone. Live it while you can.

You have to go big. Why take a single when the boundary is open? Why take a four when you can aim higher and beat away a six?

I'm not a man for regrets. I regret not punching a particular person in the face, but that time has passed, and anyway, I'm not a violent man. Let the stress and anger go.

Be happy now, not on a promise or another day. The happiest time in your life is not when you're making a million bucks. Happiness comes with freedom, with having enough to buy the food you want when you want it, with being able to move when you want to move. That is the golden time.

You can feel sometimes like you're climbing a mountain. One more push, and you're at the summit.

Trus' mi. There is no summit, only a plateau and then another climb. You will never play the perfect innings, never hit the perfect six.

But you can come close, and you can come close only by trying. And when that six sails away, when you see the crowd scatter or jump, when the umpire's arms go up, behind that gladiator's mask you are alive. You are the centre of it all. You are the Six Machine.

I sit on this balcony, and in the room behind me are Raddy Haynes and Mr Mac, and Kevin Murray and Popeye, and my dad and my brothers, and we are all together. Triple Century calls, for there is a special send-off party for Jamaica's entry to Miss World, and it would be rude not to wish a compatriot well before such a long and trying journey.

But the world never stops, not even for World Boss. Soon there will be others in the house, not just my girlfriend but the child she carries for us inside. A landmark like no other, a delivery I have never faced before. What did you expect? I always did like three figures.

So here I am, on Noah's Ark.

You might think this is the end, but I'm only just start-ing. Moving up, always moving up.

I escaped, and I took everyone with me. *Yuh cyaan stop me.* I am all you have seen and much more you have not. I am complicated. I am weird.

I am the Six Machine. And I am moving up, always mov-ing up.

The Records

Tests

103 matches

7,214 runs

Average: 42.18

Highest score: 333

Hundreds: 15

Fifties: 37

Sixes: 98

Strike rate: 60.26

Wickets: 73

Best bowling: 5-34

Catches: 96

One-day internationals

269 matches

9,221 runs

Average: 37.33

Highest score: 215

Hundreds: 22

Fifties: 47

Sixes: 238

Strike rate: 85.11

Wickets: 163

Best bowling: 5-46

Catches: 114

T20 internationals

49 matches
1,515 runs
Average: 36.07
Highest score: 117
Hundreds: 2
Fifties: 13
Sixes: 98
Fours: 129
Strike rate: 145.39
Wickets: 15
Best bowling: 2-15
Catches: 13

First-class cricket

180 matches
13,226 runs
Average: 44.83
Highest score: 333
Hundredss: 32
Fifties: 64
Wickets: 132
Best bowling: 5-34
Catches: 158

List 'A' cricket

336 matches
11,694 runs
Average: 38.21

Highest score: 215
Hundreds: 25
Fifties: 63
Wickets: 222
Best bowling: 5-46
Catches: 140

Twenty20 domestic cricket

241 matches
8,826 runs
Average: 43.69
Highest score: 175 not out
Hundreds: 17
Fifties: 55
Sixes: 637
Strike rate: 150.15
Wickets: 72
Best bowling: 4-22
Catches: 59

Records

Fastest ever hundred (30 balls, Royal Challengers Bangalore v Pune Warriors, 23 April 2013)

Joint fastest ever fifty (12 balls, Melbourne Renegades v Adelaide Strikers, 18 January 2015)

Only man to hit first ball of a Test match for six (West Indies v Bangladesh, 13 November 2012)

First man to score a World Cup double century (West Indies v Zimbabwe, 24 February 2015)

Fastest double century in one-day international cricket (West Indies v Zimbabwe, 24 February 2015)

First man to score World T20 century (West Indies v South Africa, 11 September 2007)

More one-day international centuries than any other West Indian (22; next highest Brian Lara, 19)

First batsman to score an international century in all three formats (Tests, ODIs, T20)

Only player to score a Test triple century, one-day international double century and T20 international century

One of only four men to score two Test triple centuries (others are Sir Don Bradman, Brian Lara and Virender Sehwag)

More T20 international sixes than any other man (98)

Highest ever score in T20 history (175 not out, Royal Challengers Bangalore v Pune Warriors, 23 April 2013)

Highest career total of T20 runs (8,623)

Most T20 centuries (17; next highest is seven)

Highest career T20 average (44.40)

Highest number of career T20 sixes (603; next highest is 388)

Most sixes in a T20 innings (17, Royal Challengers Bangalore v Pune Warriors, 23 April 2013)

Joint record holder for most sixes in a one-day international (16, West Indies v Zimbabwe, 24 February 2015; record shared with A. B. de Villiers and Rohit Sharma)

Most career sixes in the Indian Premier League (230; next highest 150)

Acknowledgements

I would like to thank all those who have been part of my journey: my family – dad Dudley and mum Hazel, my brothers Wayne, Andrew, Michael, Vanclive and Lyndon, and my sister Michelle, plus all the Berridges; those who gave me the love of the game, from Miss Hamilton and Paul McCallum at school to the wider family at Lucas Cricket Club like George Watson, Spike Rhoden and Briggy Breese; those who played with me on the streets in the young days, from John Murphy and Kevin Murray to O'Neill Powell (Popeye) and all the happy crew across Rollington Town; and those who have played with me on pitches across the world for Jamaica and the West Indies.

Six Machine came to be as a book from my stories and achievements and the listening and writing of Tom Fordyce. From World Boss to Word Boss, great job. Big thanks too to Joel Rickett and his dedicated team at Penguin: any time you guys want to drink champagne on the roof again, I'm your man. Thanks to my trusted adviser Simon Auteri and to David Luxton for the detail work.

Thank you to all the fans, across the continents, across the franchises, on social media and in the stands. Sorry if one of my sixes nearly sent you flying. Catch you in Triple Century any time.

And finally to Natasha and Raddy, my right hand and my left. I love you both.

One love.

Chris